Harold Janzi

THE BIBLE AND THE CHURCH

THE BIBLE AND THE CHURCH

Essays in honour of Dr. David Ewert

Edited by A.J. Dueck • H.J. Giesbrecht • V.G. Shillington

Kindred Press

Winnipeg, MB Canada   R2L 2E5   Hillsboro, KS USA   67063

Published simultaneously by Kindred Press, Winnipeg, MB,
Canada R2L 2E5 and Kindred Press, Hillsboro, USA 67063

Printed in Canada by The Christian Press, Winnipeg.

International Standard Book Number: 0-919797-88-1

PREFACE

This publication, sponsored by the Mennonite Brethren Bible College, recognizes the valued service of Dr. David Ewert to the church, particularly to the Mennonite Brethren Church. The volume comes upon the occasion of his retirement as President of the College.

As the introductory essay, "In Appreciation of Dr. David Ewert," reveals, Ewert spent almost all of his adult life in a teaching ministry, most of it at MBBC. He was a man who loved the classroom, but he equally loved the pulpit. The pulpit became an extension of his teaching ministry and, conversely, the classroom was a preparation for a ministry in the church. Dr. Ewert's unequivocal commitment to the Bible--the New Testament in particular--and to the church makes the title, *The Bible and the Church*, quite appropriate.

The essays have been arranged in two parts in keeping with the two-fold interest and commitment of the man in whose honor they are being published. The first part of the book addresses issues pertaining to church life and ministry, and the second to the interpretation of the text of Scripture. These divisions are, of course, not absolute and a few essays might well have been included in the other category. Perhaps this exigency is as it should be, for neither the Bible nor the church exists independently of the other.

The various contributions to the volume come from persons associated in some way with Professor Ewert. And the subject matter in each case reflects in some manner an area of interest exhibited in his life and ministry. Some of the contributors have been students of Dr. Ewert, and others colleagues. But all acknowledge the fine and faithful service which he has rendered in the name of Jesus Christ to the Christian community.

The Editorial Committee express their sincere appreciation to the writers of the essays for their readiness to participate in this undertaking. They have done so admirably. Indebtedness must also be recorded with respect to those who typed the manuscripts, to Fred Koop for designing the book jacket, and to Gilbert Brandt of Kindred Press for consultation and expertise in bringing the project to its completion. An expression of our gratitude is also due to the Board of Higher Education of the Canadian Conference for encouraging the Faculty to proceed with this project.

Editorial Committee

Abe Dueck

Herbert Giesbrecht

V. George Shillington

CONTENTS

Preface..v

In Appreciation of Dr. David Ewert 11
    Herbert Giesbrecht

PART I: THE BIBLE

1. History of Editing the Greek New Testament 29
    Bruce Metzger

2. Imaginative Participation in Parable Interpretation 45
    V. George Shillington

3. Discerning What is Bound in Heaven..63
    David Schroeder

4. Women in Church Leadership 75
    John E. Toews

5. Women and the Church: 95
    Herbert Swartz

6. From Text to Sermon 111
    Elmer Martens

PART II: THE CHURCH

7. The Changing Role of Biblical/Theological Education
    in the Mennonite Brethren Church 131
    Abe J. Dueck

8. Give Attendance to Public Reading 149
  Esther Wiens

9. Preach the Word 165
  David Ewert

10. Preaching that Delights 179
  John Regehr

11. Evangelical Preaching and Pastoral Care 191
  Frank C. Peters

12 .Biblical Realism and Urban Evangelism 203
  Myron S. Augsburger

13. The Church's Mission and Eschatology 217
  Victor Adrian

14. Translating God's Word as Mission 229
  Hans Kasdorf

Bibliography of Books and Articles by Dr. David Ewert:1953-1987 ...251
  Herbert Giesbrecht

List Of Contributors..275

IN APPRECIATION OF
DR. DAVID EWERT

Herbert Giesbrecht

In his play *Julius Caesar* Shakespeare has Cassius remark to his friend and compatriot, Brutus, with specific reference to the public life and achievements of the Emperor: "Honor is the subject of [my] story."[1] While "honor", in the precise sense in which these Roman compatriots conceived of it, is not the subject of our "story", there is a moral sense in which the concept of honor, viewed as a singular quality of spirit, provides a leitmotif to illustrate and illumine the person and public ministry of Dr. David Ewert, the honoree of this *Festschrift*.

I begin this essay in appreciation of David Ewert by suggesting that he has manifested himself as a "man of honor" in this moral sense by the way in which he has always viewed the key experiences of his own life and vocational ministry. Revealing glimpses into the earliest years of Ewert's life, from the days of his birth (1922) in the southern Ukraine to the time of the family's more permanent settlement in the Coaldale (Alberta) area (1930), are provided within the dramatic story recounted in an unpublished document entitled "Pilgrims and Strangers: The Story of Our Exodus from Russia and Settlement in Canada."[2] It was David Ewert who first encouraged his father, David Ewert, Sr., to set down the memorable details of this "family story" and himself translated it into the English language so that it might serve as a continuing testimonial to the grace and goodness of God as experienced by the Ewert family during those earliest and often arduous years.

David Ewert was born of David and Margaret (nee Wiebe) Ewert on December 5, 1922, upon the steppes of the southern Ukraine, in the Memrik Colony village of Alexanderhof. David, Jr. was the second son—John had preceded him by about sixteen months—and was born shortly after his parents had moved into the house of his grandparents after their untimely death as victims of the disease of typhus during the Civil War years. David's parents sought, in the aftermath of the Bolshevik Revolution and of the loss of almost everything from their paternal farm as a result of the merciless raids of Bolshevik and anarchist intruders, to eke out some sort of living from the very little which was left on the small farm. With the kind assistance of a Russian farmer and a Bulgarian neighbor, to both of whom David Ewert, Sr., had rented small parcels of land (in 1922), and by dint of very strenuous work on their own part, the Ewert family managed to survive the economic crisis of those very bleak and famine-ridden years.

Towards the end of 1923 David Ewert, Sr. resumed former duties as a manager of a Russian cooperative in the village of Galizenowka, near Alexanderhof, but returned to farming again several years later. However, the more widespread implementation of Communist rule, and the imposition of increasingly more oppressive regulations in social and economic spheres of life, induced the grandparents of David (on his mother's side), the Abram Wiebes, and a recently widowed great-aunt, Justina Wiebe, to consider emigration from the Ukraine. Their eagerness to remain united with their next of kin, David, Sr. and Margaret Ewert and family, finally persuaded the latter to grant their consent to emigration. As it turned out, however, only the Ewert family, accompanied by Aunt Justina Wiebe and her two young sons, were sufficiently healthy to receive permission to leave for Canada.

Other circumstances conspired to make it possible for the Ewert family, finally, to leave Russia, in October, 1926. In the city of Riga, in Latvia, their pilgrimage was suddenly halted:—the family was quarantined, and young David was admitted to a hospital because he had contracted chicken pox. At the time this seeming setback provided a severe test for David's parents in respect to their faith in God's providential guidance. Soon, however, the family was able to continue its journey to England by way of the North Sea. In Liverpool the family, together with a small Mennonite Brethren congregation from Siberia, boarded a steamship, "The Montclary", and crossed the Atlantic, entering the harbor of Quebec City on November 12, 1926, after a rather turbulent voyage.

It was under such circumstances that David Ewert, then a lad of nearly four years of age, reached the country in which he would live out most of his life and pursue a very active and fruitful career as teacher, preacher, churchman, and author. Ewert contends to this day that it was God's kindness and faithful guidance during those often difficult and danger-filled years which rendered it possible for him to study, and then to serve God and his own people in this land of liberty and opportunity.

Several geographical displacements, between the years 1926 and 1930, shifted the Ewert family about rather uneasily, from Winnipeg, Manitoba, to southern Saskatchewan, then to Ontario, and finally to southern Alberta where the family first settled down in the Grassy Lake area (1929) and then in the Coaldale district (1930). In the Coaldale district the family was at last able to acquire a suitable and well-situated farmstead.

It was indeed fortuitous that the Ewert family was in a position to set up a permanent household in the Coaldale area at this time. These were the years during which the young Ewert children (John, David, Margaret and Abram) grew up in the midst of what was rapidly becoming one of the most stable and active Mennonite Brethren communities within the country as a whole. It was in Coaldale that some of the most gifted and compelling preachers within the Canadian Mennonite Brethren constituency of the time–preachers like Abram J. Schierling, Benjamin W. Sawatzky, Jacob Siemens, Benjamin B. Janz, Jacob Dueck, David Pankratz, and later also Jacob H. Quiring and John A. Toews–exercised spiritual influence upon many of our people and especially challenged the awakening minds and spirits of such sensitive youngsters as David Ewert. Moreover, it was in Coaldale that a Bible School had recently been established (in 1929) by the Mennonite Brethren. Its teaching staff, though always remaining small, continued to include two or more of these leading preachers, and for this reason the school's evangelical influence soon came to be felt far beyond the immediate constituency.

David Ewert had experienced a conversion to Christ when he was about twelve years old. Several years after this experience he entered the Coaldale Bible School where he spent several winters (1939-1941) as a student, eagerly responding to the inspired teaching of such men as Abram Schierling, Benjamin W. Sawatzky, Jacob H. Quiring, and John A. Toews. The well-organized class lectures and remarkably expressive and winsome manner of Toews impressed young David especially, as he has publicly acknowledged in his biographical sketch of Toews,[3] and undoubtedly reinforced his own gradually emerging aspirations for the future. It was however the personal example and encouragement of Benjamin Sawatzky, then Principal of the Coaldale Bible School and a very intense and incisive preacher, which provided the first and most significant impetus for David Ewert with respect to a *possible* preaching and teaching ministry for himself.

David Ewert continued his Bible and religious education at the Winkler Bible School (1942-1943) and Prairie Bible Institute (1943-1944), having been attracted to these schools by his awareness of the teaching and preaching competence of Abraham H. Unruh (at the former school) and Leslie Maxwell (at the latter school) particularly. Ewert could not have known then that some ten years later (1953) he would become a young teaching colleague of Unruh, this powerful preacher so highly esteemed throughout the Mennonite Brethren constituency in Canada. From Unruh, David Ewert learned much about the art of sound expository preaching, an art which would be increasingly and singularly reflected in his own preaching ministry.

Ewert's long career as a Bible teacher and preacher actually began with a short teaching stint, during the winters of 1944 and 1945, at the La Glace Bible School. On October 12, 1944 he married Lena Hamm, daughter of Martin and Anna Hamm, to whom he had become attracted while they were fellow students at the Coaldale Bible School. Several further teaching opportunities, first at the Bethany Bible Institute (1946-1947), and then at the Coaldale Bible Institute (1948-1951), quickly followed. While these were all relatively small schools, their significance for the Canadian Mennonite Brethren constituency was quite considerable at the time. In these several schools David Ewert nurtured his own teaching and preaching abilities and so became increasingly known to the larger church constituency. When a formal invitation to teach at the recently established Mennonite Brethren Bible College was extended to him a few years later, he was already recognized as a very promising young teacher and preacher.

Meanwhile, Ewert had already begun (in 1947) to pursue studies towards a B.A. degree at the University of B.C., which degree he obtained in 1950, and was also continuing his theological education, first at the Central Baptist Seminary (Toronto) and then at Wheaton College. When, in 1953, the invitation to join the faculty at the Mennonite Brethren Bible College reached David and Lena, although they were at the time giving some consideration to the acceptance of a preaching/teaching ministry in Europe under the auspices of the Mennonite Brethren Board of Missions/Services, they did not find it difficult to reach a decision in the matter. The prospect of becoming a teaching colleague alongside such esteemed and influential teachers and preachers as Abraham H. Unruh, Henry H. Janzen, Jacob H. Quiring, and John A. Toews appealed to him immensely. In making this particular decision, David Ewert cast his lot, as it turned out, with the larger cause of theological education within the Mennonite Brethren constituency in Canada.

David Ewert's appointment to the Mennonite Brethren Bible College, in 1953, only intensified his desire to further advance his theological education although, as he was very much aware, he would need to assign a large portion of many summers to the pursuit of this long-range plan. During the next decade and a half or so, he was able to secure the following degrees: the B.D. degree from Central Baptist Seminary (Toronto) in 1953; the M.A. degree from Wheaton College in 1956; the M.Th. degree from Luther Theological Seminary (St. Paul, MN) in 1961; and the Ph.D. degree from McGill University (Montreal) in 1969. The measure of such academic achievement is enhanced by the fact that Ewert had very nearly completed a doctoral program (by the early 1960s) at the Lutheran School of Theology of the University of Chicago when he felt obliged to withdraw from it because he could not, in good conscience, subscribe to the theological position into which he felt he was being coerced by his dissertation adviser, and had therefore to begin doctoral studies anew at McGill University.

While most of his teaching ministry was carried out in Canada, Ewert also devoted a decade to seminary teaching at two Mennonite institutions in the U.S.: the Eastern Mennonite Seminary (Harrisonburg, VA) from 1972 to 1975, and the Mennonite Brethren Biblical Seminary (Fresno, CA) from 1975 to 1982. During these years Ewert was able to enlarge the scope and enrich the content of his teaching courses and also to fortify his communication skills as a teacher. Other shorter (usually summer school) teaching stints, as visiting professor, brought him to such schools as Regent College (Vancouver, BC), Associated Mennonite Biblical Seminary (Elkhart, IN), and the Canadian Theological College (Regina, SK).

There is little doubt that *classroom teaching* has always been Ewert's most cherished endeavor and pursuit. During his teaching years at the Mennonite Brethren Bible College (1953-1972 and 1982-1986), which are the years of his teaching career best known to me, Ewert increasingly gained the esteem of students and colleagues alike. The very earliest teaching years at the Mennonite Brethren Bible College were, in some respects, difficult and demanding for him in view of the slate of new teaching subjects and a heavy teaching load. But such difficulties and demands became strong challenges for him, to be confidently accepted and successfully managed by dint of hard work and personal dependence upon the Spirit of God. Highly methodical study and class preparation habits, a ceaseless curiosity about biblical and historical knowledge, and further studies (pursued during summer sessions) enabled him continually to improve and enhance his classroom teaching. The lecture has remained his preferred teaching style in the classroom but he has always welcomed discussion as a supplement to the lecture.

As the years went by his classroom lectures revealed an increasingly comprehensive and incisive knowledge of the subject matter under consideration. Moreover, they were increasingly enriched by fitting illustrations drawn from a variety of historical, biographical, and literary sources. Another identifying feature of his classroom teaching, especially of his teaching of New Testament courses, was a deeply-felt concern about the ethical and practical implications of the material under consideration. A certain aversion to the merely academic study of biblical material could frequently be sensed in his explication of specific biblical texts.

A firm and fine command of the language, an appropriate (never artificial or ostentatious) use of basic rhetorical devices, and a delicate touch of humor were other features which have characterized his teaching style. It has not been surprising, therefore, to observe that Ewert's classes--despite a certain reserve and dignity in his personal demeanor--have often been among the largest within the College program of studies. Indeed, it has been the very presence of a large and expectant group, whether in a classroom or congregational setting, which has especially stimulated David Ewert and has frequently called forth his finest and most animated efforts.

While Ewert has, in the course of many years of college and seminary teaching, taught a wide variety of courses, his strongest interests have focused upon New Testament Greek, the Pauline letters, introduction to biblical studies, and the Book of Revelation. His precise and thoroughgoing knowledge of Greek, careful exegetical study of the biblical text, and constant concern for the spiritual edification of his hearers have enabled Ewert to gain the increasing respect and affection of many eager students and church members, to help shape their theological reflection and understanding, and to influence many leaders within our Canadian constituency. Of course, Ewert's short-term teaching ministry abroad, from time to time– at the Union Biblical Seminary (now in Pune, India), the Instituto Biblico Asuncion (in Asuncion, Paraguay), and the European Mennonite Bible School (in Liestal, Switzerland)–has extended the scope of his theological influence to other Mennonite and Mennonite Brethren groups as well. A tincture of dogmatism may at times have colored his public statements–so some would contend–but about the sincerity, integrity, and abiding impact of his teaching there has always been widespread consensus.

If teaching may be said to be David Ewert's "first love", *preaching* emerges as a very close neighbor to it. Part of the appeal of the invitation to return to the Mennonite Brethren Bible College in 1982 was the prospect of more extensive preaching opportunities in Canadian Mennonite Brethren churches. Whether the influence of his earliest "mentors" was crucial for this close linkage of teaching and preaching, or whether Ewert's own abilities along these lines simply developed in natural conjunction with each other, may never be known with certainty. It is very clear, however, that his attentive response to good preaching during the years of his youth and his collegial association with notable preachers at the Mennonite Brethren Bible College, enabled him to develop unusual skills in exegetical preaching. The same scholarly care taken in his preparation of classroom lectures was also applied by him to the analysis of specific texts and to the development of the sermons themselves.

One of the local and significant preaching ministries into which Ewert was drawn while at the College, during the late 1950s and early 1960s, involved the so-called *Bibel Besprechungen* (Bible conference sessions) which were convened annually in the Elmwood Mennonite Brethren Church (Winnipeg, MB) during several days between Christmas Day and New Year's Day. It was at these Bible conferences that Ewert preached, in close partnership with such notable preachers as Henry H. Janzen, John A. Toews, Jacob H. Quiring, and Frank C. Peters, over a period of some ten years. He enjoyed a similar preaching opportunity, together with John A. Toews, at Bible Conference sessions held annually in the Scott Street Mennonite Brethren Church (St. Catharines, ON) during the Easter weekend. It was a consistent practice for these "College preachers", in preparation for these conference sermons, to assign portions of a book within the Bible (the New Testament, usually) among themselves, and each one to commit himself to the task of exegeting the assigned passage(s) carefully under the head of an overarching theme which had been mutually agreed upon.[4] It was a thoroughly sound practice from a homiletical point of view, and one which yielded rich fruit in terms of the instruction and edification of the hearers.

Although David Ewert occasionally preaches other types of sermons--topical and biographical sermons, for instance--it is the expository sermon, which is punctuated by apt illustrations drawn from a rich repository garnered through avid reading across the years, and which applies these truths to the situations of everyday living, that has come to be recognized as the hallmark of his preaching practice. What has been said about Alexander Maclaren, the great nineteenth century Scottish preacher whom Ewert much admired, might also be said of David Ewert himself:

> [His] biblical emphasis is seen in his excellent expository sermons, which he seemed never to tire of preparing and which his listeners seemed never to grow weary of hearing.[5]

Many within our larger Mennonite Brethren constituency have come to feel that Ewert is indeed a "prince" among expository preachers, a preacher well deserving of Christian honor and respect.

Much might be said as well, if space permitted, about David Ewert as *churchman*. It has often been the case, within the shifting, and sometimes unsteady course of Mennonite Brethren Conference activity, that Ewert's alertness to the need of the hour, his perceptive understanding of the relevance of biblical truth to a specific situation, and his boldness in speaking forth a much needed word served the churches of our Conference to very good advantage. Many of us can recall such moments, during conference sessions, when the well-reasoned and appropriate comments of Ewert served to clarify a specific issue in the midst of rather turbid or confused discussion, or else prodded hesitant delegates into making a necessary and wise decision. As churchman, Ewert has been at his best, I suggest, in working out specific guidelines and agenda items for study conferences and for Conference boards which have been concerned particularly with the theological orientation and spiritual well-being of our denomination as a whole. One obvious instance in which his contribution along these lines has been very substantial pertains to the subject of eschatology. The enlightened and sane teaching and preaching of David Ewert on eschatological texts and themes, his readiness to engage in open debate of controversial aspects of the entire subject and, finally, his own book, *And Then Comes the End* (1980), have all helped to focus more sharply and to unify more nearly, disparate views and convictions about this subject, especially during more recent decades. Ewert's fundamental concern throughout this process of rethinking a dispensational view of eschatology has been a concern for the integrity of biblical exposition as such and for the promotion of doctrinal unity (not uniformity) within the entire Mennonite Brethren Church. This kind of "servant" attitude and this capacity to appraise quickly and to analyze properly, theological notions and trends within our brotherhood are distinctive traits which many brothers and sisters in the Conference have recognized within Ewert. They are distinctive gifts which have gained him widespread esteem as a courageous and sagacious churchman.

Among Ewert's multifaceted contributions to the Mennonite Brethren Church, perhaps few promise more enduring significance than his *writing endeavors* across the years. David Ewert's earliest published articles, it seems,[6] coincide with his beginnings as teacher at the Mennonite Brethren Bible College (1953), and appeared in its official journal, *The Voice*. His regular and carefully prepared contributions to the pages of *The Voice*, as well as his work as chief editor for some ten years, constituted part of an earlier and significant apprenticeship, as it were, for his later writing projects. Of course, Ewert's consistent practice of writing out his lectures and sermons with diligence and care also served to strengthen and refine his writing skills.

The realization that the range of his teaching and preaching influence could be extended beyond the boundaries of classroom and pulpit, and the explicit encouragement of others induced Ewert to submit more articles for publication in denominational magazines, particularly in the *Mennonite Brethren Herald* and *The Christian Leader*. In the course of time he began to prepare some of his lecture material for possible publication in book format. The preparation of his earliest books (pamphlets, really), *Creation from a Biblical Perspective* (1966) and *An Approach to Problems of Christian Ethics* (1967), seem to have been prompted by the explicit requests of Conference boards/committees for helpful material which could offer guiding insights to our people on the topics treated therein. Ewert's third published book, *Stalwart for the Truth:The Life and Legacy of A. H. Unruh* (1975), written at the request of the Board of Christian Literature of the General Conference of Mennonite Brethren Churches, allowed him to pay warm tribute to a great teacher and preacher, Abraham H. Unruh, who had elicited his personal respect and affection.

Another booklet, *How the Bible Came to Us* (1975), arose directly from David Ewert's classroom teaching material and turned out to be a small harbinger of what was to appear in 1983–a full-fledged history of the transmission of the biblical text, *From Ancient Tablets to Modern Translations: A General Introduction to the Bible*. This latter book has received favorable reviews in numerous journals and has been adopted as a textbook in several Bible colleges in recent years. His book, *And Then Comes the End* (1980), has also received the positive acclaim of reviewers. I recall Dr. Bruce M.

Metzger of Princeton Theological Seminary remarking to me that this was a book which he regularly recommended to Seminary students and visiting pastors as one of the best brief introductions to the subject of eschatology. It is a book which, I believe, has enabled many within our Mennonite Brethren constituency to rethink their views on the subject and to become less dogmatic, perhaps, in their insistence on secondary aspects of dispensationalism which bear upon the "end times".

Other books by Ewert, such as *Die Wunderwege Gottes mit der Gemeinde Jesu Christi* (1978) and *The Church in a Pagan Society: Studies in I Corinthians* (1986), are well-written expository studies which can usefully serve pastors and preachers in their teaching ministries. To date some ten books authored or (in one instance) edited by him have been published.[7]

It comes as no surprise that Ewert's published works are marked by much the same general features which characterize his classroom teaching and public preaching. Among these features are the following: (1) a strong concern for the responsible interpretation of biblical texts and truths; (2) clarity and coherence in the outlining and organization of the material under consideration; (3) a careful use of scholarly opinion in the endeavor to understand the material; (4) a constant interest in the moral implications of the material being considered; and (5) a prose style marked by precision and simplicity in the use of words, a certain sensitivity to the enhancing values of rhetorical devices, and a pleasing fluency in regard to sentence form and movement. In summary, one might assert about David Ewert's published writings what James McGraw has said of John Wesley's books and pamphlets:

> [They reveal] an extraordinary ability to think clearly and logically and to present truth, controversial though it may be, plainly and convincingly[8]

A careful and wide-ranging study of the published writings of David Ewert suggests that their deepest inspiration and their fundamental theological lineaments derive from his personal study and diligent teaching of the New Testament, especially, and of the cultural and religious world which surrounded it during its formation. In this sense it may be said that his published work is, to a very large extent, the rich fruit of years of assiduous and faithful study and teaching of the biblical material which came within the scope of his assigned task as a Conference teacher and churchman. In this respect Ewert proved himself to many, once again, as a man of Christian integrity and honor.

I need, finally, to say something about David Ewert as an individual. To portray him as the individual that he is—in the personal contexts of family, friends, and working colleagues—is, in some respects, a more difficult and precarious undertaking than to delineate more public aspects of his life and vocation. Dr. Ewert, while being a person who thoroughly enjoys public ministry and one who readily enters into animated conversation with acquaintances, is also a rather private person. He is not much given to the public revelation of personal details about himself, whether in the classroom or in the pulpit. Moreover, his capacity for self-discipline and self-containment and his generally dignified manner, in both classroom and pulpit, have tended to foster the public image of him as a person of high dignity and aloofness. Such an image, however, obscures other more spontaneous and amiable aspects of his personality.

To speak of David Ewert as a family man, first of all, is to provide unmistakable evidence of these other facets of his personality. While his many vocational endeavors—as teacher, preacher, churchman, and writer—and his summer school studies, especially during earlier years, may have occupied much of his working time and left all too little time for family and friends, as one can assume, it is nevertheless a fact, testified to by his wife, Lena, and by family members, that David Ewert was not merely respected but thoroughly enjoyed by his children during their growing up years. Even as the children grew into adolescence, Ewert was able to retain their personal confidence and affection, although he was not one to be much preoccupied, as a young father, with small details in everyday life or to be unduly perturbed by minor misdeeds of his children. In respect to these latter happenings, he was prone to adopt a more detached and philosophical attitude than his wife in the full confidence that she was quite capable of handling these exigencies of everyday living with motherly concern and wisdom.

It may be appropriate, at this juncture, to say something about Lena Ewert herself. While Lena may be a less public and vocal person than her husband, she is by no means a languid or timorous woman. Quite the contrary: Lena possesses and manifests, as the occasion calls for it, rich resources of mind, emotion, and will. Although circumstances of family life have made it impossible for her to pursue further studies in a formal sense, her own ardent love of reading and powers of perception have enabled her to share the intellectual interests and concerns of her husband at various levels, and this without ever succumbing to a sense of inferiority or of exclusion from the exciting aspects of a College professor's life!

Both David and Lena recognized, from the very beginning of their life together, the singular importance of taking time out, each day, for family devotions, and since both enjoyed reading, they also reserved times, quite regularly, for oral reading from books to their children. David and Lena would certainly concur with the comments of Frederick F. Bruce, made in his autobiography, *In Retrospect: Remembrance of Things Past:*

> Children brought up in homes without books are deprived
> children, intellectually deprived, just as children brought
> up without affection are emotionally deprived.[9]

Such books frequently included tales of missionary exploits but were certainly not restricted to this one subject of interest in terms of their content or focus. The very positive impact of these family adventures in the world of books upon them is affirmed by David's and Lena's children to this day. Between the years 1947 and 1956, five children were born into the Ewert family, all of them now married: Eleanor, married to Raymond Martens; Marianne, married to Robert Worcester; Ernest, married to Brenda (nee Waighorn); Grace, married to Steve Bruhn; and Doreen, married to Samuel Myovich.

One can illustrate the amiable side of Ewert's personality also by alluding to some of his extracurricular interests and pursuits. While reading remains a very prominent and precious pastime for him, other interests of his include listening to classical music (while reading), attending musical concerts, traveling through new regions, jog-walking, and occasional participation in such sports as volleyball and baseball. Ewert's keen appreciation of good choral music emerged early in life and found expression in his regular participation in a singing quartet during student days at the Coaldale Bible School and in conducting a choir while attending the Prairie Bible Institute. And he continued to demonstrate this appreciation of fine choral music by way of his strong support of the music program at the Mennonite Brethren Bible College during his years as a teaching colleague and, later, as President of the College.

To speak of David Ewert's capacity to engender and sustain personal friendships is another way in which to convey something of the congenial and engaging side of his personality. Of course, his widely respected preaching ministry brought him into close encounter with many people across the years. Ewert's many articles and books have also enlarged the circle of his friends especially among those who deeply appreciated the essential thrust of his published works. Those who encountered him by way of his writings and public ministry were often quick to sense both his desire and his capacity for cordial friendships.

It was within the context of teaching partnerships, however, it seems to me, that a spirit of genuine collegiality and intimate friendship could most readily develop between David Ewert and others. At the Mennonite Brethren Bible College, his close working relationship with men like Cornelius Wall, Henry H. Janzen, and Jacob H. Quiring, brothers whom he found highly congenial in respect to their Christian character and theological orientation, allowed him to experience intimate and abiding friendships with them. Two other teaching colleagues with whom Ewert developed enriching friendships during his earlier years at the College were Dr. John A. Toews and Dr. Frank C. Peters. His working association with Peters, a person of unusual spontaneity and exuberance, served to gently soften the edges of David Ewert's more restrained and dignified demeanor and also to enlarge somewhat the boundaries of Ewert's own "social world" without ever diminishing his genuine respect for this colleague and friend.[10]

Ewert's long partnership with John A. Toews, as teaching and preaching colleague, kindled mutual respect and a lasting friendship between them. Some years after Toews had departed from the Mennonite Brethren Bible College in order to assume pastoral duties in the Fraserview Mennonite Brethren Church (Vancouver, BC) and, soon thereafter, to teach in Trinity Western College (now University), Toews reflected upon his long-standing friendship with Ewert. Having struggled in the course of years, together with Ewert and other Conference leaders, with a variety of doctrinal and ethical issues which sometimes threatened to divide churches within the Mennonite Brethren Conference, to weaken their spiritual life or to blur their theological outlook, Toews confided in a personal letter to him:

> There is no one within the Conference with whom I agree
> as genuinely and fully, in respect to matters of doctrine and
> faith, as just you.[11]

David Ewert responded to this expression of intimate confidence and trust with a deep sense of gratitude and affection.

One could enumerate the names of numerous other colleagues who have labored alongside David Ewert in teaching and preaching ministries, in a variety of colleges, seminaries, and churches, and who have been drawn into mutually enriching friendships with him. Those of us who have been Ewert's continuing colleagues during his last six years at the Mennonite Brethren Bible College (1982-1988) will recall, for many years to come, not only his orderliness and competence as a teacher, and his insightfulness and freshness as a Bible expositor and preacher, but also his warm collegiality and his desire for sincere friendship--this latter so often manifested in the eager and engaging ways in which he has participated in informal conversations with and among us. In this respect also, David Ewert remains for all of us a man of unfeigned virtue and honor, a man whom we shall continue to esteem highly and to love sincerely.

ENDNOTES

1. *Julius Caesar*, act 1, scene 2, line 92.

2. David Ewert, Sr., "Pilgrims and Strangers: The Story of Our Exodus from Russia and Settlement in Canada." Translated from the German and edited by David Ewert, Jr. Harrisonburg, VA, 1973 (Typewritten).

3. John A. Toews, *People of the Way: Selected Essays and Addresses by John A. Toews*, eds. Abe J. Dueck, Herbert Giesbrecht, and Allen R. Guenther (Winnipeg, MB: Historical Committee of the Canadian Conference of Mennonite Brethren Churches, 1981), p. 6.

4. These Bible Conference sermons were frequently published in the pages of the *Mennonitische Rundschau* soon after the conclusion of the Conference sessions. One series of sermons, presented in December 1963, was published in book form: John A. Toews, David Ewert, and Frank C. Peters, *Das Ernste Ringen um die Reine Gemeinde* (Winnipeg, MB: Christian Press, 1964).

5. James McGraw, *Great Evangelical Preachers of Yesterday* (New York: Abingdon Press, 1961), p. 110.

6. See "Bibliography of Books and Articles Authored and Edited by David Ewert: 1953-1987" in this *Festschrift*.

7. See "Bibliography..."

8. McGraw, *Great Evangelical Preachers*, p. 59.

9. Frederick F. Bruce, *In Retrospect: Remembrance of Things Past* (Grand Rapids: Wm. B. Eerdmans Publishing Company, 1980), p. 28.

10. See David Ewert's words of tribute to Dr. Frank C. Peters, "A Tribute to F. C. Peters," in the October 30 1987 issue of the *Mennonite Brethren Herald*, p. 30.

11. John A. Toews, *People of the Way*, p. 21.

PART I

THE BIBLE

"The Bible speaks to the Church but it also speaks through the Church to the world inasmuch as the whole world is claimed by the Church's Lord."

Alan Richardson

1

HISTORY OF EDITING THE GREEK NEW TESTAMENT

Bruce M. Metzger

One summer a decade ago, while at New College in Berkeley, I was pleased to be brought almost daily into the company of David Ewert. The friendship formed then has continued over the years, and my admiration for the clarity of his expository powers has increased with each new publication from his pen. One of the books that I would regularly recommend to my students in a course on the Book of Revelation was his helpful and sensible volume *And Then Comes the End*. Among his other publications (in English, German and Russian) are the solid studies on the Holy Spirit in the New Testament and on the transmission of the Holy Scriptures over the ages (*From Ancient Tablets to Modern Translations*). It is in the latter area that I wish now to contribute to his Festschrift a short overview of the history of editing the Greek New Testament (being material that also appears in the *Proceedings of the American Philosophical Society*, Volume 131).

Editions Prior to Printing

Historians are unable to say exactly when and by whom the first edition of the Greek New Testament was prepared. It is altogether probable, however, that toward the close of the first century of the Christian era someone set about to collect copies of as many epistles of the apostle Paul as could be found. According to a theory popularized earlier this century by Edgar J. Goodspeed, this unknown individual was a great admirer of Paul who, having read the account of the apostle's missionary journeys in the Acts of the Apostles, thereupon decided to search out his surviving epistles and to issue an edition of the *corpus Paulinum* at Ephesus in the last decade of the first century.[1] Subsequently Goodspeed's theory was elaborated by John Knox, who conjectured that the person responsible for making the collection was none other than Onesimus, a former slave whom the apostle had befriended and who later became bishop at Ephesus.[2]

More recently other scholars, including Hans-Martin Schenke[3] and Kurt Aland,[4] have contended that several persons independently began to assemble *corpora Paulina*, each containing varying numbers of his epistles, which at a later time, perhaps in the second century, were amalgamated into an edition of ten such epistles, to be augmented still later by the addition of the three so-called Pastoral Epistles (1 and 2 Timothy, and Titus).

In any case, whichever theory is adopted, it is noteworthy that the transmission of the Pauline epistles was in the format of a collection. Except for some stray leaves from one or another epistle, none of the more than seven hundred Greek manuscripts[5] of his epistles presents only a single epistle standing alone; all contain a collection of his epistles. The earliest such collection is the Chester Beatty Biblical Papyrus II, discovered in the 1930s and dating from the third century.[6] This collection preserves portions of nine epistles, and may originally have contained one or more other epistles. How far the unknown collector who assembled the first *corpus Paulinum* may have made editorial adjustments in copies of the individual epistles at the time of assembling them, we have no way of knowing--but that there were such adjustments is virtually certain.[7]

The four gospels were probably collected early in the second century. At any rate, evidence in the writings of Justin Martyr of Rome shows that by the middle of the second century he knows of the existence of at least the three synoptic gospels, and perhaps was acquainted also with the Gospel according to John.[8] By about the year 170 Justin's pupil, Tatian, wove the four gospels into a composite edition called the *Diatessaron*, a fragment of which (in Greek) turned up earlier this century at Dura-Europos,[9] a city on the Euphrates River that was destroyed A.D. 256 by the Persian armies of King Shapur I.

As long as Jewish Christians continued to use the time-honored scroll for transmitting sacred books, it was impracticable to collect the New Testament documents within one roll. But by the beginning of the second century of the Christian era, the codex or leaf-book came into favor among Christians, and thus it became possible to produce editions that contained the four gospels in one volume, as well as copies of the Pauline epistles in one volume. By the middle of the fourth century huge parchment codices, called pandects, containing both the Old and New Testaments, were written, two of which have survived until today, *Codex Sinaiticus* and *Codex Vaticanus*.

During the early centuries special features were added to manuscripts of the New Testament.[10] In order to assist in the study of the gospels, Eusebius of Caesarea, in the fourth century, devised a useful system of cross-references to parallel passages in the four gospels. Each gospel was divided into numbered sections, a bit longer than our verses but considerably shorter than our chapters. Eusebius then drew up in columns the section numbers arranged so that those which refer to similar passages in different gospels stood in the same horizontal line across the columns. Soon this system, called Canon Tables, was adopted also in manuscripts of early versions of the gospels in Latin, Syriac, Coptic, Armenian, Georgian, and Gothic.

An edition of helps for the study of the Acts and the epistles was prepared by another fourth-century scholar, named, it seems, Euthalius or Evagrius.[11] These helps included a chronology of the life of Paul, and a system of references to quotations from other parts of the Bible. Euthalius also divided the text of Acts and the epistles into chapters, and provided summary headings of their contents. In order to assist in the public reading of the Scriptures, copies were produced written in longer or shorter cola, i.e., in lines according to sense.

There was developed also, perhaps as early as the second century, a special system of writing the *nomina sacra*. These were contractions of sacred names and titles, such as the Greek words for God, Jesus, Christ, Spirit, heaven, Jerusalem, etc. Eventually, fifteen such words were regularly treated thus by scribes.

Still other editions, called lectionaries, were prepared that present the several passages of the gospels appointed to be read on each Saturday and Sunday,[12] and on other days as well, each lection being set forth in chronological sequence according to the ecclesiastical calendar. Lectionaries are sometimes furnished with *neumes*, a system of hooks, dots, and oblique strokes, written usually in red (or green) ink, in order to assist the lector in chanting or cantillating the Scripture lesson. The most ancient system of *notation ekphonetique*, as it is called, is thought by Devreesse to have originated in the early centuries of the church.[13]

Something needs to be said now concerning the titles of the several books of the New Testament. After the several gospels and epistles had been gathered together, it became desirable to attach titles in order easily to distinguish one from the other. Instead of identifying a gospel as The Gospel of Matthew, The Gospel of Mark, and so forth, the prevailing custom was to use "The Gospel" as a generic title and to offer a four-fold explication of it, as The Gospel according to Matthew, The Gospel according to Mark, and so forth.

In the case of the Pauline Epistles, which were sent originally to one or another congregation or individual, the earliest titles were simply "To the Romans", "To Philemon", and so on. The Catholic or General Epistles, however, being addressed to Christians generally, were identified by the name of the author, as The Epistle of James, The Epistle of Jude, and so forth.

Another feature that needed attention when the several books of the New Testament were collected was the sequence of the parts of the New Testament as well as the sequence within each part. It is natural that the section containing the four gospels should stand first. Within this section the order of Matthew, Mark, Luke, and John is found in nearly all Greek manuscripts. It was followed by Eusebius in his Canon Tables, and was adopted by Jerome for his Latin Bible. Among six other sequences of the four gospels,[14] the next most widely distributed one was the so-called Western sequence, in which the gospels attributed to the two apostles, Matthew and John, take precedence over the two written by followers of apostles (Mark, a follower of Peter, and Luke, a companion of Paul). This order is presented in two fifth-century manuscripts, the bilingual Greek-Latin codex Bezae, now at the University of Cambridge, and Codex Washingtoniensis, now in the Freer Art Gallery, part of the Smithsonian Institution. It is also the sequence in several Greek minuscule manuscripts, in a considerable number of Old Latin manuscripts, in the Gothic version made by Ulfilas in 364, and in several of the older Peshitta Syriac manuscripts.

As for the rest of the books of the New Testament, the "Book of Acts" forms a natural link between the gospels and the epistles. Almost all Greek manuscripts that contain the gospels, Acts, and epistles place the Catholic Epistles after Acts and before the Pauline Epistles. In many Latin manuscripts, on the other hand, the Pauline Epistles follow immediately upon

Acts and before the Catholic Epistles. The latter is the sequence followed in modern European and American vernacular translations.

The order within the several groups of epistles (whether Pauline epistles to congregations, or to individuals, or Catholic epistles) was one dictated by length. As is the case also of the tractates in the Jewish Mishnah and the suras (except the first) of the Koran, the epistles in each group stand in the sequence of decreasing length--but with 1 and 2 Corinthians, and 1 and 2 Thessalonians, brought side by side.

Here and there during the second, third, and fourth centuries, many other gospels and epistles were drawn up, and several of these were for a time included in editions of the New Testament. In Armenia the New Testament was enlarged by the inclusion of the so-called Third Epistle of Paul to the Corinthians, while among the Western churches Latin manuscripts frequently contained the spurious Epistle of Paul to the Laodiceans. This epistle was composed probably in the second or third century when someone noticed that at the end of Paul's Epistle to the Colossians (4:16) the suggestion is made that, when the Christians at Colossae have read that epistle, a copy should be sent to the church in the neighboring town of Laodicea, and a copy be obtained of the epistle in the possession of the Laodiceans. Assuming that the epistle in question had been addressed to the church at Laodicea, and not finding any trace of such a document, someone composed a brief epistle, of quite second-rate character, made up of sentences derived from Paul's genuine epistles, chiefly the "Epistle to the Philippians". It is a curious fact that all eighteen editions of the complete German Bible that were published prior to Luther's German Bible contain the Epistle to the Laodiceans following the Epistle to the Galatians.

Yet another feature of special editions of the Greek New Testament which developed, perhaps in the sixth or seventh century, was the provision of portraits of the four Evangelists, placed at the beginning of the respective gospels. Iconographic models for these were supplied, it seems, from traditional portraits of classical poets and/or philosophers.[15] Portraits of Paul and other apostles were sometimes included. Other artistic illumination was also occasionally provided, and deluxe editions for royalty or high ecclesiastics were prepared by using parchment dyed purple and writing with silver or gold ink.

Printed Editions

Turning now to printed editions of the Greek New Testament, we are struck by a certain delay in producing such editions. As is well known, Johannes Gutenberg[16] produced at Mainz in (or shortly before) 1456 the first book printed in Europe[17] with moveable type. It was the complete Latin Bible, and during the next fifty years at least one hundred other editions of the Latin Bible were issued by various printing houses. In 1488 the first edition of the complete Hebrew Bible came from Soncino Press in Lombardy. Before 1500, Bibles had been printed in several of the principal vernacular languages of Western Europe--in Bohemian, French, German, and Italian. Except for several short extracts, however, the Greek New Testament had to wait until 1514 to come from the press. Why was there such a long delay? Two reasons may be suggested.

In the first place, the production of Greek type necessary for a book of any considerable size was both difficult and expensive. The attempt was made to reproduce in print the appearance of minuscule Greek handwriting, with its numerous alternative forms of the same letter, as well as its many ligatures that combine two or more letters.[18] Instead, therefore, of producing type for merely twenty-four letters of the Greek alphabet, printers prepared about 200 different characters (of these there remain today only two forms of the lower case sigma).

The principal cause that retarded the publication of the Greek text of the New Testament was doubtless the prestige of Jerome's Latin Vulgate Bible. Translations into the vernacular versions were not derogatory in respect to the supremacy of the Latin text from which they were derived. But the publication of the Greek New Testament offered any scholar acquainted with both languages a tool with which to criticize and correct the official Bible of the church.

The first edition of the Greek New Testament to come from the press was that contained in the Complutensian Polyglot Bible. Having been planned as early as 1502, by the cardinal primate of Spain, Francisco Ximenes de Cisneros, the Polyglot was placed under the editorial care of several scholars, of whom Diego Lopez de Zuniga (Stunica) is perhaps best known. When completed the editions were a monument both of learning and of typographical excellence.[19] Volume 5, containing the New Testament, was the first to come from the press; its colophon is dated 10 January 1514. Volume 6, containing a Hebrew lexicon and elementary Hebrew grammar, was printed next, in 1515. The four volumes containing the Old Testament appeared last, the colophon of volume 4 bearing the date 10 July 1517. Sanction for publication of the six volumes was given by Pope Leo X on 22 March 1520. The explanation of the delay in granting permission may be connected with the requirement that all manuscripts borrowed from the Vatican should first be safely returned.

Although the Complutensian was the first printed edition of the Greek New Testament, the first published edition was that of Erasmus, issued by the printer Froben of Basel on 1 March 1516. At the importunity of Froben, who perceived that the market was ready, indeed eager, for an edition of the Greek New Testament, Erasmus began in July of 1515 to gather material for such an edition, the printing of which began on 2 October 1515. Owing to the haste in producing the volume--Erasmus himself declared later that it was "thrown together rather than edited" (*praecipitatum verius quam editum*)-- the volume contains hundreds of typographical errors.

Since Erasmus could not find a manuscript that contained the entire Greek Testament, he made use of several that contained various parts of the New Testament. For most of the text he relied on two rather inferior manuscripts of the twelfth century from a monastic library in Basle. For the "Book of Revelation" only one manuscript was available to Erasmus, and this lacked the final folio, containing the last six verses of the book. Rather than taking time to search for a complete copy, Erasmus translated the missing portion from the Latin Vulgate into Greek. It is understandable that his edition contains several words or forms of words that have never been found in any of the some 250 known manuscripts of that book--but which are still perpetuated today in the printing of the so-called "Textus Receptus" of the Greek New Testament. And this was not all. In other passages as well, Erasmus took the liberty of correcting or supplementing his text from the Latin. The result is that, in a considerable number of cases (generally speaking, not of much importance), the reading of the common English version (the Authorized or King James Bible of 1611) is supported by no known Greek manuscript.[20]

In four subsequent editions of his New Testament, Erasmus made many needed typographical corrections. In his third edition (1522) he introduced into I John 5:7-8 (but on entirely inadequate textual grounds) the famous *Comma Johanneum.* He did so, he wrote to Stunica, with whom he had extensive correspondence,[21] "so that no one would have occasion to criticize me out of malice."

Subsequent editors, though making a number of alterations in Erasmus's text, essentially reproduced this rather debased Byzantine form of the Greek New Testament. Among such early printed editions of the Greek New Testament that deserve to be mentioned here are the four editions issued by the scholarly Parisian printer and publisher, Robert Estienne (Stephanus, 1503-59), and the ten editions produced by Calvin's successor at Geneva, Theodore de Beze (Beza, 1519-1605), an eminent classical and biblical scholar. Stephanus's third edition (1550), a folio sumptuously printed with type cast at the expense of the French government, contains on the inner margin of the page occasional variant readings from fifteen Greek manuscripts. Stephanus's fourth edition (1551) is noteworthy because in it, for the first time, the text was divided into numbered verses.[22] Beza's editions are important, not only for introducing in his annotations evidence from the Syriac and Arabic versions, but chiefly because many of the translators appointed by King James I made large use of Beza's editions of 1588-89 and 1598 in producing the so-called Authorized Bible of 1611.

In 1624 the Dutch printers Bonaventure and Abraham Elzevir issued at Leiden a small and convenient edition of the Greek New Testament, the text of which was taken mainly from Beza's smaller 1565 edition. The Latin preface to the second edition, which appeared in 1633, contains a statement addressed to the reader: "Thus you have the text now accepted by everyone, in which we give nothing changed or corrupted."[23] From this rather boastful comment (what modern publishers might call a "blurb") there arose the designation "Textus Receptus" or commonly received, standard text. The textual basis, however, as can be appreciated from what has been said already, is essentially a handful of late and haphazardly collected Greek minuscule manuscripts, and in several passages the text is supported by no known Greek witness.

During the following two centuries efforts were made to collect evidence of variant readings from increasing numbers of manuscripts of the Greek New Testament, from early versions, and from quotations of the text cited by Church Fathers. Strangely enough, however, virtually all editors of the

Greek New Testament during this period were content to reprint the time-honored but corrupt *"Textus Receptus"*,[24] relegating the evidence for the earlier readings to the apparatus. An occasional brave soul who ventured to print a different and better form of Greek text was either condemned or ignored.[25]

The rise of scientific textual criticism of the New Testament began with Johann Jakob Griesbach (1745-1812), who was professor of New Testament at the University of Jena from 1775 until his death. Following hints of earlier scholars, Griesbach investigated the transmission of the New Testament text in antiquity by identifying the several groups or families of texts. He elaborated fifteen canons of criticism to be followed in evaluating the relative worth of variant readings. His first canon, for example, was, "The shorter reading (unless it lacks entirely the authority of the ancient and weighty witnesses) is to be preferred to the more verbose, for scribes were much more prone to add than to omit." On the other hand, however, Griesbach recognized that "the longer reading is to be preferred to the shorter (unless the latter appears in many good witnesses), if the occasion of the omission can be attributed to homoeoteleuton [similar ending of two lines]."[26]

The importance of Griesbach for New Testament textual criticism can scarcely be overestimated. For the first time in Germany, a scholar ventured to abandon the "Textus Receptus" at many places and to print the text of the New Testament in the form to which his investigations had led him.

The man to whom modern textual critics of the New Testament owe the most is without doubt Lobegott Friedrich Constantin von Tischendorf (1815-74), who sought out and published more manuscripts and produced more critical editions of the entire Greek Bible than any other single scholar. The total number of his books and articles, most of them relating to biblical criticism, exceeds 150.

The year 1881 marked the publication in Great Britain of a critical edition of the Greek New Testament, prepared by two Cambridge scholars, Brooke Foss Westcott (1825-1901) and Fenton John Anthony Hort (1828-1892), that was destined to enjoy long and widespread use. This edition, along with the publication the same year of a second volume containing a full account of the critical methodology followed by the editors,[27] was a "first" in more than one respect. Never before had an edition of the Greek New Testament been prepared by the collaboration of two editors, working independently as well as conferring periodically to resolve differences. Never before had the textual principles underlying the formation of an edition been set forth with the same clarity and fullness of detail. And never before was a set of principles applied in the construction of a text with such thoroughgoing consistency. For twenty-eight years, while also pursuing other duties, the two collaborated. Adopting the methodology of Griesbach, they identified four principal types of New Testament text, the so-called "Neutral", the "Alexandrian", the "Western", and the "Syrian" or "Byzantine". Readings supported by witnesses of the Syrian type, being essentially the "Textus Receptus", were almost always set aside, and a choice was made among readings found in one or more of the other text-types. It goes without saying that the editors did not apply their principles mechanically, but, along with external evidence, they also took into account both transcriptional and intrinsic probability of readings.

Epoch-making though the edition of Westcott and Hort was, it was inevitable that, owing to the ever-increasing acquisition of still earlier manuscript evidence, and with the consequent development of critical analysis that scholars brought to bear upon the documents, the need for a new edition became ever more apparent. Early in the twentieth century an attempt to meet this need was made by a Berlin pastor, Hermann Frieherr von Soden.[28] With the financial assistance of a wealthy patron, Elise Koening (who deserves special recognition--may her tribe increase!), von Soden sent out nearly forty students and colleagues to examine manuscripts in the libraries of Europe and the Near East. These helpers secured partial or complete collections of a very great number of hitherto unexamined manuscripts of the New Testament. (That almost all of them were of late, Byzantine origin was not the fault of the project.) Utilizing this newly-acquired information, von Soden divided the witnesses into three main groups, which he called the "Hesychian", the "Jerusalem", and the "Koine" recensions. Each of these was further subdivided, the "Koine" recension undergoing the greatest amount of division, resulting in seventeen sub-groups for this text. According to von Soden's analysis (set forth in 2,203 pages of prolegomena), the three recensions go back to a lost archetype, used by Origen, but already corrupted in the second century by Marcion, in the case of the Pauline Epistles, and by Tatian, in the case of the Gospels. Unlike Westcott and Hort, who rejected readings supported by only the "Syrian" or "Byzantine" text (von Soden's "Koine" text), von Soden tended to give preference to readings supported by two of the three main texts, thus elevating the "Koine" type of text to a rank coordinate in importance with the other two types of text. As a consequence, the edition approaches the "Textus Receptus" somewhat more closely than other modern editions.[29]

Among other twentieth-century editions of the Greek New Testament mention should be made of three that were prepared by Roman Catholic scholars, who also supply the Latin Vulgate text on facing pages, namely those by H.J. Vogels (Duesseldorf, 1920; 4th ed., Freiburg, 1955), by A. Merk (Rome, 1933; 9th ed., 1964), and by J.M. Bover (Madrid, 1943; 5th ed., 1968). Most recently at Madrid a triglot edition was published in 1977, with Bover's Greek text slightly modified by Jose O'Callaghan, accompanied by the Neo-Vulgata and a Spanish version. Each of these, along with the most widely used pocket edition (prepared by Eberhard Nestle in 1898; 26th ed., 1979),[30] offers at the foot of the page an apparatus of selected variant readings.

It will have been noted that, with the exception of the edition prepared by Westcott and Hort, all of the editions mentioned above were prepared by a single editor--and, in fact, in many respects Westcott and Hort shared the same text-critical views. In the second half of the twentieth century, however, and for the first time in the history of New Testament scholarship, a critical edition of the Greek New Testament was prepared by an international and interconfessional committee of textual scholars. Brought together in 1955 by the American Bible Society, the committee comprised (in alphabetical order) Kurt Aland of Muenster, Matthew Black of St. Andrews, Bruce Metzger of Princeton, Arthur Voeoebus, formerly of Tartu, Estonia, and later of Maywood, Illinois, and Allen Wikgren of Chicago. After four years of work with the Committee, Voeoebus, feeling the pressure of other duties, resigned from the Committee, and his place was taken several years later by Carlo M. Martini, S.J., of Rome.

In keeping with its distinctive purpose of providing for students and for Bible translators throughout the world a basic text of the Greek New Testament, the Bible Society's edition was to have the following special features: (1) a critical apparatus restricted for the most part to variant readings significant for translators or necessary for establishing the text; (2) an indication of the relative degree of certainty for each variant adopted as text; (3) a full citation of representative evidence for each variant selected; and (4) a second apparatus giving meaningful differences in punctuation.

After ten years of work that involved five weeks each summer of face-to-face discussions, with private work being done by individuals between committee meetings, the edition was published in 1966.[31] A second and a third edition, published by the United Bible Societies, followed in 1968 and 1975, each involving the correction of minor errors in the text and in the apparatus. A companion volume, providing a summary of the Committee's reasons for adopting one or another variant reading, was published in 1971.[32] Plans are underway for a fourth edition (projected for 1990) which will contain a thorough revision of the textual apparatus, with special emphasis upon evidence from the ancient versions, the "Diatessaron", and the Church Fathers. In addition, the evidence from Greek manuscripts will be carefully checked by direct comparison with manuscript readings. This latter work is being done at the Institut fuer neutestamentliche Textforschung in Muenster/Westphalia.

Over the years, owing to the acquisition of new documentary evidence and the refinement of textual analysis, New Testament scholars have been able to make, here and there, an advance in the attempt to ascertain still more precisely the original text of the New Testament. In all candor, however, it must be acknowledged that such advances have been made only because of what our predecessors have achieved. In the field of textual criticism, as elsewhere, one is reminded of the saying attributed to the twelfth-century philosopher, Bernard of Chartres:

> We are like dwarfs, sitting on the shoulders of giants, in order that we may see things more numerous and more distant than they could see, not, certainly, by reason of the sharpness of our own vision or the tallness of our bodies, but because we are lifted and raised on high by the greatness of the giants.[33]

ENDNOTES

1. *New Solutions of New Testament Problems* (Chicago, 1927), and "The Editio Princeps of Paul," *Journal of Biblical Literature*, 64 (1945): 193-204. The fact that the book of Acts nowhere mentions that Paul wrote any epistles apparently seemed unimportant to Goodspeed. On this point, see the comments by John Knox, "Acts and the Pauline Letter Corpus," *Studies in Luke-Acts*, ed. by Leander E. Keck and J. Louis Martyn (New York, 1966): 279-87.

2. *Philemon Among the Letters of Paul* (Chicago, 1935; 2nd ed.1959), esp. ch. 5.

3. *Einleitung in die Schriften des Neuen Testaments; I. Die Briefe des Paulus und Schriften des Paulinismus* (Guetersloh, 1978).

4. "Die Entstehung des Corpus Paulinum," *Neutestamentliche Entwuerfe* (Munich, 1979): 302-50.

5. For statistics on Greek manuscripts of the New Testament, see Kurt and Barbara Aland, *Der Text des Neuen Testaments* (Stuttgart, 1982), p. 92.

6. Edited by Frederic G. Kenyon, *The Chester Beatty Biblical Papyri*...; Fasc. iii Supplement, *Pauline Epistles* (London, 1936).

7. For a critical study of the transmission of selected epistles, see G. Zuntz, *The Text of the Epistles; a Disquisition upon the Corpus Paulinum* (London, 1953).

8. For a recent discussion of the evidence in Justin, see Metzger, *The Canon of the New Testament, its Origin, Development, and Significance* (Oxford, 1987), pp. 143-8.

9. Edited by Carl H. Kraeling, *A Greek Fragment of Tatian's Diatessaron from Dura* (London, 1935). For a survey of the extensive research on Tatian's Diatessaron as transmitted in secondary versions, see Metzger, *The Early Versions of the New Testament; Their Origin, Transmission, and Limitations* (Oxford, 1977), pp. 10-36.

10. For fuller information, see the chapter "Special Features of Biblical Manuscripts" in Metzger, *Manuscripts of the Greek Bible, an Introduction to Greek Palaeography* (New York and Oxford, 1981), pp. 33-48.

11. The most recent study of the Euthalian materials is by L. Charles Willard, "A Critical Study of the Euthalian Apparatus," Ph.D. dissertation, Yale University, 1970.

12. For the organization of the contents of Greek lectionaries, reference may be made to Metzger, "Greek Lectionaries and a Critical Edition of the Greek New Testament," in *Die alten Uebersetzungen des Neuen Testaments, die Kirchenvaeterzitate und Lektionare,* ed. by Kurt Aland (Berlin, 1972), pp. 479-97. For instances of the influence of lectionary manuscripts on the text of non-lectionary manuscripts, see Metzger, *The Saturday and Sunday Lessons from Luke in the Greek Gospel Lectionary* (Chicago, 1944), pp. 14-18.

13. See Robert Devreesse, I*ntroduction a létude des manuscripts grecs* (Paris, 1954), pp. 197f.

14. For information about the several sequences of the gospels, see Appendix II in Metzger's *The Canon of the New Testament: Its Origin, Development, and Significance* (Oxford, 1987).

15. See especially A.M. Friend, Jr., "The Portraits of the Evangelists in Greek and Latin Manuscripts," *Art Studies* 5 (1927):115-47; 7 (1929): 3-29.

16. What is not as well known is that the name of Gutenberg's father was Gensfleisch ("Gooseflesh") and that in adult life Johannes preferred to be known by his mother's maiden name, Gutenberg.

17. Moveable bronze types made from molds were used in Korea a half century before they were used in Europe, but there is no evidence that the European invention was not independent; see Pow-key Sohn, *Early Korean Typography,* new ed. (Seoul, 1982), pp. 126-59.

18. See Richard P. Breadon, "The First Book Printed in Greek," *Bulletin of the New York Public Library,* 51 (1947), pp. 586-592; also Robert Proctor, *The Printing of Greek in the Fifteenth Century* (Oxford, 1900) and Victor Scholderer, Greek Printing Types 1465-1927 (London, 1927).

19. For the story of the making of this famous Polyglot Bible, see Basil Hall's monograph, *The Great Polyglot Bibles* (San Francisco, 1966), part of which is condensed in his essay, "The Trilingual College of San Ildefonso and the Making of the complutensian Polyglot Bible," *Studies in Church History,* 5 (Leiden, 1969):114-46. Of the original 600 copies, the locations of 97 are known today; see Mariano Revilla Rico, *La Poliglota de Alcala, estudio historico-critico* (Madrid, 1917). Cf. also J.H. Bentley, "New Light on the Editing of the Complutensian New Testament," *Bibliotheque d'Humanisme et Renaissance,* 42 (1980), pp. 145-156.

20. Examples cited by Ezra Abbot, in *The Authorship of the Fourth Gospel and other Critical Essays* (Boston, 1888), p. 218, include Acts 9:5, 6; Rom. 7:6; 2 Cor. 1:6; 1 Pet. 3:20; Rev. 1:9, 11; 2:3, 20, 24; 3:2; 5:10, 14; 15:3; 16:5; 17:8, 16; 18:2.

21. For a magisterial edition, with introduction and explanatory notes, see Henk Jan de Jonge, *Desiderii Erasmi Roterodami, Apologia respondens ad ea quae Iacobus Lopis Stunica taxaverat in prima duntaxat Novi Testamenti aeditione* (Amsterdam, 1983). See also de Jonge, "Erasmus and the Comma Johanneum," *Ephemerides theologicae lovanienses*, 56 (1980), pp. 380-389.

22. For a detailed list of slight divergencies among subsequent editions of the Greek New Testament, see Ezra Abbot "De editionibus Novi Testamenti Graece in versuum quos dicunt distinctione inter se discrepantibus," in Caspar Rene Gregory's Prolegomena, being vol. 3 of Tischendorf's *Novum Testamentum Graece*, ed. Octava (Leipzig, 1884), pp. 167-182; an English translation is in Abbot, *op.cit.*, pp. 464-477.

23. *Textum erqo habes, nunc ab omnibus receptum; in quo nihil immutatum aut corruptum damus.* The author of this Latin preface, as de Jonge has detected, was in all probability none other than the current University Librarian, the learned Daniel Heinsius (H.J. de Jonge, *Daniel Heinsius and the Textus Receptus of the New Testament*...[Leiden, 1971]).

24. For a comprehensive list of several hundred editions of the Textus Receptus, classified in accord with minor differences of text and typography, see Eduard Reuss, *Bibliotheca Novi Testamenti Graeci*... (Brunswick, 1872).

25. For a little known edition by a learned printer, see "William Bowyer's Contribution to New Testament Textual Criticism," in Metzger's *Chapters in the History of New Testament Textual Criticism* (Leiden, 1963), pp. 155-60.

26. Johann Jakob Griesbach, *Novum Testamentum Graece*, Ed. Sec. Vol. 1 (Halle/London: 1796), pp. LIXSV.

27. *The New Testament in the Original Greek*, [volume 2], *Introduction* [and] *Appendix* (Cambridge, 1881).

28. *Die Schriften des Neuen Testaments in ihrer aeltesten erreichbaren Textgestalt hergestellt auf Grund ihrer Textgeschichte*, I. Teil, *Untersuchungen* (Berlin, 1902-10); II. Teil, *Text mit Apparat* (Goettingen, 1913).

29. For an assessment of the limitations and deficiencies of von Soden's edition, see Metzger, *The Text of the New Testament, its Transmission, Corruption, and Restoration*, 2nd ed. (Oxford, 1968), pp. 141-3.

30. The text of the United Bible Societies' third edition (see below) was adopted by Aland for the 26th edition of the Nestle (now Nestle-Aland) *Novum Testamentum Graece* (Stuttgart, 1979).

31. *The Greek New Testament* (London, 1966).

32. *A Textual Commentary on the Greek New Testament*, prepared by Bruce M. Metzger (London, 1971).

33. Cf. F. E. Guyer, "The Dwarf on the Giant's Shoulders," *Modern Language Notes*, 45 (1930):. 398-402.

2

IMAGINATIVE PARTICIPATION IN PARABLE INTERPRETATION

By George Shillington

Some parts of the Scriptures have received greater attention than others in the life and ministry of the church. And of those parts none has been put to greater use in the teaching of the church than the parables of Jesus. There is something very compelling about a parable-story, something that draws the reader or hearer into its world. But in the case of the parables of Jesus, no sooner are we captivated by the drama of the story than we want to modify its world of meaning. We feel the need to do so, I think, because the world of the parable that seems to line up with our own world at first glance, takes a turn out of our world, beckoning us all the while to follow if we dare.[1] But following is not an easy matter when it comes to the parables of Jesus; hence the urge, unconscious almost, to alter "the turn" in a direction that we can follow. This tendency to make the movement of the story fit our under-standing of how it should move is demonstrated in the way the church has used the parables of Jesus in sermons and commentaries throughout its history.[2]

We can be grateful for the modern interest in "story", and the concomitant investigation of the parables of Jesus.[3] One could say that the power of the parables of Jesus is being rediscovered in our own time, and in such a way that some interpreters are now beginning to create parables from within their own horizon to project an image of another way, another world; in short, to signal the inbreaking of the kingdom of God in our time.

My primary intention in this chapter is to promote an audience-response approach to the parables of Jesus in keeping with the form and thrust of the parables themselves. But I hope to do so with sufficient caution, recognizing the ever present tendency in parable interpretation to blunt the sharp edge of the parable to accommodate the world of thought and life into which we as interpreters have been socialized, often quite unwittingly. More pointedly, I am here proposing to serious interpreters of the parables of Jesus that they participate as fully as possible in the lifeblood of the parable before attempting to weave its "meaning" into another form of speech, namely a sermon with the standard introduction, three points and conclusion. By participating imaginatively in the parable, by allowing its mood and movement and drama and characters to take hold of our wills and emotions, we encounter the paradoxical kingdom of God, the kingdom for which we yearn but are not ready to receive on its terms.[4]

It may help to focus the thrust of the discussion more sharply to begin with an overview of the history of the interpretation of the parables of Jesus with particular emphasis on the present century.

Directions in Parable Interpretation

The church has had to learn to live with the parables of Jesus. Strange as that may sound, it has to be said. Parables are memorable and inviting; but parables are also puzzling, even shattering. Yet it was by means of the puzzling parable, above after all, that Jesus proclaimed the good news of the inbreaking of the kingdom of God.

Jesus presented the parables in oral form to an audience of Palestinian Jewish people. The disciples remembered them and passed them down to the post-Easter community of believers. Eventually the Synoptic Evangelists (Matthew, Mark and Luke) incorporated them into the context of their Gospels.[5] Even before the end of the first century of Christian witness in the world the parables were already being subjected to a kind of manageable interpretation that was to take hold and last for more than fifteen hundred years.

Allegorical interpretation of Scripture had been adopted by Jewish leaders even before the first century CE.[6] It was advocated, for example, by Philo, a Hellenistic Jewish philosopher of Alexandria, as the only appropriate method by which to interpret the Jewish Scriptures.[7] And the Christian church, living as it did in the midst of a Hellenistic environment, found the allegorical method ready to hand for the interpretation of the parables of Jesus.

Allegorical interpretation seeks a meaning beyond the literal form of the text, a "hidden" meaning available only to those whose spiritual insight, purportedly, has been enlightened by education and the grace of God. Allegorization paid little attention to the history associated with the text, cared only slightly about actual characterization in the narrative and used the words merely, together with some details, as pointers to a "deep" meaning that an ordinary reading of the text would miss completely. Why did the church adopt and develop such a method? How did it serve a purpose in the life of the church?

The church began to use the allegorical approach to the parables as it sought to bring the teaching of Jesus into new situations in the life of the church in the world. This approach accommodated the parables to the contemporary concerns facing the church on its march through the conflicts of the ages. Moreover, we should not be too quick to condemn the method to death, at least not before we pay attention to the church's quest to hear the voice of Jesus speaking anew through the interpreters to the contemporary concerns of the community of believers.[8] What other options did the church of those early years have? How else could it make sense of the parables told so many years earlier in the temple period of Palestinian Judaism, and directed as they were to issues of that time and situation? Efforts to take the literal reading seriously failed to speak pertinently to the vital issues of society and church. Allegorization, then, was the instrument by which the message of Jesus in the parables was brought to life again in the new and changing circumstances of the church in the world.

Nevertheless, we cannot revert naively to the allegorical approach of the interpreters from another time. We cannot afford simply to recapture in our time the interpretive mode of Irenaeus of the second century who interpreted the parable of the laborers in the vineyard[9] in terms of three periods of world history. The first workers are the beginning of the created world, the second the old covenant, and the third the ministry of Christ. Nor can we become again an Origen[10] of the third century who took the same parable to mean entirely different periods, five in all: the first shift of workers is the period of people from creation to Noah, the second from Noah to Abraham, and the third from Abraham to Moses, the fourth from Moses to Joshua, and the fifth from Joshua to Christ. The owner of the vineyard in Origen's allegorical rendering is God and the denarius-wage is salvation. Nor yet again can we imitate Augustine of the fourth/fifth century who provided even more elaborate allegorical embellishments.[11]

This way of dealing with the parables held sway in the church's teaching until the Reformation. And even with the biting critique of the Reformers against the method, allegorization persisted into the early twentieth century. But the work of the Reformers, of Martin Luther especially, helped diminish the stronghold that allegorization had in the hermeneutics of the church.[12] Luther criticized the earlier allegorists severely, calling them "clerical jugglers performing monkey tricks."[13] Interestingly enough, Luther himself fell prey to the influence of allegorization, apparently without realizing it. Of the parable of the great supper Luther says that in it we find the gospel is preached and published throughout the world, but few receive and embrace it. Supper in the parable, so he says, means the rich and sumptuous feast which God made through Christ in the gospel.[14] Luther's interpretation may not be quite as elaborate as those of earlier allegorists, but the kind of interpretation illustrated here with the parable of the great supper can hardly be called by any other name than allegorization.

A critical turning point in the interpretation of the parables came at the end of the nineteenth century with the publication of Adolf Juelicher's two volumes under the title, *Die Gleichnisreden Jesu.*[15] Juelicher, in condemning the allegorical approach to the parables, set forth the thesis that a parable of Jesus has one point, and only one point to make. This was an important step away from allegorization of the parables, but Juelicher's conclusion about the nature of the single message of the parable reflected the thinking of theologians and biblical scholars of the time.[16] The idea that Jesus was a great moral teacher in his time was widespread, and it is not surprising to find Juelicher proposing that each parable contains a moral maxim that applies to people in every age.

In 1912 Juelicher found a critic in Paul Fiebig, a rabbinic scholar.[17] Fiebig insisted that Jesus' parables were spoken as allegories and were intended to be interpreted as such. Juelicher ignored the Aramaic background of Jesus in favor of an Aristotelian one which would have been foreign to Jesus. The rabbis told stories similar to those of Jesus, and they contained allegorical elements without question. So also the parables of Jesus, according to Fiebig.

If Fiebig's assessment should be correct--that the parables of Jesus were first spoken as allegories--then certainly they should be interpreted allegorically. But his judgment in this respect fails to account for the distinctive use of the parable in the ministry of Jesus as reflected by the Synoptic Evangelists.

The next major effort to understand the parables of Jesus came in 1935 with the publication of C. H. Dodd's book, *The Parables of the Kingdom*[18] Dodd, following Schweitzer,[19] believed that eschatology was central to Jesus' ministry, and that the parables should be interpreted accordingly. Jesus told parables about the coming of the kingdom in his own time, that the kingdom was being realized in his calling people of all classes to renewed faith in God. And the call came in the form of parable primarily. In drawing attention to realized eschatology in the teaching of Jesus, Dodd also sounded a hermeneutical note that had been muted since the parables first appeared in manuscript, namely that interpreters must ask what the parable would have meant on the lips of Jesus in the presence of a Palestinian Jewish audience.

Not long after Dodd's publication in English, Joachim Jeremias published a book that has since become a classic in the field, *Die Gleichnisse Jesu (ET The Parables of Jesus).*[20] His principal concern was to cast the parables in the Aramaic pattern of thought they must have had when they were first spoken by Jesus. His aim was to hear them just as they were heard first in the particular situation of conflict in Palestine. The assumption underlying this aim was that the parables had undergone a degree of transformation by the time they were finally incorporated into the context of the Synoptic Gospels. Having noted ten laws of transformation, Jeremias concludes his chapter on the "the setting" of the parables with a pastoral, if not emotional, tone thus:

> These ten laws of transformation are ten aids to the recovery of the original meaning of the parables of Jesus. They will help us lift in some measure here and there the veil, sometimes thin, sometimes almost impenetrable, which has fallen upon the parables of Jesus. How great the gain if we succeed in rediscovering here and there behind the veil the features of the Son of Man! Everything depends on his word. To meet with him can alone give power to our preaching.[21]

Whether the task of returning to "the living voice of Jesus" can be achieved fully remains a question. We have the *texts* of the Synoptics. That is all we have of the actual living voice of Jesus of Nazareth. From these texts we can have an understanding of what Jesus would have meant in the telling of the parable, and so far as I can see we shall have to content ourselves with an on-going understanding of Jesus as we find him in the context of the Gospels.

Jeremias also grouped the parables, as did Dodd before him, under several headings, as if to suggest that any one of the parables may carry one of the themes (e.g. "now is the day of salvation", "God's mercy for sinners", "the great assurance").[22] This result is not altogether satisfactory. The parables do not fit easily into categories of thought. Rather, they present various angles of vision, one could say, on the breakthrough of the kingdom of God. The task facing the interpreter and preacher is to get into the appropriate position to catch the vision at that moment of the breakthrough.

Dan Via, Junior (1967) approached the parables from a strictly literary perspective.[23] Influenced by certain theories of language structure developed by anthropologists, Via sought for the meaning of the parable in the inter-relation of the various literary/linguistic parts. While the focus of Via's work was needed, it tended to play down the importance of historical under-standing in the interpretation of the parables. By comparison, Robert Funk,[24] who has likewise demonstrated remarkable insight into the nature of lan-guage and literary creation, recaptures with utmost diligence the setting of Jesus' telling of the parables, the audience of the first telling, etc.

On another front, and with persuasively creative insight, John Dominic Cros-san (1973)[25] took serious account of previous work. His vision in writing his book, *In Parables*, was to open up the parables of Jesus for a freer exis-tentialist interpretation. His paradigm for the interpretation of parables is striking. He writes:

> The basic attack of Jesus is on idolatry of time and that this is the center whence issued forth what Yeats called that "Galilean turbulence" which set Jesus against all the major religious options of his contemporaries.... The one who plans, projects, and programs a future, even and especial-ly if one covers the denial of finitude by calling it God's future disclosed or discloseable to oneself, is in idolatry against the sovereign freedom of God's advent to create one's time and establish one's historicity. This is the central challenge of Jesus.... In their totality then, the parables proclaim the kingdom's temporality and the three simultaneous modes of its presence.[26]

Crossan claims there are three kinds of parables and all of them relate in some

way to this central challenge: 1) parables of advent, 2) parables of reversal, 3) parables of action. All of them, in one way or another, shatter the constructs of life we take for granted; to use Crossan's categories, they shatter the very concept "world."[27]

Some interpreters have resorted to a psychoanalytical model for understanding the parables of Jesus. Mary Ann Tolbert (1979),[28] for example, applied psychoanalytic hermeneutics to the parable of the prodigal son. The prodigal represents the id of Freudian theory, the elder brother the superego, and the father the ego uniting the two in appropriate psychological balance.[29] One senses here that we have an up-dated allegorical interpretation, and indeed Tolbert speaks favorably of the allegorists, recognizing in her own efforts a kinship with them.

One final perspective deserves recognition, and could prove helpful in discovering the significance of the parables of Jesus for our own time. David Granskou[30] pinpointed an element in the parables that had been somewhat neglected. He calls it prophetic irony. Granskou cites three components that should be kept in focus in the interpretation of the parables of Jesus. One is humor. As he remarks, "There is a laughter which leads to repentance and change just as there is a cry of sorrow which leads to new life."[31] This ironic element cannot go unnoticed as it often has been. Perhaps it is in this prophetic irony (or humor) that we are confronted with that "turn" we mentioned earlier. If we miss the irony we may also miss the turn in the road and the kingdom to which it leads. Another component, says Granskou, is "open-ended communication".[32] The parables are conversational; we can enter into dialogue with them. And each time we meet them they prompt us to ask new questions of them. A final characteristic of the prophetic aspect of the parables is their situational character. They speak to concrete realities in the life of the community.

From the foregoing it becomes evident that parables do not yield their meaning immediately to the reader. They baffle the interpreter at times, and this should not discourage us from reading them and using them in ministry. On the contrary, we may have a clue to their usefulness in the very fact that they are baffling. Interpreters want to say something *about* the parable; the parable simply wants to be heard, and in the hearing, in the participation, (not in the explanation) we sense the call of the kingdom. We need to test our signals of hearing, let us say, lest we miss the sound of the inbreaking kingdom. We could begin by asking what a parable is.

The Form "Parable"

Form does matter. To treat form (or structure) as if it has no inherent relation to content (or meaning) is to run the risk of falling prey to a hermeneutical error similar to that of the earlier allegorists.[33] Form and content are linked inextricably in literature, and biblical literature is no exception. The parable is a distinct form and should not be confused with other forms. A parable is not an allegory. It is not a letter, and not an argument within a letter. It is not a sermon, a note worth making when we incorporate an interpretation of a parable into the structure of a sermon. Neither is it a proverb, although some of the parables have become proverbial, exemplified recently in the command of my brother as we motored past a steaming roadside vehicle: "Be a good Samaritan and pull over", he said. Nor is the parable simply an example story, an illustration of good moral sense, as in Aesop's "Fables."

The term in English is a transliteration of the Greek *parabolé*, a word used by the translators of the LXX to render the meaning of the Hebrew *mashal*.[34] Both the Hebrew and the Greek words are open-ended. They were used to designate a simple story, but also a riddle and a proverb. In the case of the parables of Jesus, perhaps the clue to determining what is meant by the term *parabolé* in the Synoptic Gospels is in their own statements about the function of this form of speech. We shall cite Mark to illustrate:

> With many such parables he spoke the word to them, as
> they were able to hear it; he did not speak to them without
> a parable, but privately to his own disciples he explained
> everything (Mark 4:33f).

This statement follows the explanation of the parable of the sower. The implication is that parables are not self-explanatory; they are therefore more in keeping with the idea of riddle or puzzle. They reveal and hide simultaneously. Hence the puzzlement.

A parable is a kind of story, but not an historical narrative, not even a narrative illustration of history. In a sense a parable is a comparison, a close comparison; it is a mental image of specific history. In John Dominic Crossan's words:

> The parables of Jesus seek to draw one into the kingdom,
> and they challenge us to act and to live from the gift which
> is experienced therein. But we do not want parables. We

want precepts and we want programs. We want *good* precepts and we want *sensible* programs. We are frightened by the lonely silences within the parables. We want them to tell us exactly what to do and they refuse to answer. They make us face the problem of the grounding of ethics and we want only to dicuss the logic of ethics.[35]

The parables do answer, in fact, but they do so in a way we least expect, in a way that evokes wonder, surprise, and quite possibly anger. They confront the participant/reader/hearer starkly with the condition of that person's own fractured world. Parables expose the fractures we have learned to accept, fractures that have simply become part of the scheme of things. The scheme bursts open in the parable like old wineskins when new wine ferments inside. I am convinced that the critical jolt of the parable was more pronounced in its telling-hearing than in its reading-hearing, and more pronounced still than in its interpreted state in a well-crafted sermon. The sermon thus crafted tends to muffle the power of the parable-form. I am more and more convinced that we must learn to tell parables of our own, perhaps within sermons, to our modern congregations on the model of the parables of Jesus.

C. H. Dodd's description of the parable form may help to clarify the parameters of the model, should we try to emulate it.

The parable is a metaphor or simile drawn from nature or common life, arresting the hearer by its vividness or strangeness, and leaving the mind in sufficient doubt about its precise application to tease it into active thought.[36]

I have not found a better description of the parable form. The metaphorical image is drawn from common life, but it is not quite common in the end. And this is the "tease." True, the hearer's attention is arrested by the vividness, but the strange element amidst the common, catches the reader/hearer off guard and throws the imagination into some confusion about how to act out the implications in life. But the impact is forceful, unforgettable, even painful at times.

Some parables are short imaginative flashes, not narratives. The parable of the so-called "salt" of the earth, is an example. But even here the sharp point of the metaphor can be missed if our hermeneutical hearing is impaired. Is the "salt" sodium chloride we use to season food? Or is it a fertilizing, life-promoting substance used on "the land" rather than the table? I think it is the latter. On this hearing the various parts of the parable hold together meaningfully. But even then, we can be sidetracked if we focus on one part of the parable, the part we like, the part we can live with. For example, I could construct a sermon (I did in fact),[37] extending the significance out of first-century Palestinian Judaism, to followers of Jesus in our own time who are fertilizing, life-bearing agents in a sterile society. But would that sermonizing actually capture the impact of the parable as it was first told by Jesus and heard on Palestinian *holy land*? I must confess otherwise. The turn, even in this short parable, comes at the end after the probing question on how the lost potency of the chemical substance could be restored: "It is no longer good for anything except to be thrown out and trodden under the foot of men" (Matt. 5:13). No need to explain. Think of it in context. Think of the religious condition in Palestinian Judaism from the perspective of the ministry of Jesus. Imagine it, shall we say, and in so imagining we are also caught, not knowing where we stand. Has our potency also been lost? If so how shall it be restored? But it is more manageable to talk about the qualities of salt, and then to moralize in general about how we all should be active agents of good in the world. Where then is the parable?

Now if the short parables present difficulty to the reader and preacher, how much more the longer narrative ones. To the latter we must now turn our attention more specifically.

Imaginative Participation in the Narrative World
Parables are verbal images of reality. They project a world beyond the ordinary, yet one not altogether removed from it. Interpretation of a parable has to be imaginative. By that I mean the reader must enter into the world of the parable before any responsible translation of the parable's significance can be captured for our own situation in the world. Imaginative *participation* means really entering into the literary fabric of the narrative, moving along with its every up and down, feeling its curves, laughing and crying with its characters. In short, it means allowing ouselves to be caught by the drama and drawn into the world of the kingdom of God. It will mean going to the marriage supper or not going; it will mean being hired at the beginning of the day or at the end of the day; it will mean being beaten and left half dead; it will mean walking away with the prodigal and returning, or standing outside with the elder brother as he utters our words for us. And we can do it all in our minds, if we would but permit ouselves the risk of being captured by the new world of the kingdom of God.

There can be no guarantee that our feelings will not get hurt in the process as we live within the dynamics of the parable. The world of the narrative parables of Jesus is a strange new world, puzzling, moving, surprising.

Imaginative participation does not mean that our minds are free to roam at will. There can be response, even reaction; there must be such in fact. The reaction could be adverse or congenial, rejecting the kingdom as projected in the parable or accepting it. But the shape and direction of the narrative cannot be changed. We are not free to advise the owner of the vineyard to pay more wages to the workers who worked more hours than other workers. The image in our minds comes under the control of the narrative structure of the parable, not the converse. Of course responsible interpreters would not actually attempt to change the phenomena of the words or phrases in the text as we read. But in our imagining, in our receiving of the signals from the text, we can easily make mental shifts, use other language forms, not at all defiantly, but perhaps defensively to shield our person from the unfamiliar other world of the parabolic kingdom of God. Imaginative participation in the parables, to be authentic, involves making our personal beings vulnerable, open to the new, surprising realm of meaning that Jesus brings.

Participation in the action imaged in the narrative parables encounters other obstacles as well. We read the parables from within an historical setting quite alien to the setting of their first telling and hearing.[38] The features of the original setting, or even of the setting in any one of the Synoptics, is removed from us. Thus removed, we tend to treat the features that are foreign to us— but native to the parable-setting—in a distanced, academic manner. To illustrate, the fact that the first audience was a Palestinian Jewish one with all the attending sociological, religious and political implications is observed using all the necessary critical apparatus for the investigation. The procedure passes as an objective handling of the data of the text, an idea that is applauded for its alignment with the scientific age in which we live.[39] And this should be the case, no doubt, but it does not necessarily lead to imaginative participation in the thought world of the text. Imaginative participation demands what Bernard Lonergan calls "a conversion."[40] It will mean moving consciously into the pattern of life that we perceive in the structure of the parable, identifying, as far as we are able, with the audience who first felt the impact of the parable. Granted, North American Christians cannot become first century Jewish people in Palestine and actually feel as they must have felt when they heard the parables on their soil. But I believe our efforts to do so can be improved beyond what we have done so far.

For example, in the parable of "the good Samaritan," was the man who was beaten and left to die in the ditch a Jewish man or any man? What assumption would the audience make? It would hardly occur to them that he was anything other than Jewish.[41] He is one of them; they identify with him as one of them; they expect one of their own leaders in the story to stop and help. Surprise! A Samaritan stops and lavished compassion on the Jewish victim. A Samaritan! How would the Jewish listener have felt in the middle of the story when the Samaritan was introduced as the one who brings grace and mercy to the broken Jewish man in the ditch? How does the parable challenge the Jewish attitude toward outcast Samaritans? To answer these kinds of questions from the parables (and there are many others as well) we must try to think and feel with the Jewish audience who first heard them. I think we shall find that we are also caught as they were: not ready for the grace of the kingdom on its terms. The grace of God comes in ways we do not expect and do not want. But the kingdom does come and its coming calls forth a response.

Element of Response

Part of parabolic communication (a major part in my opinion) involves an element of response. Responses occur within the narrative itself, but the listeners also respond personally with the respondents internal to the parable structure. In some parables the listeners are so tied in with the structure of the parable that they become co-creators of the parable.[42] Perhaps the best example of this aspect of the parable-form comes from the Old Testament in II Samuel 12. The prophet Nathan tells a parable to David who had committed adultery with Bathsheba and had murdered her husband Uriah. At the climax of the story, when the rich sheep owner has taken the one little lamb of the poor man, David enters into the story, angry at the injustice, and pronounces the judgment of death upon the offender. Nathan returns with the indictment: "You are the man." What irony!

In one way or another the parables of Jesus reflect this mode of audience response. His Jewish audience, who listened in on the story of the good Samaritan (perhaps priests, levites, lawyers, ordinary Jewish people), are asked to decide: "Which of these three, do you think, proved neighbor to the man who fell among robbers?" There is no escaping the implications of this inevitable response. Nothing more needs to be said, no moralizing, no allegorizing. The specific point is made, the point that really needs to be made in that setting.

The point is always specific. Jesus does not teach a new morality in the parables. Nor are the parables designed to pronounce truth where it is not known. They elicit response in relation to a specific situation where morality is well known but inoperative in the actuality of living within specific human relationships.[43]

Consider, for example, the parable of the two debtors, recorded in Luke 7:41-43. The creditor forgave the one who owed much and the one who owed little. Then comes the question in which the respectable pharisee is drawn into the unfolding of the parable: "Which of them will love him more?" And the pharisee is bound to answer as the parable dictates: "The one, I suppose, to whom he forgave more." The parable did not teach the pharisee a lesson on love and forgiveness in general. He knew the principle of forgiveness quite well, as any self-respecting pharisee would. But he was not able to see how the dynamics of the principle of forgiveness operate in the specific situations of his own life, in his own country, from his own religion. Here again the pharisee becomes a participant in the plot of the parable, like it or not, and in the process has his own standard of righteousness turned on himself in judgment.

The same kind of response mode of the parable-form can be detected in other parables as well, where the response does not turn on an explicit rhetorical question. The parable of the prodigal son, for example, ends with an invitation to the elder son to rejoice with the forgiven prodigal. Implicit in that ending is a question that the hearer has to ask imaginatively: Who has the prodigal attitude and action in the end? Again, this parable is not simply a parable of grace in general, but one that challenges the status quo morality of the social and religious establishment of that particular time and place.

In another way the parable of the workers in the vineyard (Matt. 20:1-6) seizes the response of the listeners, draws them into the attitude and action, and summons a response in relation to the responses given in the narrative. We need to get into the line to pick up the wage for the work done. The ones who worked only one hour are paid first. They receive one denarius. They receive the wage gladly. And there is no complaint from the others in the line; that is worth noting in the narrative. Next come the three-hour workers, then the six-hour, then the nine-hour ones. And there is no complaint until the twelve-hour workers come to the table and are paid the same as the others before them. The complaint is not about the injustice of paying the nine-hour workers the same wage paid to the one-hour workers. They are concerned only about the injustice done to themselves as a special category. It is in relation to these first workers, the complainers, that the audience is expected to respond. Moreover, the parable is not merely highlighting grace over against merit, as Jeremias proposed. It directs the hearers to ask: Do the twelve-hour workers really exhibit justice and grace?

To conclude, we can be thankful that the parables of Jesus have become the focus of much research in recent times.[44] Our understanding has been enhanced by the results of the various avenues of investigation. Attention to the accomplishments in parable-interpretation and awareness of the pitfalls can only facilitate our efforts to bring the parables to life in our time and situation. The particular plea that was made throughout the discussion called for an imaginative participation in the plot of the parable, not merely an objective statement about the structure, the characters, the situation of the time, the identity of the hearers, the context in the Synoptics, etc. I mean by this that we cannot be satisfied with *a statement about* the parable. The statement about the parable has to become transformed into *a response to* the implications of the parable. In other words, if we expect to come to an understanding of meaning embedded in the parable-form we have to join the hearers, imagine what it would be like to be a Jew who confronts the grace of the kingdom of God in the person of a Samaritan; what it would be like to be faced with the question put to the pharisee about the two debtors. Imagination, in the sense in which I have used the term throughout, calls for a first-person kind of involvement. It happens often in interpretation that the interpreter either ignores the idea of a hearer in a particular setting or treats the first hearer as a third party, someone to talk about, even to criticize.

In the end we may decide to create some parables of our own, not to abandon imaginative participation in the dynamics of the parables of Jesus, but to enhance the same. But in our parable, character figures will not be a Samaritan or a pharisee or a tax-collector; the wage will not be a denarius; the containers of wine will not be animal skins. Our parable, to be modeled after the parables of Jesus, will exchange the characters and other narrative elements of the parable to conform to the contemporary concerns of our church and society and world. If interpreters and preachers should choose this option, they should also be aware that the creation of parables after the manner of the parable-form of Jesus in the Synoptic Gospels holds out a great challenge and carries a great risk. But I am convinced both are worth taking.

ENDNOTES

1. See Robert Funk's section on "The Narrative Parables: The Birth of a Language Tradition", *Parables and Presence*. (Philadelphia: Fortress Press, 1982), pp. 19-28.

2. Cf. David Granskou, "The History of Parable Interpretation", *Preaching on the Parables*, (Philadelphia: Fortress Press, 1972), pp. 8-53.

3. As in this sampling of modern publications: Charles H. Dodd, *The Parables of the Kingdom*, (New York: Charles Scribner's Sons, 1960); Joachim Jeremias, *The Parables of Jesus*, (New York: Charles Scribner's Sons, 1972); idem, *Rediscovering the Parables* (1966); A. M. Hunter, *Interpreting the Parables*, (London: SCM Press, 1960); David Granskou, *Preaching on the Parables*; John Dominic Crossan, *In Parables*, (New York: Harper and Row, 1972); Robert Funk, *Parables and Presence*; Mary Ann Tolbert, *Perspectives on the Parables*, (Philadelphia: Fortress Press, 1979); Kenneth E. Bailey, *Poet and Peasant: A Literary Cultural Approach to the Parables in Like*, (Grand Rapids: William B. Eerdmans Publishing Company, 1976).

4. Further on this aspect of Jesus' proclamation of the kingdom of God see Crossan, *In Parables*, pp. 53-78.

5. On the contextualization of parables in Luke see Bailey, *Poet and Peasant*, pp. 79-206.

6. Jeremias, *The Parables of Jesus*, pp. 66-79.

7. See e.g. Philo's treatment of Genesis 2 and 3 in *Legum Allegoria*, II and III, *The Loeb Classical Library*, Vol. 1, (Cambridge: Harvard University Press, 1929), pp. 224-473. "When Philo wished to fashion the Old Testament into something its authors had not intended the allegorical tool lay ready to hand", so Charles K. Barrett, *The New Testament Background: Selected Documents*, (New York: Harper and Row, 1961), p. 180.

8. Acknowledged rightly by Tolbert, *Perspectives*, pp. 62f: "Allegorical interpretation...was the dominant interpretive procedure from the time of Origen to the Enlightenment. It allowed the church...to apply an historically conditioned text to all the detailed and complex circumstances of existence" (p.63).

9. *Against Heresies*, Book IV, xxxvi, 7.

10. Especially Origen's *De Principiis*, 4.2; cf. Archibald M. Hunter's comment on Origen in *Interpreting the Parables*, (London: SCM Press, 1960), p. 25.

11. "The Works of Augustine", in *A Select Library of the Nicene and Post-Nicene Fathers of the Christian Church*, edited by Philip Schaff, (Grand Rapids: Wm. B. Eerdmans Publishing, 1956), pp. 374f.

12. See Robert M. Grant, *A Short History of the Interpretation of the Bible*, (Philadelphia: Fortress Press, 1984), pp. 92-99.

13. Quoted in Hunter, *Interpreting the Parables*, p. 32.

14. Ibid.

15. Adolf Juelicher, *Die Gleichnisreden Jesu*, (Tuebingen: J.C.B. Mohr, 1910).

16. Grant, *Short History*, pp. 110-118; Granskou, *Parables*, pp. 12-16.

17. Paul Fiebig, *Die Gleichnisreden Jesu im Lichte der rabbinischen Gleichnisse des neutestamentlichen Zeitalters*, (Tuebingin: J.C.B. Mohr, 1912). See further discussion in Jack Dean Kingsbury, *The Parables of Jesus in Matthew 13*, (Richmond: John Knox Press, 1969), pp. 3ff.

18. The original work of the 1930s underwent revision in 1961, Charles H. Dodd, *The Parables of the Kingdom*, (New York: Charles Scribner's Sons, 1961).

19. Especially Schweitzer's work, *The Quest of the Historical Jesus*, ET W. Montgomery, (London: Adam and Charles Black, 1954; German 1906).

20. This work has also undergone several revisions, the latest in German in 1970 under the same title.

21. Jeremias, *The Parables*, p. 114.

22. Ibid. pp. 115-229.

23. Dan O. Via, Jr., *The Parables*, (Philadelphia: Fortress Press, 1967).

24. In particular, Robert W. Funk, *Parables and Presence*, pp. 19-54; and his more extensive work on language and interpretation, *Language, Hermeneutic and the Word of God*, (New York: Harper and Row, 1966).

25. John Dominic Crossan, *In Parables: The Challenge of the Historical Jesus*, (San Francisco: Harper and Row, 1973).

26. Ibid., p. 35.

27. Ibid., p. 27.

28. Mary Ann Tolbert, *Perspectives on the Parables: An Approach to Multiple Interpretations*, (Philadelphia: Fortress Press, 1979).

29. Ibid., pp. 93-114.

30. David M. Granskou, *Preaching on the Parables*, (Philadelphia: Fortress Press, 1972).

31. Ibid., p. 42.

32. Ibid., p. 43.

33. "In a literary work form and content, though distinguishable, are inseparable", Tolbert, *Parables*, p. 71.

34. See the discussion on this point in Jeremias, *Parables*, pp. 11-22.

35. Crossan, *Parables*, p. 82.

36. Dodd, *Parables*, p. 5.

37. A sermon delivered at the Canadian Conference of Mennonite Brethren Churches assembled in Saskatoon in 1981.

38. Whether we consider strictly the setting of Jesus behind the Synoptic contexts as in Jeremias, *Parables*, pp. 96-114, or the setting in the given Synoptic Gospel, the circumstances are the same.

39. Cf. J. G. Davies, "Subjectivity and Objectivity in Biblical Exegesis", *Bulletin of the John Rylands University Library of Manchester*, Vol. 66, No. 1 (1983), pp. 44-53.

40. Bernard J. F. Lonergan, *Method in Theology*, (New York: Herder and Herder, 1973), pp. 52, 155, 161, 246.

41. See Funk, *Parables*, pp. 29-34.

42. Observed especially by Granskou, *Preaching*, pp. 42ff.

43. Ibid., p. 58ff.

44. See further on recent developments in approaches in biblical interpretation in Daniel J. Harrington, "Biblical Hermeneutics in Recent Discussion: New Testament", *Religious Studies Review*, Vol. 10, No. 1 (1984): 7-10.

3

DISCERNING WHAT IS BOUND IN HEAVEN:
Loosing and Binding

David Schroeder

The recent use of the ban in the exercise of church discipline has shocked the main line churches, and has raised a whole new set of questions. Those who practice the ban see it as a matter of obedience to the Word of God. They accept Matthew 18:15-20 as the biblical way of dealing with a "brother" who has "sinned against you." The procedures to be followed in such cases are clearly outlined and should be followed. Their attempt to follow these procedures has been seen as misconceived and as simplistic or naive.

Those of us who are shocked by the use of the ban in a free country, have to ask ourselves whether it is not a worse indictment of the church, that it is no longer a moral community. Ethical questions are left untouched for they are considered to be private and personal. Ethical relativism has become the norm, and the practice of the ban is seen as an intrusion into the lives of people, into a sphere of life that is "none of the church's business."

The church that practices the ban is at least seeking to be a moral community; it is saying that some things are right and others are not; it is seeking to assist its members to abide by acceptable Christian norms, and it is making a statement about what it means to be Christian in the modern world. The churches that make no attempt to speak to moral issues and make no overt moral demands on its members, are also communicating a clear message. They are saying that ethics is relativistic; that each person has his or her own understanding of what is right or wrong; and that the church has no right to discipline anyone.

Both of the stated approaches may in fact be extremes, but they raise important questions for us. What is the understanding of God, of Jesus, of the Church and of being Christian, that lies behind the passages of Scripture that refer to functions of loosing and binding? Why did Jesus outline this procedure? How was it understood by those who heard his words, and by the evangelists who recorded them? What are we to make of these passages today? Where does it fit into our understanding of biblical theology? How can we come to terms with the texts in Scripture that define the task of the church in terms of loosing and binding?

The Texts

The texts are basically three: Matthew 16:13-20; Matthew 18:15-20; and John 20:19-23. These passages presuppose the same background of understanding even though they are set in three very different contexts.

Matthew 16:19 : "I will give you [Peter] the keys of the kingdom of heaven, and whatsoever you shall bind on earth shall be bound in heaven, and whatsoever you loose on earth shall be loosed in heaven." [RSV]

This passage is set within the context of the confession of Peter. The revelation has broken through to the disciples that Jesus is in fact the Messiah. They now know and confess that he is the Christ, "The Son of the living God" (cf. Matt. 8:27-30). Jesus affirms that they have come to know this truth through a revelation from God, and not from other humans ("flesh and blood").

This confession that Jesus is the Messiah calls forth Jesus' statement to Peter. "I tell you, you are Peter (*petros*), and on this rock (*petra*) I will build my church, and the powers of death (the gates of hades) shall not prevail against it"(Matt.16:18). Jesus then addresses the above words about "loosing and binding" to Peter. He is given the keys to the kingdom of heaven with the power to loose and to bind.

The confession of Peter in Matthew 16:13 ff. is set in the same context as in the Gospel of Mark, except for the omission of the healing of the blind man

(Mark 8:22-26). Both are preceded by Jesus' statement and warning about the leaven of the Pharisees (Mark 8:14-21; Matthew 16:5-12). Both are followed by Jesus' announcement of his suffering (Mark 8:31-33; Matthew 16:21-23). The strong rebuke to Peter for responding negatively to the announcement of Jesus' suffering, however, is omitted by Matthew. Not only does Matthew omit the incident wherein Jesus rebukes Peter, but gives in its place the bestowal of the keys of the kingdom.

Matthew 18:18: " Truly, I say to you whatever you bind on earth shall be bound in heaven, and whatever you loose on earth shall be loosed in heaven."[RSV]

This passage is obviously related to the Matthew 16:19 passage, but it is given an entirely different context. It is placed in the context of human sin and temptation. Notice the phrases, "Woe to the world for temptations to sin!" (18:7) and "If your brother sins against you" (18:15). It is followed by Jesus' teaching on forgiveness. The power to loose and bind is related very directly to human sin, even sin against a fellow believer. The power received by Peter (Matthew 16:19) to loose and to bind is here seen as exercised, not only by Peter, but by the other apostles as well. The reading is even more general in that it refers to every Christian. The "you" in Matthew 18:15 is singular, and the two or three witnesses (18:16) refer to any fellow Christian. The context indicates that this commission to loose and to bind belong to the church - to individual members and to the corporate fellowship.

John 20:23 :" Receive the Holy Spirit. If you forgive the sins of any, they are forgiven; if you retain the sins of any, they are retained." [RSV]

In one sense this is a different word from the Matthew passages, and stands in an entirely different context. This word is spoken by the resurrected Lord on Easter Sunday. Jesus suddenly appears to the disciples with his "Peace be with you" (20:19). He identifies himself by calling attention to his hands and his side. Once they know who he is, he repeats his word of peace, and gives to them the commission "As the Father sent Me, even so send I you." The word about forgiving and retaining is related directly to the commission of the church in the world. It is as though Jesus confirmed the prayer he prayed to God in the garden, "As thou didst send me into the world, so I have sent them into the world" (John 17:18).

The words "loosing" and "binding" are not used here. This passage speaks of "forgiving" and "retaining" the sins of others. What is remarkable, however, is that in the contexts of both passages in Matthew, the loosing and binding function is related to forgiveness. Note Peter's question in Matthew

18:21 about how many times it is appropriate to forgive. This passage states that the loosing and binding is related to the forgiveness of sin.

The commission is given to all who were then in the room the disciples, certainly, and perhaps some others. It is a commission to all, not only to Peter.

The same context of understanding applies to all three passages. One passage interprets the other. Several things can be highlighted: 1) The disciples seem to know what Jesus means with the "keys to the Kingdom" and with the "loosing" and "binding" injunction bestowed on them. 2) Peter and the disciples receive a place of primacy in the carrying out of the commission Jesus has given them. 3) The loosing and binding function is integral to the task of being the church in the world. 4) Forgiveness is central in the understanding of what it means to loose and bind. 5) In order to loose and to bind the church has to become a community engaged in doctrinal and moral discernment.

Understanding The Basic Terms
It is amazing how the terms that occur in these passages have been understood (or misunderstood). They have been used to advocate the primacy of the Pope, autocratic authority over the church by its leaders, the excommunication of people from the church for disagreeing with the church, and many other similar things. But how are the various terms to be interpreted?

1) It is clear that in Matthew 16:13-20, Peter is the central figure. To him were given the keys of the kingdom of heaven, and he also figures in Jesus' granting of the name *Petros* (Peter) to Simon. The question is, what does Jesus mean when he says "on this rock (*petra*) I will build my church"? Will it be built on Peter or on the foundation rock of the confession that Jesus is the Christ? It is clear that the reference to *Petros* and *petra* is a play on words. It makes sense only if petra refers to Peter. Peter, as an apostle, a sent-one of Christ, is given a special place of significance as the first to confess that Jesus is the Christ. The church is thus built on Peter and the other Apostles for whom he spoke. Thus Paul can say that the church is built on the "foundation of the apostles" (Eph. 2:20 cf. Rev. 21:14).

2) What is meant by the "keys" of the kingdom of heaven?
The biblical references are fairly clear. In Rev. 3:7 Jesus is the chief steward of the house of David in that he has the keys. This calls to mind Isa. 22:22 where the keys to the house of David were given to Eliakim. He became the chief steward. He had the authority, baring none, to open doors and to shut

them. Jesus is clearly the lord of the house. In giving the keys to Peter he is making Peter the chief steward of the house. Peter is to execute the will of the Master. In Matthew 18:18 the same injunction is given to the other apostles, so we must conclude that this special task related to the keys was conferred on all the apostles. Peter represents the apostles in this respect.

3) The words "loose" and "bind" in this context can hardly be understood apart from their background in Judaism. In Judaism it was the Scribes who interpreted the law for the people, i.e. who had the keys. They opened and shut the doors to the Kingdom (Lk.11:52). The terms loose (*luein*) and bind (*dein*) were words that described the Scribes' function and service to the people. They interpreted the meaning of the law. They translated the general commands of the law into the specifics of everyday life. If the law indicated that people ought not to work on the Sabbath, then they had to spell out specifically which works one was permitted (loosed) to do and which works one was obliged (bound) to do. The disciples no doubt understood Jesus to say that they were to take over the function that the Scribes had had in Judaism. They were to be the guardians of the tradition (*paradosis*) about Jesus and to lay the foundation for the church.

The disciples were, however, asked to follow Jesus and to learn from him. Jesus had told them that they were not to function as rabbis in the sense of calling disciples and teaching them in the pattern of the scribes (Matthew 23:8). Jesus himself would remain the teacher. He gave to the disciples the Holy Spirit (John 20:23) and through the Spirit they were to continue to learn from him.

4) What is to be bound? The scribes exegeted the Scriptures and the interpretation agreed on by an authentic majority became binding, and wasconsidered to be ratified in heaven. This was so because they considered their interpretation as true to the law of Moses, which was given by God. But the disciples were not to be rabbis in the same sense. Jesus remains the teacher. What then was a binding word for them?

The translation "whatever you bind on earth shall be bound in heaven" seems to suggest that anything that the disciples would bind on earth would automatically be bound in heaven. Such is not the case, for it would make God subject to human caprice. It is a problem of translation. How is the Greek periphrastic future perfect to be translated? Derritt suggests that the meaning is "shall be (already) bound". This would imply that they are to bind on earth what is already bound in heaven. It could thus not be exercised apart from the revelation of God and the message of the Gospel. It is significant that Jesus remains the teacher, and that we are given the Holy Spirit to discern what is already bound.

Ethical discernment is an essential function of loosing and binding. The will of God needs to be discerned.

The Larger Biblical Pattern
The Acts of God

Loosing and binding constitute what God does. They are related to the character of God and the will of God. These become known to us through the revelation of God to Israel and through Jesus Christ and reveal to us that which is already bound in heaven.

God has revealed His purposes in creation. God created order out of chaos and created all forms of life. Those things, therefore, that sustain the created order, and that support fullness of life, must be seen as already bound in heaven. The beginning of creation tells us something of the end (*telos*) God has in mind for the created order.

The character of God, as a saving and redeeming God is revealed most clearly in the exodus event. The descendants of Abraham were slaves in Egypt. God set them free by God's mighty works. By this Israel knew God to be a loosing, liberating, saving God.

But God did not simply free the people in order to abandon them in the desert. To be set free is not yet to be responsible, or to have chosen what is already bound. To be set free is to have all hindrances and compulsions removed, but they still need to commit themselves to that which promises life. God, therefore, made a covenant with the people He had freed.

God promised to be their God, if they would be God's people. To covenant is to bind. God revealed to the people the will of God by giving them the law. The law indicated which actions would lead to life and which actions would lead to death. God then appealed to the people to bind themselves to life (Deut.30:19).

Through the exodus and the covenant, the people experienced God to be a loosing and binding God. But both the loosing and the binding were such that they might have life in God. Both actions were in the direction of what is already bound.

Jesus, A Pattern for Life

Jesus did the work of God. Jesus manifested the character of God in his earthly ministry. He came to loose and to bind in obedience to God. Jesus saw his commission in the words of Isaiah 61:1-2:

> The Spirit of the Lord God is upon me, to bring good tidings to the afflicted; he has sent me to bind up thebrokenhearted, to proclaim liberty to the captives, and the opening of the prison to those who are bound; to proclaim the year of the Lord's favor, and the day of vengeance of our God (Luke 4:18-19 RSV). Jesus announced his mission as that of setting people free. He came to liberate people who were in bondage. Jesus set people free to become fully responsible persons. This message was gladly received by the oppressed and rejected, but it was also intended for the oppressors.

Jesus freed people from bondage to the law. He viewed the scribes as binding people with heavy burdens (Matthew 23:4) but did nothing to set people free. Jesus came to set people free to do the will of God. This will of God they would know through following Jesus; through binding themselves to him; through becoming his disciples.

Jesus freed people from sickness and from possession. He set them free to respond to the revelation he gave of himself and of God. Jesus raised the dead, and thus liberated people from the bonds of death. He revealed that he had overcome all principalities and powers that enslaved people and was able to save those in captivity to the powers.

Jesus liberated those who were outcasts, publicans and sinners. He set them free from rejection and prejudgment. They were given moral choice and responsibility. They were set free to respond to his call to follow him. Some people were enslaved by the structures of society. Women were free to follow Jesus; the Samaritan woman was regarded as a responsible person by Jesus, and as a witness to him; the Good Samaritan was an example of being a neighbor. People were freed from the walls that separated the pious from sinners; the Jew from the Samaritans; and men from women. Persons were liberated to respond personally to Jesus' call.

Jesus did not only free people. He bound them to himself. In him they would find life. He took the place of the law and called people to follow him and to bind themselves to him. In him was life. He was the way, the truth and the life. Jesus did not just set people free; he indicated by his call the direction that would lead to life.

The incarnate Son revealed in his body both the character of God and what God intended for all people on earth. He was the new Adam. He was the one who revealed what life in obedience to the will of God looks like. He manifested the will of God in the flesh just as the law had been a manifestation of the will of God. He could therefore truthfully bind people to himself and so to the will of God.

Jesus, Savior and Lord

The apostles, after the resurrection and Pentecost, saw and experienced the loosing and binding power of God in a new light. They now understood that it was precisely through Jesus' life and death that he had overcome the principalities of sin and death.

They now proclaimed that sinners were set free from sin by Christ's atoning death on the cross. They now understood and could say with Paul:

"He delivered us from the domination of darkness and transformed us to the kingdom of his beloved Son, in whom we have redemption, the forgiveness of sins" (Col. 1:13 RSV).

Jesus was the Savior, the one who loosed or freed them from sin. Through the resurrection, the power of death had been broken (I Cor. 15:54 ff).

The early Christians confessed that Jesus Christ is *Lord*. They now realized how fully God has revealed the will of God through Jesus' life and death. They recognized Christ as Lord. They bound themselves to know his will; they became followers in the true sense of the word.

The names given to Jesus by the early Christians indicate the central concepts of loosing and binding. He was called Savior (loosing, freeing, forgiving, saving) and Lord (binding, following, abiding in). This was the basic confession of the early Church.

The Commission To Loose And To Bind

Those who follow Christ are to be like him. Jesus sent the apostles into the world as he was in the world (Jn. 20:21). They were to continue the work of loosing and binding in the world. This commission was given to the church through the apostles, who were the link between Jesus and the early Church. The apostles retained and transmitted the tradition about Jesus to the church until such time as it should be retained for all time in the New Testament.

All loosing and binding is thus to be done on the basis of the Scriptures and through the ministry of the Holy Spirit.

We ourselves have participated in what we are enjoined to do for we have experienced the loosing and binding work of God in conversion, in the new birth. When we turned to God in repentance and faith, we experienced the forgiveness of our sins. We were set free. At the same time, we became followers of Jesus; we bound ourselves to do his will. We turned to the Scriptures to know more about Jesus so that we could become more like him.

The moment we turned to Christ in faith we were freed from one set of relationships (the communities of unbelief) to bind ourselves to a new fellowship, to the people of God. We were freed from associations that constrained us to serve idols and could now bind ourselves, together with others, to do the will of God.

Those who are in Christ are freed (loosed) from the spirit of this age; from the idols of this generation; from the principalities and powers that rule the present age. The spirit liberates them from the power of materialism that determines so much of present human endeavors; from the spirit of individualism that determines so much of our personal lives and the life of the nation; from militarism that is the idol of the rich and powerful, sweeping the rest of the world into its orbit; from authoritarianism that mistakes power for what is right; and from other powers. At the same time, the Spirit of God binds them to the Spirit of Christ. He binds those who know Christ to the love of Jesus and to the power of selfless love; he binds them to the spirit of overcoming evil with good; he binds them to a willingness to suffer for what is right; he binds them to the power of the cross. He binds them to Christ to form a new community in the world, a new humanity .

The church as a corporate body has also received the commission to loose and bind (Jn. 20:23). This task is to be carried out in a variety of ways.

Through the proclamation of the Gospel we participate in God's work of salvation. When we proclaim Christ, we participate in his life, death and resurrection; we proclaim that he has atoned for the sin of the world, and will forgive those who turn to him in faith and trust. Proclamation participates in liberation, and at the same time invites people to bind themselves to Christ and to the will of God.

The proclamation of the Gospel is also a warning to the unbelievers. It makes it known that if they bind themselves to the work and will of Satan, and not to Christ, they will suffer the consequences of sin -- separation from God.

Loosing and binding is also action. It consists of healing the sick, freeing those enslaved by poverty, and forgiving those who have sinned. To forgive is to free people from estrangement and to open to them new possibilities for life. To illustrate, let us suppose a young woman, who seeing no future for herself, or for her child, considers having an abortion. Rather than condemning her, and insisting that it is wrong to have an abortion, why not hold out to her forgiveness and the promise that we will see to it that she and the child will not be disadvantaged? We promise to share with her our lives. Then she will be free to bind herself to a new life, and to do what is right.

Discerning What Is Already Bound

It is evident from what we have said that if we are going to loose and to bind what is already bound in heaven, then we need first of all to discern the will of God. The church needs to become a discerning community. This requires careful study of the Word of God, careful attention to the world and the situation in which life is lived, and reliance on the Holy Spirit, who leads us to know what is already bound in heaven.

All persons need to be heard in such deliberations; all have something to contribute. All ethical questions from the most ordinary to the most technical and complex need to be evaluated. There is to be no area or arena of life not subjected to the Lordship of Christ.

But how do we know we have reached a binding word? That depends not so much on the procedure used, and certainly not on a democratic vote. It comes to us more in the way in which we know God in Christ. If we are desirous to know the will of God, earnest in our deliberation, willing to commit our lives to a clear word from God, and rely on the leading of the Spirit, there will come in the midst of our deliberation the moment when "it seemed good to the Holy Spirit and to us" (Acts 15:28) that we should do thus or so. There will come a moment where we will know what is of God.

There could still be instances where a fellowship could be in error and where a member who dissents could be right. The church must therefore always be prepared to examine critically and reexamine what is binding on the community. Only so can there be growth and a deeper understanding of the will of God.

Where the discernment of what is binding is clear, and where, after reexamination, the community has found a binding word, then that word applies to all members in the community. Should someone then deliberately, after repeated admonishment (Matt. 18:15-20), refuse such a word, that person has declared him or herself as no longer being one with the community. Excommunication in this sense is the recognition of what has already happened. The church then seeks to win such a person back to the faith.

The study outline presented by John Howard Yoder touches on many of the implications that the task of loosing and binding has for the congregation. Once the congregation takes this commission seriously, it will find that it will grow and mature in its knowledge of and relationship to Christ. It will experience in a new way what it means to be the church in the world.

ENDNOTES

1. The Holdeman Church in Manitoba and Alberta.

2. Our perceptions may have more to do with an accommodation to our culture than to a careful reading of the text.

3. The significance of Peter and the apostles is removed if the emphasis is placed only on the confession. See E. Schweizer *The Good News According to Matthew*, (Atlanta: John Knox Press 1975), p. 341. cf. William G. Thompson, *Matthew's Advice to Divided Community,* (Rome: Biblical Institute Press, 1970) esp. p. 175-202.

4. Colin Brown, *Dictionary of New Testament Theology*, Vol 2, p. 732, cf. "Keep" in *Theological Dictionary of the New Testament*, Vol III, p. 744 ff.

5. "Binding and Loosing" *The Jewish Encyclopedia*, Vol. III p. 215. cf. Colin Brown, p. 171-72 and *Interpreters' Dictionary of the Bible,* Vol. I p. 438.

6. *Jewish Encyclopedia*, p. 215.

7. J. Duncan, M. Derritt "Binding and Loosing" (Matthew 16:19; 18:18; John 20:23)" *Journal of Biblical Literature,* 102 (1983): 112-7. cf. J. A. Emerton, "Binding and Loosing - Forgiving and Retaining" *Journal of Biblical Studies* 13 (1962): 325-31.

8. This was discussed in two articles by J. R. Mantey, "The Mistranslation of the Perfect Tense in John 20:23, Matthew 16:19, and Matthew 18:18" *JBL* 58 (1958): 243-9) and H.J. Cadbury ("The Meaning of John 20:23, Matthew 16:19 and Matthew 18:18" *JBL* 58 (1958): 251-60).

9. Derritt, op.cit., p.112.

10. The word *"lutron"*, translated "Ransom" in Matthew 20:28 and Mark 10:45 is related to *"luein"* to loose. In this way, loosing is basic to atonement. *TDNT* Vol. 4 p. 340 ff.

11. John Howard Yoder, *Concern* No. 14 (1967): 2-32. See also David Schroeder "Binding and Loosing: The Way of Communal Ethics", *Seeds,* Vol. 3 (1984): 5-8.

4

WOMEN IN CHURCH LEADERSHIP: *I Timothy 2:11-15, A Reconsideration*

John E. Toews

Introduction

The question of women in church leadership has been an issue of growing interest in the Mennonite Brethren Church since the early 1970s. Professor Ewert was one of the first Mennonite Brethren teachers to open the door to a more liberating reading of the New Testament texts that speak about the ministry of women in the church. In 1974 and in 1980 he acknowledged the complexity of the issue, and warned the church that it always tends to read the Bible in light of its own practices. The church is tempted, he observed, to accuse scholars who question such teaching and praxis with unfaithful interpretation. Ewert exhorted the church not to "absolutize prohibitions" that were designed to address local first century excesses. And he urged the church to free women for the exercise of their gifts. The only restriction on the ministry of women he saw was the ordained pastoral ministry.[1] Professor Ewert's exegesis troubled many in the church because it opened new understandings and new opportunities for women. I can think of no greater honor for a teacher than to push beyond his teaching in an attempt to interpret the same Bible as faithfully and carefully as he did.

Everyone who addresses the issue recognizes that the most critical biblical text for the question of women in ministry is I Timothy 2:11-15. The interpretation of the text is filled with serious problems, and very different readings of the text are proposed. Interpretive consensus has not been achieved even among those with a similar view of biblical authority.

This chapter will review two existing interpretations of the text, and then propose an alternative reading.

The Traditional Interpretation

The traditional reading begins with two assumptions: 1) that the thrust of the passage is proper order in the church, and 2) that the main point of the text is the subordination of women. The core instruction is found in vv. 11-12.

Vv. 11-12

The subject of these verses is "woman". The instruction is that women are: 1) to be silent in the church, 2) to be subordinate to men, 3) not to teach in the church, and 4) not to exercise authority over men.

Two reasons are given in this interpretation for women to be silent and not teach. First, teaching involves the exercise of authority. It is a governing function that gives direction to individuals and communities. This gift is restricted to selected men rather than available for all believers in the church. Secondly, women are not to exercise authority over men. This reading of v. 12b assumes that the word *authentein*, this being its only occurrence in the New Testament, means "to exercise authority". As such it can mean "to exercise authority without authorization", or "to usurp authority", or "to domineer". If the reference is to the exercise of authority, the word prohibits women from exercising any authority over men. It forbids women from taking authority in an improper way if the reference is to the usurpation of authority. Or, if the word means domineer, it forbids the autocratic exercise of authority. In other words, the term is understood to have two possible meanings: 1) to forbid women to exercise authority over men, or 2) to forbid women to usurp authority from men or to use authority improperly over men. Despite the acknowledged ambiguity in this single usage in the New Testament, traditional interpreters understand the word to forbid all exercise of authority.

The issue in vv. 11-12 then, according to this interpretation, is the proper relationship of men and women in the church. Women are to be silent and not to teach in the church because such activity constitutes "exercising authority" over men.

Vv. 13-14

These verses provide the rationale for the order of vv. 11-12. The reasons are rooted in creation and the fall.

V. 13 is believed to assert that priority in the order of creation means superiority throughout history.

V. 14 states the cause of the fall. Eve was deceived. Her deception, according to this reading, changed the nature of womanhood and made all women more susceptible to deception than men. Therefore, it is inappropriate for women to teach and exercise authority.

V. 15

Beyond agreeing that v. 15 is added as a qualification to vv. 13-14, there is no consensus about the meaning of this verse. The interpretive options are legion. Most evangelicals struggle between reading it as a reference to the birth of the child, the Messiah, or the salvation of women through childbirth as a statement about the proper sphere of women's activities and the good works of v. 10. The problem of the latter view, of course, is that it involves a theology of salvation by works that runs contrary to the center of Paul's thought. V. 15 is a very difficult verse, and its meaning remains uncertain.

Summary

I Timothy 2:11-15 is traditionally interpreted as a rule of church order that prohibits women for all time from teaching men and exercising authority over men in the church because they are women. The issue is the relation of women and men in church leadership. Men teach and exercise authority. Women are subordinate and silent in the church. The grounds for the restrictions on women's ministries are the way men and women were created and woman's causative role in the fall. The prohibitions are universal and transhistorical; they are not a function of women being untrained or disorderly or a response to some specific circumstance in the church Paul is addressing.[2]

The Problems with the Traditional Interpretation
The traditional reading has been challenged for a variety of reasons.

1) It assumes that I Timothy is a manual on church order. The agenda is an establishment church issue of how properly to order the church, especially a church that is struggling with problems of false teachings. The answer to the problem of heresy is proper church order. The church for all time must be ordered according to the principles of the manual.

If, however, I Timothy is addressing a missionary situation, and is written to assist Timothy in fighting false teachers in Ephesus, as 1:3 states, then everything in the letter concerns this purpose. The letter speaks to new churches in a missionary setting about how to deal with problems of false teachings among new Christians.

2) It ignores the multivalent meaning of the critical words in the text. The key words on which the interpretation of this text hinges have multiple meanings, as the standard Greek dictionary by Arndt and Gingerich indicates. The traditional interpretation reads each word in the most restrictive way possible, even when it is a secondary meaning, or is consistently used differently by Paul, and/or the rules of Greek grammar call for a different meaning. This restrictive reading is simply assumed without any acknowledgment that other meanings are possible.

3) It creates contradictions with other teachings of Paul. At least six such contradictions must be resolved in the traditional interpretation. a) The radical differentiation between men and women contradicts the principle of the mutuality of the sexes in I Corinthians 7 and Ephesians 5.

b) The prohibition of women teaching contradicts Colossians 3:16 and I Corinthians 14:26, which state that the teaching ministry is open to all qualified believers. The word "teach" in Colossians is the same as in I Timothy 2. The teaching ministry is open to all on the same basis as the other ministries listed in Colossians 3: forgiveness (v. 13), love (v. 14), admonishment and music (v. 16). None are restricted on the basis of sex. Vv. 18-19 differentiate instructions on the basis of gender. Thus, the context makes it clear that this is done if necessary. If a ban on women teachers was important for all the churches, a reminder of this restriction in this context of a general invitation to sharing in Christian ministries, including teaching, would have been in order. The absence of such a reminder creates tensions with I Timothy 2.

c) The prohibition of teaching contradicts the freedom for women to exercise the more authoritative ministry of prophecy. The most authoritative ministries in the New Testament are apostle, prophet, and teacher. In every catalog of the gifts--Romans 12, I Corinthians 12, Ephesians 4--teaching is always listed after prophecy. Women are free to prophesy (I Corinthians 11:5; Acts 2:16-18; 21:9). Prophecy is teaching by inspiration rather than from tradition. It is a more authoritative ministry than teaching. Apostles and prophets constitute the foundation of the church, whereas teaching is not so defined. If I Timothy 2 forbids all women from any teaching, while they otherwise are free to exercise the more authoritative ministries in the church, we have a problem in the consistency of Paul's teaching.

d) The reading of the Adam/Eve illustration contradicts Paul's other uses of Adam and Eve. Adam's creation before Eve is used in only one other instance in the New Testament, I Corinthians 11:8-10. The chronological priority is declared meaningless because "in the Lord" both are mutually and reciprocally interdependent. Therefore, the woman can worship God independently of the man (as long as she is appropriately dressed). In I Corinthians woman's subsequent creation is to her advantage, but here it is to her disadvantage. Here Eve is held accountable for the fall of the human race. But in Romans 5 and I Corinthians 15 Adam is held responsible. Paul sounds discordant in the traditional interpretation of I Timothy.

e) An equally serious problem is that if the ban on women teaching is a retribution for the fall, then Adam's responsibility for the fall should involve a restriction for men. Men should be barred from teaching, according to this logic. To prohibit women from teaching as a retribution for the fall means that the doctrine of salvation by grace and the new creation must be reformulated to say that women are excluded from God's forgiveness and salvation because of Eve's sin, but men are included despite Adam's responsibility. Furthermore, if the ban on teaching is a function of the fall, there is no explanation for the choice of this particular ministry as the means of penalization rather than the more authoritative ministry of prophecy.

f) Finally, this interpretation contradicts Paul's own practice of including women in his ministries. Paul names sixteen different women as "coworkers" in his ministries (Romans 16; Philippians 4:2-3; Colossians 4:15; Philemon 2; Acts 16:14-15). The terms used to describe the activities of these women are normally associated with leadership roles: "minister" (Romans 16:1); "ruler" (Romans 16:2); "my fellow worker in Christ Jesus" (Romans 16:3; Philippians 4:3); "apostle" (Romans 16:7); "worked hard in the Lord" (Romans 16:6, 12); "contended at my side for the cause of the gospel" (Philippians 4:3); "explaining the way of the Lord more accurately" (Acts 18:26).

These contradictions create serious problems for a coherent reading of Paul. Any over-all interpretation of the ministry of women in the church, and of the I Timothy 2 text, must create a more consistent interpretation of Paul.

4) The singularity of the prohibition is problematic. The exclusion of women from a significant ministry is a major stance that should be repeated in other writings dealing with the exercise of ministries in the church. The texts dealing with such ministries--Romans 12, I Corinthians 12, Ephesians 4--do not hint at the exclusion of women. In fact, it is clear that women are gifted and empowered for diverse ministries of the church. The gifts and ministries of the Spirit are never differentiated on the basis of gender.

5) The problem of v. 15 calls the entire interpretation into question. A key statement in any text unit that cannot be integrated into the overall meaning of the text, as well as the other teachings of the Scripture, means the text unit has not been properly interpreted. The inability to understand v. 15 in any meaningful way means we have yet to interpret properly the whole of vv. 11-15.

An Alternative Interpretation

A series of evangelical scholars are attempting an alternative interpretation of the text to resolve some of the problems of the traditional interpretation.[3] A summary of this alternative follows.

The Historical Context

The historical context of I Timothy is critical for an understanding of the text.

First of all, the Pastoral Letters were written to address problems of false teaching in young missionary churches (I Timothy 1:3-11, 19-20; 4:1-10; 6:3-4, 20f.; II Timothy 1:15; 2:14, 16-18, 23; 3:1-9, 13; 4:3-4; Titus 1:10-16; 3:9-11). I Timothy was written to stop false teaching (1:3). It is clear that women were involved in the false teachings (I Timothy 3:11, 5:11-15; II Timothy 3:6-7), and that some women were going from house to house spreading these teachings (I Timothy 5:13). Young widows especially were among those influenced by the false teachers.[4]

Secondly, Ephesus was one of the main centers of female religion in the ancient world. It was known as the bastion of the female spiritual principle. One major temple was dedicated to Artemis (or Diana) and a second to Aphrodite (Venus). The goddess Artemis represented the most powerful expression of the Great Mother. She took second place to no other god. In the religious culture of Ephesus, woman was prior to man in the creative order.

The generative role of the male was unimportant. Descent was claimed through the mother. The genealogy of the mother, not the father, provided a person with rank.[5] Furthermore, women were thought to possess special affinity for the divine and served as mediators between the human and the divine. Sacred prostitution was a special feature of religion in Ephesus and of the divine-human mediation. Temple prostitution effected a union with the goddess, thus bringing about salvation and fertility. Ephesus boasted thousands of prostitutes.[6] By the end of the first century a gnostic cosmology was taught in Ephesus which stated that female activity was responsible for the creation of the universe. Eve was the potent force. She pre-existed Adam, who was created from her side. She could procreate without Adam and she was the instructor of Adam.[7] In addition, laws in Ephesus forbade women, except prostitutes, to wear the adornment forbidden in chapter 2:9.[8]

Thirdly, there is a general link between teaching and sex in the ancient world. Male teachers engaged in homosexuality with male students. Female teachers concluded their teaching by announcing their availability for sex with their students.[9]

I Timothy is written to a church in this kind of cultural environment to correct false teaching that involves women serving as false teachers and acting immorally, women dressing as prostitutes, and arguments about questions of origins (genealogies).

The Literary Context

Chapter 2 begins with "therefore" (*oun*). What follows is a direct consequence of the concern for combating false teaching in chapter 1. In other words, chapter 2 contains instructions that respond to the problem of the false teachers.

The thesis of chapter 2 is that the gospel is for all people (vv. 1:4-6, 7). Therefore, the first order of business is offering prayers for all people, including the authorities.

In v. 8 the concern shifts from the universal to particular controversies in Ephesus that are impacting the credibility of the gospel. The issue is improper conduct. The first problem is that men are gathering for prayer but engaging in controversies and strife. The second problem is that women are dressing inappropriately, teaching before they are knowledgeable, and linking their teaching to sex.[10]

The issue of teaching is preceded by an exhortation regarding proper dress. Adornment and submission to the husband are linked in common instructions in the ancient world, Jewish and Greco-Roman. They are two sides of the same coin. The adornment texts speak uniformly in favor of modest clothes and of a woman's submission to her husband. Expensive adornment was indicative of sexual infidelity.[11] In Ephesus the adornment question was also linked to prostitution. The critical concern of the adornment texts is fidelity in marriage.

The Meaning of the Words in vv. 11-15

The standard New Testament Greek dictionary indicates that important choices of meaning must be made for the key words in this text.[12] The optional meanings will be indicated in the order of preference given in the dictionary.

The word translated "silence" in vv. 11 and 12 means 1) quietness as in peace or harmony or 2) quiet as in silence. The word "subjection", also in v. 11, is a military term that means "in order". The term is concerned with the right "lining up" or alignment of the troops for battle. Properly ordered troops are said to be "in subjection".

"I am not allowing" in v. 12 is the primary meaning of *epitrepo*. But the secondary meaning, "order" or "instruct", is to be preferred when the word is used with infinitives. "To teach" and "to sexually seduce" ("to exercise authority" in the traditional interpretation) are infinitives. So in v. 12 the word has something to do with proper ordering or lining up.

The critical word in v. 12 is *authentein*, traditionally translated as "to exercise authority". It is a compound word from "self" and "thrust". The basic meaning is "to thrust oneself". The word went through three stages of meaning in the ancient world. The earliest meaning is to "commit murder or suicide", that is, to thrust a weapon into someone. The second stage of meaning, from 300 B.C. to A.D. 300 (the period of our text), is to "thrust oneself sexually" or to "desire sexually". It is so used in the Wisdom of Solomon 12:6. John Chrysostom, one of the earliest church fathers to comment on I Timothy 2:12, translates the text as "I forbid a woman to teach and to engage in fertility practices with a man". The word is used with the same meaning by another early church father, Clement of Alexandria, around A.D. 200. The third stage of meaning, which begins around A.D. 300, is to "thrust oneself to rule" or to "usurp authority." The traditional interpretation has taken a later meaning and read it back into the New Testament.[13] The word must be defined by the usage of its period, and thus refers to sexual intercourse.

The "for" at the beginning of v. 13 is normally an explanatory term, not a causal word as in the traditional interpretation. That is, it introduces an explanation or illustration, not a statement of cause or reason; it means "for example" not "because". The other "double meaning" word in v. 13 is the word "created". It can mean 1) to create something or 2) to form with understanding. Thus, it can refer to Adam's creation by God or to his education by God.

The word "saved" in v. 15 normally means "preserved for good" or "preserved from disaster and affliction". In the New Testament, and especially in Paul, it most often refers to "salvation from sin and death", but it can still be used in its secular sense.

The Meaning of vv. 11-15

V. 11 - "Let a woman be discipled peacefully in all orderliness".

Women are to be discipled and taught. This instruction represents a radical stance in the ancient world. With a few exceptions, women were not taught. But in the church women are to be taught.

The learning of the women is to be characterized by two things. They are to learn peacefully or harmoniously. The connotation of silence is not present. Secondly, the learning is to be orderly. Submission is not the issue, but orderliness in learning. Women are to be learners in the instructional times; they are not to assert themselves prematurely as teachers.

This teaching addresses the style of female worship in the ancient world. The worship of women was distinctly different from that of men. They often worshiped different gods in different temples on different days and in different ways. Women were noisy and abandoned in worship while the men were sedate and silent. The worship of women was often indecent, indecorous and indiscreet. When these women became Christians they had to learn an entirely different mode of worship. Paul says they are to be discipled, and exhorts them to be properly ordered learners.[14]

V. 12 - "And I am not lining up (or I am not permitting) a woman to teach or sexually to seduce a man, but to be in peacefulness".

Paul is instructing women in Ephesus not to teach. The verb used here in the first person does not refer to a continuing state. Paul, more than any other New Testament writer, distinguished his personal advice for a particular situation from permanently valid instruction. A command of the Lord he identifies as such (e.g., I Corinthians 7:6, 10, 12, 25, 40), or a command to be observed in all the churches is explicitly stated (e.g., I Corinthians 11:16; 14:33, 34, 36). In contrast, when Paul gave personal advice, he used the first person singular present active indicative verb form (e.g., I Corinthians 7:6, 7, 8, 12, 17, 25, 26, 28, 29, 32, 35, 40). In v. 12 Paul uses the typical verbal form for giving personal counsel. It is his advice for the particular situation in Ephesus, and cannot be generalized into a command for all time. Paul could have written "I will never permit" by using the future tense or the aorist subjunctive. Paul's usage is consistent with the use of the verb *epitrepo* in the LXX. The verb refers to permission for a specific situation, never to a universally applicable command. Furthermore, when Paul does use the present tense to specify a timeless instruction he usually indicates this with phrases such as "in behalf of all" (I Timothy 2:1) or "in every place" (I Timothy 2:8). He gives no indication that the instruction for women not to teach is to be understood as a continuing prohibition. Rather, he is offering instruction for the particular situation in Ephesus.[15]

The word "teach" can refer to authoritative Christian teaching, teaching one another, human teaching, or Jewish teaching. The teaching described here is teaching one another. Paul does not want unlearned women to be teaching men. More specifically, Paul does not want women to be teaching men and sexually seducing them. Such in fact was the practice in the church in Thyatira (Revelation 2:20). Instead, the women are to be peaceful or harmonious. They are to be in the community as gracious learners, not seductive teachers.

The instruction of vv. 11-12 is that women be peaceful learners. That is clear because it is the first thing said in v. 11 and the last thing said in v. 12. A literal translation of the poetic structure of the text (following the word order of the Greek) underlines this emphasis:

A woman in *peacefulness* let learn

   in all orderliness

      to teach not I am lining up

      nor to seduce sexually a man

   but to be in *peacefulness*.

Vv. 13-14 - "For example, Adam was formed with understanding first, and then Eve. And Adam was not deceived, but the woman was deceived having become a transgressor".

The example of Adam and Eve offers a Jewish commentary (a midrash) on the creation story. It is a reading of the story in terms of the contemporary situation. Furthermore, the example makes one point, not two as in most commentaries. The issue is education as a safeguard against deception, not creation and then fall as two different events and causes. Adam was taught first, his understanding was formed first, and then Eve's. In other words, vv. 13-14 present a statement about the order of education, not the order of creation.[16] Adam was not deceived because he knew better. Eve was misled because she was not learned. Adam's chronological priority makes him more knowledgeable, not more righteous.

The point of the illustration is that women must be taught or they will again be led astray, as in fact was happening (5:15). The interpretation fits the one other reference to Eve's being deceived, II Corinthians 11:3. There Eve is an illustration of the dangers of being led astray by unauthorized teachers.

V. 15 - "And she will be saved by means of childbearing if they remain in faith and love and holiness with reasonable judgment".

"Saved" is used here in its non-theological meaning, to preserve from natural dangers and afflictions, to keep in good condition.

But from what will the woman be preserved in childbearing? Two proposals have been made. First, she will be preserved from the theological condition that outlaws her from teaching. In childbearing woman demonstrates her divinely ordered preeminence over man, even as man's prior creation and education shows his preeminence over woman. Paul's argument here is interpreted as similar to I Corinthians 11:8-9. Woman is saved from her subordinate status by bearing children. Woman assumes a prior position to the man as his source. While woman is second in being created and educated, she is first in the birthing sequence. Childbearing then serves the healing function of counterbalancing man's prior creation and education.[17]

Although such reasoning seems strange to us, it shows that Paul was struggling to express a fundamental equality between the sexes in categories that were understandable at the time. Each sex is logically prior in equally significant, but different, ways.

The second proposal interprets salvation to mean protection in the intensified pain of the birthing process. That is, salvation addresses the pain of the curse in Genesis 3.

Whatever the precise object of the salvation, the verse concludes by promising woman's full restoration if women and men—"they" (plural, not singular as at the beginning of the verse–live faithfully.

Meaning - Vv. 11-15 teach that women are to be educated before they teach, women are forbidden to teach as unlearned teachers and as teachers who link teaching with sexual seduction. The restriction on teaching by women is condition specific–the problem of heresy involving unlearned teaching and sexual seduction.

An Assessment of the Interpretive Debate

The non-traditional interpretation provides an historical context for the concern of the text; it takes seriously the nuanced nature of the language used, and it resolves the problem of contradictions with other Pauline teachings. The interpretation of v. 15 offers more hope in respect to contextual meaning. On strictly interpretive and exegetical grounds this reading is preferable to the traditional one.

But the interpretative debate illustrates a critical hermeneutical problem. Evangelical scholars are unable to agree on what Paul is saying. This lack of interpretive consensus is an evangelical family affair; it is not an evangelical-liberal dispute. The struggle to interpret I Timothy 2:11-15 is an evangelical enterprise that is deeply divided over the real meaning of the text. Are women only prohibited from teaching men, or are they prohibited from teaching anyone? Does the prohibition apply to women everywhere in all times, or only to women addressed in the culturally specific situation of first century Ephesus? The wide and intensive disagreements among evangelical scholars indicates that both readings are problematic. When two alternative readings of the text are so diametrically opposite, they usually share a common assumption which, if challenged, creates the possibility of a different reading.

Another Possible Reading

The Common Assumption

The traditional and the non-restrictive interpretations are built on one common assumption. They both assume that vv. 11-15 concern public worship. The basis for this assumption involves two more assumptions. First, vv. 1-7 refer to prayer in public worship. Secondly, the exhortation for men to pray with hands lifted refers to public prayer. "In every place" in v. 8 means "every place where the church gathers for worship". On the basis of these assumptions the rest of the chapter is read as a discussion of public worship. The question of adornment and women teaching addresses questions of dress and teaching in the public gatherings of the church.

A Challenge to the Common Assumption

The common assumption ought to be challenged on at least six grounds. First, in the Old Testament and Judaism the father, as the head of the family, would lead prayers for the household and teach the members of the extended family. Everything exhorted in chapter 2:1ff. is instruction given to fathers.

Secondly, "in every place", *en panti topó,* is used three other times by Paul, and never means "whenever the church gathers for worship", nor is it a synonym for "in every church". The three uses are: 1) I Thessalonians 1:8– an affirmation that the faith of the Thessalonians is known everywhere; 2) I Corinthians 1:2–a reference to Christians everywhere in the world who call on the name of Jesus; 3) II Corinthians 2:14–a description of Paul's ministry all over the world. The phrase refers to the world, to every place where the action described is occurring. In I Timothy 2:8 Paul is talking about men praying wherever they are. Nothing suggests a public worship context.

Thirdly, the subject of the submission in v. 11 has never been clear. The Adam and Eve illustration suggests the referent is the husband. But scholars have assumed it must be men in general or established church authorities. Nothing in the context, however, suggests the reference is anything other than the husband of the Adam illustration.

Fourthly, the singular "she" in vv. 11-15a has always puzzled scholars. It should be plural for women in public worship.

Fifthly, the adornment, sexual fidelity and marital submission linkage of the adornment texts has been ignored by nearly all interpreters.

Finally, the shift from the singular "she" to the plural "they" in v. 15 has given scholars endless trouble. The common assumption is that the shift is from woman as singular to women as plural. Thus, if women as a collective body will live by faith, love, and holiness, they will be saved.

An Alternative Reading

Ward Powers, in the Australian InterVarsity magazine, *Interchange*, suggests that I Timothy 2:8-15 refers to family relationships.[18] His thesis deserves consideration and development.

V. 8 - The lifting of hands in prayer is a common practice in Judaism whether in public or private prayer. Husbands are exhorted to pray with proper posture and disposition.

Vv. 9-10 - The concern for adornment of women is a family concern in the ancient world, especially a concern for husband-wife relationships. Wives are not to engage in prostitution but to live monogamously with their husbands.

V. 11 - The words translated "woman" in vv. 11 and 12 and "man" in v. 12 are the common words for wife *guné*) and husband (*anér*). The only exhortation for women" to be submissive", "to order themselves appropriately", in the New Testament is to married women (Ephesians 5:24; Colossians 3:18; I Peter 3:1). Husbands are to teach their wives. Wives are to learn peacefully and without the use of sexual manipulation.

It is hard to imagine how radical this teaching was in the ancient world. The home was the private domain, literally, the "domain of the idiot". The public assembly, called the *ekklésia* (the Greek word for "church"), was a place of higher education. The home was the center of the woman's power, the public place was the center of the man's power. The two did not intersect in the ancient world. Besides Paul, only a few like Musonius Rufus, a Roman philosopher of Paul's time, issue a radical challenge that women be treated as fully equal with men and that they be educated. Both assert that the public should be moved into the private. Paul wants to give content to the marital relationship. That also is a radical stance. It was common for men to be thirty or more years of age at the time of marriage and for women to be in the teens. Paul's exhortation for the husbands to teach their young wives is revolutionary. The need for the wives to learn peacefully, and also to be properly ordered is more understandable.

Vv. 12-13 - The relationship between husband and wife is illustrated from that of Adam and Eve. When Eve, who was uninformed because of her subsequent creation, taught Adam, she led herself and Adam astray.

V. 15 - The reference to salvation through childbearing is a promise either that the wife will be saved from her subordinate status by childbearing or that she will be preserved from disaster in childbearing. The plural of v. 15b refers to the husband and wife, picking up the idea of Adam and Eve from the previous statement. The wife will be preserved in childbirth if the husband and wife together live by faith, love and holiness. Christian discipleship is the equal responsibility of the husband and wife together.

Proposed Translation of vv. 8-15

V. 8 - I wish, therefore, the husbands to pray in every place lifting holy hands without anger or disputation.

V. 9 - Likewise, also wives dress with good taste and modesty and dress with good judgment, not with plaited hair and gold or pearls or expensive clothes,

V. 10 - but as fitting wives who promise godliness through good works.

V. 11 - Let a wife be discipled peacefully in all orderliness.

V. 12 - And I am not permitting a wife to teach or sexually to manipulate her husband, but to be in peacefulness.

Vv. 13-14 - For example, Adam was formed with understanding first and then Eve. And Adam was not deceived but the woman was deceived, having become a transgressor.

V. 15 - And she (the wife) shall be saved through childbearing if they (husband and wife) remain in faith and love and holiness with good judgment.

Meaning - The focus of the text is on the husband-wife relationship, not on public worship. Therefore, this text ought not to be used to address the question of women's roles in public ministry. The point of the text is that the unlearned wife is to be taught by her husband, thus giving theological content to the marriage relationship. She is not to teach her husband or to link teaching him with sexual manipulation. Furthermore, the wife should not participate in prostitution, sacred or otherwise, but live faithfully with her husband as together they seek to be true disciples of Jesus.

Relation to Titus 2:1-10

If this reading of the text is correct, the concern for the proper ordering of the home is parallel to a similar concern in Titus 2, another Pastoral Letter. Paul is concerned that the cause of the gospel not be hindered by family life that discredits the gospel and/or advances the cause of false teaching.[19]

Conclusion

Two alternative interpretations of I Timothy 2:11-15 have been outlined. The traditional interpretation asserts that women are by definition subject to men, and are to be silent in the church. This interpretation is based on an inadequate understanding of the nuanced language in the text, and creates major contradictions in Paul's teachings. The second interpretation argues for the education of women and for the disengagement of teaching from sex as a condition for their teaching. The restriction on the ministry of women is limited until the particular problem in Ephesus is solved. A third interpretation offered here suggests that the text is concerned with family questions rather than with church ministry questions. It is a family order text rather than a church order text. If the latter interpretation is correct, the text should not be used to restrict the public ministry of women.

ENDNOTES

1. See "The Christian Woman in the Church and Conference," *Yearbook of the Canadian Conference of Mennonite Brethren Churches, 63rd Convention, July 6-9, 1974* (Vancouver, BC: Canadian Conference of Mennonite Brethren Churches, 1974), pp. 30-43; and "The Place of the Woman in the Church," Unpublished Paper, "Board of Reference and Counsel Study Conference, May 8-10, 1980, Clearbrook, BC" (Typewritten).

2. This summary is based on Stephen B. Clark, *Man and Woman in Christ* (Ann Arbor: Servant Books, 1980); Donald Guthrie, *The Pastoral Epistles*, in *The Tyndale New Testament Commentaries* (Leicester: Tyndale Press, 1957); James B. Hurley, *Man and Woman in Biblical Perspective* (Grand Rapids : Zondervan Publishing House, 1981); Douglas J. Moo, "I Timothy 2:11-15: Meaning and Significance," *Trinity Journal* 1 (1980): 62-83. There are versions of the traditional interpretation that are less restrictive than the one taken by these authors. The difference, however, is one of degree, not kind.

3. See the following studies: Gilbert G. Bilezikian, *Beyond Sex Roles: A Guide for the Study of Female Roles in the Bible* (Grand Rapids: Baker Book House, 1985); Mary J. Evans, *Women in the Bible* (Downers Grove: Inter Varsity Press, 1983); Alvera Michelsen, ed., *Women, Authority and the Bible* (Downers Grove, IL: Inter Varsity Press, 1986); Gordon D. Fee, *I and II Timothy, Titus,* in *Good News Commentary* (San Francisco: Harper and Row, 1984); N.J. Hommes, "Let Women Be Silent in Church," *Calvin Theological Journal* 4 (1969): 5-22; Walter C. Kaiser, "Shared Leadership," *Women in Leadership* (Carol Stream: Christianity Today Institute, 1986), p. 12; Catherine C. Kroeger, "Ancient Heresies and a Strange Greek Verb," *Reformed Journal* 29 (March 1979): 12-15; Catherine C. Kroeger, "The Apostle Paul and the Greco-Romans Cults of Women," *Journal of the Evangelical Theological Society* 30 (March 1987): 25-38; Catherine C. Kroeger, "A Classicist Looks at the 'Difficult' Passages, *Occasional Papers No. 10. Perspectives on Feminist Hermeneutics* (Institute for Mennonite Studies, 1987), pp. 10-15; Richard and Catherine C. Kroeger, "May Women Teach? Heresy in the Pastoral Epistles," *Reformed Journal* 30(1980): 14-18; Alan Padgett, "Wealthy Women at Ephesus, I Timothy 2:8-15 in Social Context," *Interpretation* 41 (1987:19-31; Philip B. Payne, "Libertarian Women in Ephesus: A Response to Douglas J. Moo's Article, 'I Timothy 2:11-15:

Meaning and Significance'", *Trinity Journal* 2 (1981): 169-197; Mark D. Roberts, "Woman Shall be Saved: A Closer Look at I Timothy 2:15," *TSF Bulletin* (November/December 1981): 4-7; David Scholer, "Women's Adornment," *Daughters of Sarah* 6 (January-February, 1980): 3-6.

4. See Stephen Davis, *The Revolt of the Widows* (Carbondale: Southern Illinois University Press, 1980) for evidence that false teachers were funded by widows in Asia Minor.

5. See Catherine C. Kroeger, "I Timothy 2:12 - A Classist's View," *Woman, Authority and the Bible*, edited by Alvera Michelsen (Downers Grove: Inter Varsity Press, 1986), p. 232

6. See Richard and Catherine C. Kroeger (1980), pp. 15-16.

7. See Kroeger (1986), pp. 234-38.

8. See Scholer (1980), pp. 5-6.

9. See Richard and Catherine C. Kroeger (1980: Catherine C. Kroeger (1987); James G. Sigountos and Myron Shank, "Public Roles for Women in the Pauline Church: A Reappraisal of the Evidence," *Journal of the Evangelical Theological Society* 26 (1983): 283-95.

10. See Fee, *I and II Timothy, Titus* (1984), pp. 25ff., for a discussion of the literary context.

11. See Scholer (1980).

12. William F. Arndt and F. Wilbur Gingerich, *A Greek-English Lexicon of the New Testament and Other Early Christian Literature.* Second Edition (Chicago: University of Chicago, 1979).

13. See Kroeger (1979).

14. See Kroeger (1987), p. 14.

15. See Payne (1981), pp. 170-73.

16.. See Kaiser (1986).

17. See Roberts (1981).

18. See "Women in the Church: The Application of I Timothy 2:8-15," *Interchange* 17 (1975): 55-9. Robert Banks, "Paul and Women's Liberation," *Interchange* 18 (1976), 96, agrees with Powers.

19. See Alan Padgett, "The Pauline Rationale for Submission: Biblical Feminism and the *hina* Clauses of Titus 2:1-10," *Evangelical Quarterly* 59 (1987): 39-52.

5

WOMEN AND THE CHURCH:
Biblical And Theological Perspectives

Herbert Swartz

In spite of the fact that the church speaks of conversion and teaches that change is central to the meaning of the gospel, the history of the church illustrates how painful change is. If that is true with reference to the church's relationship to a changing world, it is just as true with reference to the church's interpretation of the Scriptures. The willingness to explore new ways of discipleship, specifically in the case of women and the church, is made doubly difficult when the prophetic claims in the church seem to be more in harmony with the claims of a counter-culture, than they are with the established ways of the church.

David Ewert's life speaks of change. The trek from Russia to Canada was only a beginning. This is not the place to recall that story, except to say that as a pastor, teacher and administrator in the Mennonite Brethren Church his life reflected the turmoil of an immigrant people who confessed their pilgrim status and faithfulness to the Scriptures as interpreted within the Anabaptist-Mennonite tradition. In recent years this involved facing the issue of the role of women in the church as Moderator of the Canadian Conference of Mennonite Brethren Churches, as a professor of New Testament at Eastern Mennonite Seminary and Mennonite Brethren Biblical Seminary, and as President at the Mennonite Brethren Bible College. This essay reflects a continuing dialogue with a beloved colleague.

As with all current topics, our publishers have served us too well in supplying us with such tantalizing titles as "Are Women Human?" and "Was Jesus Married?", or the predictable "Woman Liberated" and "Woman in a Man's Church", to mention only a few. In fact, so prolific is the literature that one is tempted to debate the views and to despair of writing anything that hasn't been written before. A few years of teaching experience, however, soon convinces one how little we read of the much that is written, and how many times we need to hear a new idea, before it can stir us enough to change our way of seeing, and our style of living.

This essay considers biblical and theological perspectives on women and the church by relating the biblical message to culture in terms of a salvation history perspective. Not only is it important to consider Old Testament insights, or to reflect on Jesus' or Paul's view, but the ancient Near East and the Greco-Roman world also bear witness as the setting for ideas and a lifestyle, whose implications we are still trying to fathom in the Church in our age. In this task one needs not only honesty and humility, and a generous measure of wisdom, but also the grace to accept one's humanity with humor. After all, the biblical picture of God creating woman from the rib of man is not only awe-inspiring, but profoundly funny.

I. Old Testament Observations

The writers of the Gospels assume Jesus' respect for and use of the Scriptures (our Old Testament), which fact, in turn, obligates us to consider its message seriously. (This same stance was readily followed by the early Church). Jesus' freedom in interpreting the text according to its fullest intention (Matthew 5:17-48) suggests that the pivotal meaning of the Old Testament reverberated in His life and teachings. His response to the test of the Pharisees on the question of divorce (Matthew 19:3-9) is a good illustration of this principle. We too are to read the story of the people of God in the Old Testament being mindful of that same "hardness of heart" which Moses recognized in a people that were difficult to teach. Three contexts from the Old Testament may be considered for an understanding of the male-female relationship in ancient Israel: the creation narrative, the patriarchal pattern, and the prophets' pronouncements.

A. The Creation Context

Matthew and Paul use part of the creation narrative as a basis for interpretive comments germane to the male-female relationship, which is itself the basis for a consideration of the theme of women and the church. While both Matthew and Paul use the combined narrative from Genesis 1:27 and 2:18-25 (Matthew 19:4-5; I Corinthians 11:7-9), Paul in I Timothy 2:13-14 alone uses the single narrative from Genesis 2:18-25. The pattern of repetition, which is so characteristic of the creation account from the general statement in Genesis 1:1 to its expansion in the account of the six days of creation, continues in the primary statement of the creation of Adam (man), "In the image of God he created him; male and female he created them" (1:27), with its expansion in the detailed account of the creation of woman (2:18-25). Since the primary statement in such a parallelism establishes the determinative kernel of truth, the meaning of Genesis 1:27, which, first, designates sexuality as a part of what it means to be made in the image of God, and second, implies a male-female partnership in the fellowship of life, as God is a fellowship in Himself, cannot be ignored in order to interpret Genesis 2:18-25 as a model for hierarchy. The narrative of chapter 2 is silent as to why God created woman from man's rib; therefore, it is sheer speculation to suppose that the act symbolizes that the woman is to stand under the man in any way, or even to affirm that this proves that woman is of the same substance as man and thus is intimately related to him.

Rather, the passage becomes a unique explanation, first, of the relation of the woman to the man as his helper (2:18, 20), and second, of the meaning of marriage as an ultimate unity described as "one flesh" (2:24). Because the patriarchal society of ancient Israel demanded that the woman leave her family to become a member of her husband's family, the inverse demand in Genesis 2:24 could suggest that rather than first being the lord and ruling over his wife, the husband is to leave all for the sake of the worth of the woman. The overall emphasis is on relatedness and not physical differences or subordination. In fact, the Hebrew word for "help," as used here, is used twenty-one times in the Old Testament, but never to designate a subordinate. Its most familiar use is in Psalm 146:5 (cf. I Samuel 7:12; Psalm 33:20) where God is described as man's "help" in time of need.

Thus, the total creation account implies that man and woman are partners in the fellowship of life. This conclusion means the rejection of an androgynous ideal whereby true humanity is defined as transcending sexuality, and the subordination of the traditional view which subsumes human sexuality under marriage. Even though marriage is viewed as the most intimate form of human fellowship, all people are primarily related as men and women by virtue of God's intent in creation. Paul K. Jewett, in *Man as Male and Female*, concludes: "To be in the image of God *is* to be male and female. Not only do men and women alike participate in the divine image, but their fellowship as male and female is what it *means* to be in the image of God."[1]

We have concluded that the creation account does not support the idea of a chain of command, and that God's primary design is not that man and woman should live in a hierarchical relationship. Now we must account for the later patriarchal pattern, and respond to the claim that it is simply a fulfillment of God's promise to the woman in Genesis 3:16b: "Your desire shall be for your husband, and he shall rule over you."

B. The Patriarchal Pattern

It is worth noting that the authority-subordination motif, which in the Genesis account is expressed in the man's naming the animals (2:19, 20), and also in God's giving a name to humankind (5:2), is absent when the man designates the newly-created woman by her gender (2:23), but is introduced again after the fall when the man calls the name of the woman "Eve" and thus asserts his authority over her (3:20). Both are involved in the rebellion and guilt of the fall which results in alienation for the man and the woman from God and each other. There seems to be very little difference between the woman, who is here ruled by her husband, and all women who are subordinate to men. The Old Testament's social and cultic restrictions express male domination in respect to woman. This can finally be traced to the sinful hardness of the human heart, but in the immediate setting must be related to the cultural similarities between Israel and her neighbors.

From one perspective the Old Testament is a record of the disastrous spread of sin's results in respect to the status of the woman. She could be given by her father to a man as a possession, and if found with "some indecency" (Deuteronomy 24:1), could be divorced. The inability to present her husband with a son meant she was viewed as a failure and treated harshly (Genesis 16:1-6 and I Samuel 1:3-8). If a woman's husband died, and she was sonless, she could not refuse a Levirate marriage (Deuteronomy 25:1-10), even though under reverse circumstances the man could. Women also played a minor role in Israel's public worship and religious life. Only the males of Aaronic descent qualified for the office of priest, partly due to the patriarchal pattern, but also because their presence might encourage Israel to follow the Canaanites in their fertility rituals.

From another perspective the Old Testament allows women a role in the rituals associated with worship. Though women were debarred from officiating in the Jerusalem temple services, they participated fully as worshippers. The law made no distinctions between male and female in regulations concerning basic redemptive offerings (Leviticus 1-7), even though distinctions were made in laws regarding ceremonial cleansing for men and women as they apply to the distinctive functioning of their reproductive systems (Leviticus 15:16-33). Men were required to participate in the three great annual festivals, while women were permitted to do so (Deuteronomy 16:16). The example of Hannah in I Samuel 1:1-2:21 informs us that women participated in prayer and in sacrificing on their own behalf. Women like Rebekah were also free to seek personal direction and guidance from God (Genesis 25:22-23). That God revealed Himself to women in their quest for His redemptive purposes (Judges 13:3-7), also is proof of a special role.

In one area of Israel's religious life women held equal rank with men. Women shared with men in the prophetic gift which involved the reception and declaration of divine revelation. Miriam is specifically identified as a prophetess (Exodus 15:20-21), and with Moses and Aaron as one of the great leaders in the redemptive exodus from Egypt (Micah 6:4). Deborah is identified, almost incidentally, as prophetess (Judges 4:4-5), though her memorable contribution lay in delivering Israel from the oppression of the Canaanites. Huldah is acknowledged as the outstanding prophetess of her day (II Kings 22:14-20). When Josiah ordered the priest Hilkiah to determine God's will, he consulted with Huldah, through whom the word of the Lord then came to the King and people. Lest we think that Huldah was called because there were no male prophets available, we need to be reminded that Jeremiah was her contemporary (Jeremiah 1:2). These almost casual references to the exercise of the prophetic function by women point to the fact that they were no anomaly among God's people.

C. The Prophetic Pronouncements

If the patriarchal pattern, with reference to women, is like a dark cloud with a silver lining, the prophets' pronouncements could hardly be different. From Amos' "cows of Bashan" (4:1), to Jeremiah's provocative description of a faithless people as harlots (3:2ff.), the status of women remained bleak.

But there are bright spots which suggest the dawning of a new day. Hebrew words are distinguished by gender; words designating the deity are masculine. Moreover, the patriarchal culture naturally turned to the masculine gender to express value and to honor an object. It is not too surprising then that the two milk cows of I Samuel 6:10, which are yoked to a cart which is to carry the ark of the covenant, are converted to the masculine gender in I Samuel 6:12 when they are in holy service. But some prophets dared to go beyond the sexual meaning in language to the personal. Isaiah sees God revealing "herself" like a mother (49:15; 66:12-13), and likens the saving activity of God to a mother giving new birth (46:3-4). Joel sees sons and daughters prophesying, and God's Spirit being poured out upon menservants and maidservants (2:28-29). These few illustrations suggest that they hoped for better days ahead in God's time.

II. New Testament Considerations

The history and theology of the New Testament are marked by both continuity and uniqueness when viewed against the background of the Old Testament thought and practices. The Christ event was a fulfillment of the hopes of the pious priests, princes, prophets and people who looked for God's Messiah. That Jesus would be a Suffering Servant, and in that role challenge the cultural and religious interpretations of Judaism, was a source of amazement and fear to the crowds, the disciples, and the religious and political establishments. Only from the perspective of the resurrection, and in the power of the Spirit, could a new people of God begin to fathom the meaning of holiness as freedom. A converted Paul shared with the Church clear statements pertaining to the principles of freedom; the applications to the Hellenized culture of the early Church were not so clear.

A. Judaism's Injustice

The record is a sad one. In the struggle with Hellenism, Judaism found it easier to imitate Greco-Roman dress, language, and attitudes towards women, than to find new ways of interpreting the unique truths in their religious heritage. Rather than taking the opportunity to witness to the true meaning of God's creation of humanity as male and female, they followed their pagan neighbors in treating women as objects. The implications of this for religious practices can be seen from a few illustrations.

Although women were not circumcised, seemingly they were considered part of God's covenant community in the Old Testament. Nevertheless, a real exclusion occurred in the temple and synagogue services. Josephus, in his *Antiquities*, mentions the separation of men and women in Herod's temple, with the women's court being designated the "harem." In the synagogue, the women were expected to observe strict silence and were not counted as members. It was in this world that Jesus was born, lived, and taught.

B. Jesus as a Radical

If the Judaism of Jesus' day considered the male as the superior person in the human family, with every right to rule, and the female person as inferior, with the obligation to obey in all things, one could expect that Jesus would react to this situation and challenge the misinterpretation and practices of a wayward people. We have no record that Jesus specifically taught a new doctrine relative to woman's place in society. Luke tells us that Jesus took the liberty to include women in the illustrations of the Kingdom of God (Luke 13:20-21), whether in parables (Luke 15:8-10) or when pointing out an example of sacrificial giving (Luke 21:1-4).

The revelation of God in Jesus Christ, as shown especially by the cross, is not manifested by words alone, but by means of a life-style open to needy women (John 4), and to friends (John 11). Jesus lived so radically that we still ponder the meaning of the revelation that came through him. How thoroughly Matthew had grasped it is shown in his development of Jesus' genealogy when he includes the four women, Tamar, Rahab, Ruth, and Uriah's wife (Matthew 1:1-6).

The male arrogance of Jesus' countrymen was severely challenged by him. He challenged a double standard of morality on the question of adultery; he exhibited intimacy and openness in relationships which included women of every social class. Matthew 5:28 defines the man who looks in lust at a woman as already guilty of adultery; and John 8:3-11 portrays Jesus as unwilling to condemn a woman taken in the act of adultery, obviously because of the accusers' forced interpretation of singular guilt in a very contrived situation. Luke 8:1-3 mentions the twelve, and a number of women, who were with Jesus. The latter include Mary Magdalene, Joanna, and Susanna, "and many others who provided for them out of their means." Some of these women dared to remain at Jesus' crucifixion until the end (Mark 15:40-41), and were the first witnesses to His resurrection (Mark 16:1-8). In spite of this openness on the part of Jesus, the disciples are evidently not prepared for His freedom to talk openly and intimately with a Samaritan woman (John 4:27).

The suggestion, that Jesus' ministry quite naturally included women, is reinforced by some of the many illustrations from His healing activity (e.g. Mark 1:29-31--Peter's mother-in-law; 5:21-43--the woman with an issue of blood and Jairus' daughter; Luke 7:11-17--a widow's son; and 13:10-13--a woman with a bent back), with the final proof given in the picture of His personal relationship with Mary and Martha at Bethany (Luke 10:38-42; John 11:1-

44). The love-hate result of such activity on the part of Jesus may be seen in the two incidents where women openly show their love for Him. At the house of Simon a sinner-woman anoints Jesus in love, and the Pharisees blame Jesus for accepting her (Luke 7:36-50); and at the home in Bethany, Mary's anointing of Jesus' feet with costly ointment is condemned by Judas Iscariot as a waste (John 12:1-8).

Jesus showed the same intimacy and esteem towards women as He did towards men. The truly thoughtful person will appreciate the thoroughly radical character of Jesus' behavior for His time, but perhaps even more importantly for our time as well.

C .Paul as a Test

Our attempt to portray Jesus as a radical may have suggested that He totally ignored the realities of the historical situation. The fact of the incarnation as the unique revelation of God in history, as a man rather than a woman, suggests that this is not so. Since Christians seemingly acknowledge Jesus as Lord without the encumbrance of sexuality, we are reminded that salvation is only incidentally and not necessarily of the male. This suggests that to proclaim this truth in the Greco-Roman world of the first century, which defined the relationship between a man and a woman only in terms of headship and submission, the apostles must be males. The tentative character of even this form is immediately evident at Pentecost and in the development of the early Church. In the letters of the apostle Paul we face the ultimate test of formulating a principle which states the meaning of God's act in Jesus Christ relative to the relationship of male and female for the community of God's people, and its practical application to Christian witness and worship in the world.

The promise of the prophet Joel found fulfillment at Pentecost. Included in the group of those who "were all filled with the Holy Spirit and began to speak in other tongues, as the Spirit gave them utterance" are "the women and Mary the mother of Jesus" (Acts 1:14). This event is important, because it stresses both the unique thing that God is doing in making the Holy Spirit equally available to all believers, and the continuity between the old and new covenants in ministry, as being, not in the exclusive male priesthood, but in those who are prophets. Acts 2 designates all of God's people as prophets, and I Corinthians 12:10 and Ephesians 4:11 speak of a special gift of prophecy. Philip's four daughters (Acts 21:9) and Priscilla (Acts 18:26) are mentioned almost incidentally as involved in prophesying.

The only fair conclusion to be drawn from this early picture is that in the first enthusiasm of God's presence among His people in the Holy Spirit, it is understood that His gifts of grace are for both men and women. All believers are to share in the task of bringing God's rule to realization in the Church and among all peoples. The almost casual way in which women are seen as a part of the experience of the New Testament Church as reflected in the book of Acts (e.g. chapter 16) and in Paul's letters (e.g. Romans 16), must always be considered in the context of the times, and also in the context of Paul's advice relative to the relationship of men and women. Those translators who explain the "diakonos" of Phoebe at Cenchreae according to Romans 16:1 as being that of a deaconess, are fair to her ministry in the Church only if they will allow for its definition according to I Timothy 3:8-13, and the parallels found in Stephen and Philip who as deacons administered and preached. This openness in ministry reflects a real desire and eagerness in the early Church to express the will of Christ.

We now move to a consideration of the specific Pauline texts which seem to be difficult to harmonize with our previous statements relative to the creation ideal, the prophetic promise, and the example of Jesus. It would appear that the patriarchal pattern was revived and sanctified in the name of the gospel by Paul. For some people the hissing hate-sound in the term misogynist is an apt label for Paul on this account. For others, the teachings of Paul provide a platform to propagate a westernized approach to the subordination of the female to the male with love-games and manipulation. Perhaps Hedy Martens best echoes the sentiment expressed by many of today's Christian college students: "The role of the Christian woman has been a tremendous problem to me. I have been endlessly torn between biblical passages seemingly forbidding women to speak in the church, and passages saying that in the last days they shall prophesy."[2] Is there any way we can read Paul without denying the new freedom we have in Christ?

We begin our investigation of Paul's thought on this subject with a safe text Galatians 3:28, if there be such a one. It has been seen as the most decisive word in favor of woman's liberation. In the context of a pericope which draws the strongest contrast between confinement under the law and the status of those who in Christ Jesus "are all sons of God, through faith" (3:26), Paul speaks of oneness or unity in three categories--race, class and sex.

The distinction between Jew and Greek is a dichotomy which tears at Paul in his letter to the Romans. As a converted Jewish person, appointed to be an apostle to the Gentiles (11:13), Paul claims that the gospel is "the power of God for salvation to every one who has faith, to the Jews first and also to the Greek" (1:17). He can assert that "there is no distinction between Jew and Greek" (10:12a). But Paul also must witness to a God who has not "rejected his people" (11:1-2), and although he cannot tell how, he can accept the inscrutability of God's ways because of his conviction that God will have mercy upon all (11:32-33). For human fellowship, the Jew-Gentile distinction, a potential source of hostility, is removed in Christ. So insistent was Paul that this truth was to be realized within the fellowship of the Church, that he dared to challenge Peter publicly on a false application of this principle (Galatians 2:11ff.).

The distinction between slave and free has also deeply divided people. Our text states that in Christ such socio-economic class barriers are to be non-existent. How does Paul apply this principle within the Church? The abundant textual evidence is proof enough of its importance. If there is really "neither slave nor free," how can Paul, urge: "Slaves, be obedient to those who are your earthly masters" (Ephesians 6:5; cf. Colossians 3:22; Titus 2:9)? The guiding rule, Paul tells the Corinthians, is, "let every one lead the life which the Lord has assigned to him, and in which God has called him" (I Corinthians 7:17, 20); we should add that he also urges, "If you can gain your freedom, avail yourself of the opportunity" (v. 21). The slave's primary orientation is his service to the Lord (Ephesians 6:5-7; cf. Colossians 3:23; Titus 2:10), as is the master's (Ephesians 6:9). It is important to recognize that Paul clearly states principles, and in their application, makes unity and fellowship in the Church the first priorities. This is a radical understanding which defines life in the Church as exemplary, and the Christian way of life in the world as witness.

The final appeal for a Christian is never a statement of law, but rather the compulsion of love. So Paul urges Philemon to accept Onesimus, possibly a runaway slave, as a brother (v. 16), "for I have derived much joy and comfort from your love" (v. 7). Our temptation is to judge this approach as inadequate, and to condemn Paul for not advocating a more revolutionary stance. But surely this is to deny both Jesus' example and the primary function of the people of God in every age. That we witness most adequately to the world in the character of our spiritual unity and the nature of our socio-economic fellowship in the Church, and in our acceptance of a servant role to the oppressed and afflicted of every race and class, has meant for some the pursuit of the legal abolition of slavery. But let us not be deceived by a system change in an evil society. The master-slave relationship remains, and Christians are still being called to serve.

We have now reached the most pertinent part of our safe text. The sex distinction is also one that Paul claims is removed in Christ. A literal rendering of the Greek text as "No male and female" suggests an affinity with the first creation narrative in Genesis 1:27 (especially in its Septuagint translation). Freely interpreted, this is sometimes taken to mean that in Christ maleness and femaleness are done away with. However, this androgynous ideal both misrepresents the creation account and dehumanizes man. We have previously asserted that to be in the image of God is to be male and female in fellowship. Oneness in Christ, therefore, means male and female in unity and fellowship. Again, this is the radical principle which is to define the exemplary life of the Christian in the Church, and a way of life to which the Christian witnesses in the world. The Scriptural texts in Ephesians, Corinthians, and Timothy must be interpreted from this perspective.

To move from Galatians 3, where the principle of the full equality of the man and the woman in fellowship is asserted, to Ephesians 5 and I Corinthians 7 is to ask whether it is possible to defend the subordination of the wife to the husband; or to I Corinthians 11 and 14 and to I Timothy 2, is to ponder the subordination of the female to the male in the congregation. Paul knows what it means to say, "There is no male and female; for you are all one in Christ Jesus," but this knowledge must be fitted into the context of the witnessing Church of his day.

Another text to be considered, Ephesians 5:21-33, is part of the "table of rules" for a Christian household. All the rules are listed under the injunctions: "Be filled with the Spirit...Be subject to one another out of reverence for Christ" (5:18, 21). Our text is instructive because it establishes the principle of subordination which is to govern the interaction of believers. Paul's experience in the Church had taught him that in the application of this principle to the special problems of a Christian marriage in a pagan culture, the wives needed to be reminded to "be subject to your husbands as to the Lord" (5:22; cf. Colossians 3:18), and the husbands needed the admonition, "love your wives, as Christ loved the church" (5:25; cf. Colossians 3:19). Within the definition of a reciprocal subordination there can be no room for a patriarchal or hierarchical control of the one partner over the other.

Paul's use of the term subordination in the middle voice implies a voluntary "surrendering of one's own rights or will." Just as Christ did not demand His own rights as the Son of God among human beings, so in the marriage relationship the partners witness to the world in their mutual subordination. Where the freedom of the gospel sometimes divided family relationships in the Church, Paul appealed to the way of love in the application of the principle of "no male and female."

So, Paul warns, in the Christian household the headship of the husband and the subordination of the wife are analogous to Christ's headship over the Church and the church's subordination to Christ. To conclude the analogy Paul pictures the unity of marriage as reflective of the great mystery inherent in speaking of the relationship between Christ and the Church (5:31, 32). The discussion then defines the debts and duties which are to be exercised in a Christian marriage where there is a unique unity and a reciprocal subordination made possible by the Spirit of God.

I Corinthians 11:2-16 moves us along in our discussion from the relation of the partners in marriage to their particular functions in worship. These functions, Paul says, can also be understood by the analogy of relationship: "The head of every man is Christ, the head of a woman is her husband, and the head of Christ is God" (11:3). The later explicit mention of the origin of woman from man (11:8), as stated in the Genesis 2 account, suggests that the use of the term "head" does not imply hierarchy but rather "source" or "origin." Paul affirms the partnership and interdependence of male and female by adding: "Nevertheless, in the Lord, woman is not independent of man or man of woman" (11:11).

But Paul knows the Church must not needlessly offend the society to which it witnesses, since in cultural matters it is not to be the agent of revolutionary destruction. It is one thing to exercise total freedom in worship and have both men and women prophesying (11:5); however, the uncovering of the woman's head would suggest a lack of subordination in the culture of Corinth. The example of Jesus declares that the goal of the discipleship is not first freedom and change, without the radical component of suffering love.

The pericope, I Corinthians 14:33b-36, seems to contradict what Paul has just stated in I Corinthians 11. How could women both pray and prophesy, and "keep silence"? Throughout chapter 14 Paul urges a restrained use of tongues in public worship. The general context could suggest that for the sake of peace and order, in this setting, it is better that the women be silent. Or, since the immediate context deals with asking questions, it may be more appropriate to apply the keeping silence, not to praying or prophesying, but rather to the practice of disrupting the services by asking questions. In a society where only a few wealthy young women received an education, and all others learned by asking questions of their male associates, Paul appeals for order and decency (14:40) according to social custom and propriety.

The text of I Timothy 2:8-15 contains an injunction similar to the one we have just considered. While the difficulties in interpretation of the other Pauline passages can be resolved contextually, a seeming lack of information hampers the exegete here. Nevertheless, there have always been those commentators, beginning with Chrysostom, who have bravely suggested that the force of the "in like manner" invites a repetition of the idea that both men and women are to pray in public (2:8, 9), and that the language of verse 11 suggests the husband-wife relationship. But the text states plainly that in worship a woman is not "to teach or to have authority over men; she is to keep silent" (2:12). The explanation that the woman, as the second to be created, was deceived by the tempter (2:134, 14), seemingly increases the problem.

Theologians are still tempted to blame the woman for the fall of the man, and to claim her necessary subordination to the man on the basis of her assumed display of inferior moral integrity and intellectual ability. But this is a crass denial of the biblical view that men and women equally bear the image of God. The difficulty here suggests that even if a resolution based on the extremity of the disorder demanding a radical remedy is proposed, we are still left with a fundamental issue: does Paul in I Timothy 2:8-15 teach that the Creator assigned different roles to the man and the woman?

David Ewert, in a paper presented to the Canadian Conference of Mennonite Brethren Churches in July 1974, after evaluating the Pauline material, states:

> Clearly the creation account gives no reason to believe that the woman has less dignity than the man. However, it does suggest that the Creator assigned different roles to each of them. To say that the order of redemption has annulled the order of creation is to overlook the New Testament passages which refer to creation when the respective roles of man and woman are discussed. Redemption reverses the curse of sin, but not the creation order. That the difference of function is not simply a biological one (which, of course, everyone recognizes) seems evident from the fact that the creation order is referred to in passages that deal with the public meetings of the church. Which means, on the one hand, that there is as much worth and dignity attached to being a woman as to being a man, but, also that

when equality of function is pushed too far, the Creator is dishonored (pp. 17-18).[3]

Brother Ewert is careful not to limit the woman's role by defining it solely in terms of subordination, or the exercise of only certain gifts within the Church. However, he is also conservative in assessing the newness which Christ brings to the interpretation of male and female roles.

Paul K. Jewett, in *Man as Male and Female,* rejects all arguments for female subordination

as being incompatible with (a) the biblical narratives of Man's creation, (b) the revelation which is given us in the life of Jesus, and (c) Paul's fundamental statement of Christian liberty in the Epistle to the Galatians. To put matters theologically, or perhaps we should say hermeneutically, the problem with the concept of female subordination is that it breaks the analogy of faith.[4]

Our dilemma then is to find definitions which do not fall short of the revealed intent of our Creation, while demanding that life in the Church based on these definitions be exemplary, so that our way of life can be a witness to the world. Finally, it may be asking too much of the biblical text to demand that it give us all the answers without any problems. The clarity of the principles of our being created as man and female in the image of God, and the removal of all the perversions of that ideal in our redemption in Jesus Christ, along with our calling to live in mutual subordination and to recognize the Holy Spirit at work in all God's people--these are sufficient to call us to adopt the radical lifestyle of Jesus, and to model it in the Church with boldness.

Conclusion

What does this glance at biblical and theological perspectives imply for women in the church? It sometimes seems that the best we can do is to announce "we do not favor the ordination of women," and in so doing to assume that we have clarified our position on the role of women in the church. Do I hear the apostle Paul chuckling at that understanding of his injunctions? There are members of the body of Christ who feel deeply that this is playing games when the Spirit is calling us to a new vision.

What does it mean to see more clearly the intent of the creation account when it defines humanity created in the image of God as male and female? Is it possible to deny the complementary reality of male-female fellowship when most of our intellectual and spiritual interchange is with only one part of the image and to succumb to the molding pressure of the world when the patriarchal pattern is allowed to define superiority and inferiority in respect to male and female, or to condition our way of life relative to the new roles we are supposed to fill under the guidance of God's spirit? Dare we ponder the implications for our knowledge of a transcendent and holy God when we adopt only the male images of our culture, when the biblical narrative uses freely both male and female images?

The gifts of the Spirit are sovereignly given by God to His people for mutual edification. As members of the body of Christ we need not only to understand more fully the implications of "no male and female" for those with us in the Church, and to learn about mutual subordination, but also to recognize specifically that the paucity of Bible teachers in the Church is a tragedy overshadowed only by the waste in the Church when women, who no longer need to learn solely from men, are not encouraged by all of us to take up the high calling of biblical scholarship.

Thanks be to God that Jesus Christ, who still walks among us and challenges us as the Creator God, made us male and female, empowers us by His Spirit and calls all of us to service and unity in His body, the Church. Amen.

ENDNOTES

1. Paul K. Jewett, *Man as Male and Female: A Study in Sexual Relationship from a Theological Point of View* (Grand Rapids: Wm. B. Eerdmans Publishing, 1975), p. 24.

2. Hedy Martens, "To Men as To Women," *Mennonite Brethren Herald* , 15 (February 6, 1976), p. 7.

3. David Ewert, "The Christian Woman in the Church and Conference," a paper presented to a study conference of the Canadian Mennonite Brethren Churches, in *The Yearbook of the Mennonite Brethren Churches*, July, 1974, p. 39.

4. Jewett, *Man as Male and Female*, p. 134.

6

FROM TEXT TO SERMON:
A Case Study, Isaiah 40:1-11

Elmer A. Martens

G. F. Handel's *Messiah* has immortalized the poetic power of Isaiah 40:1-11 in music. I have heard Isaiah's stirring words sung at Advent and Christmas, and at funerals. The message of Isaiah 40 is appropriate for Easter, Sunday morning sermons, ordinations and mission conferences. In this essay I wish, first, to display the exegetical method by which one arrives at the message of the text, and then to show how one moves from text to sermon. Two styles of sermons will be illustrated. In the person of David Ewert, my valued teaching colleague and friend, to whom this essay is to be a tribute, love of music, skill in exegesis, and good preaching come together.

Getting at the Message

How should an orderly and balanced investigation into the text proceed? One plan is to follow six steps. Three of these six steps are analytical and three are synthetical in nature. The analytical steps involve 1) establishing the literary unit, 2) preparing a structural outline, and 3) investigating key words and concepts. The synthetical steps consist of 1) relating the parts, 2) stating the thrust, and 3) examining the larger context of the thrust. [1] We can illustrate these six steps in our consideration of Isaiah 40:1-11.

Our text has one major textual variant, which can be illustrated by comparing English versions. The Hebrew in v. 6 reads, "Then He said," (so NASB). Both Syriac (a more eastern text) and the Greek and Vulgate (western texts) use "I" instead of "He." The reading, "And I said," (NIV) is preferable and is confirmed by structural analysis of the unit.

Step One: Determine the Unit

A sentence is a unit. So is a paragraph, and for that matter, a book. When we prepare to teach or preach from a text of Scripture, we select a bite-sized passage, but not any random bite-sized passage. The bite-sized passage is a coherent block of material with a distinct beginning and ending, encompassing appropriately the intervening material.

The unit in our text begins with v. 1 because v. 1 is poetry, whereas the preceding is prose. The unit ends with v. 11, because the next verse not only begins with a question but introduces a different theme. More importantly, the opening note on comfort (v. 1) is sounded again with the Shepherd carrying lambs in his bosom (v. 11). The comfort theme is a wrap-around signaling the close-out of a unit.

Setting the limits of a unit is important, for the message is skewed if material that "belongs" to a passage is omitted. Those who preach on Isaiah 6 frequently center on God's call and Isaiah's ready response, "Here am I, send me." The unit, however, does not end with v. 8, but with v. 13. Isaiah 6:1-13 speaks more to the issue of audience obstinacy and "programmed failure" for the messenger than to a divine call. That conclusion is confirmed by Jesus' use of the text (Matt. 13:14-15). We need to take care, then, to establish the unit.

Step Two: Prepare a Structural Analysis

To come to a text is like coming to a new building. Our instinct is to explore its rooms. Similarly, the interpreter tries first to grasp the text according to its plan or format. One can lay bare the structure of the text by outlining the text *formally*; that is, by identifying and formally labeling its parts, as for example, "command," "accusation," "announcement," "question." It is as though the interpreter steps back and asks, figuratively speaking, is this a door or a panel, a window or a mirror? It is an elementary step, but nevertheless essential. It would be a gross error to mistake a mirror for a painted portrait.

Careful attention to shifts in speaker and sensitivity to formal language characteristics and changes in content yields the following outline for Isaiah 40:1-11.

I. Divine Speech vv. 1-2

  A. Identification v. 1aB

  B. Commission vv. 1-2

    1. Command vv. 1-2a

      a. Comfort. 1a

      b. Speak tenderly v. 2a

      c. Call out v. 2aB

    2. Content v. 2b-d

      a. bondage fulfilled v. 2b

      b. penalty paid v. 2c

      c. sins forgiven v. 2d

II. Voice (Speech) vv. 3-5

  A. Introduction v. 3a

  B. Content v. 3b-5

    1. Commands v. 3b-c

    2. Announcements vv. 4-5b

      a. re valley/mountain v. 4a-b

      b. re rough/rugged v. 4c-d

      c. re God's glory v. 5a-b

  C. Closing Formula v. 5c

III. Voice (Speech) v. 6a

  A. Introduction v. 6aA

  B. Content v. 6aB

IV. Prophet's Speech vv. 6b-7c

    A. Question v. 6b

    B. Observation v. 6c-7c

V. Voice (Speech) v. 7d-8

    A. Affirmation v. 7d

    B. Observation v. 8a

    C. Affirmation (Word of God) v. 8b

VI. Voice (Speech) vv. 9-11

    A. Commands v. 9a-3

        1. Ascend mountain

        2. Lift up mighty voice

        3. Do not Fear

        4. Say to the cities of Judah

    B. Content (Announcements) vv. 9f-11

        1. Basic (Behold your God) vv. 9f-10a

        2. Specifics vv. 10b-11

            a. re king v. 10b-c

            b. re judge v. 10d-e

            c. re shepherd v. 11

This step of labeling the parts and recognizing what parts are subordinate to others is a painstaking process. It usually requires several draft outlines beginning with a straightforward listing of format parts without, on the first round, setting the major headings. The headings make it clear that our text consists of several speeches. Before we see how these speeches fit together, it is best to investigate the content.

Step Three: Study Key Words and Concepts

Now with the literary blueprint of the text before us, we are prepared to examine the details of content: the meaning of selected words, phrases or concepts, etc. We get out our tools such as concordances (preferably an Englishman's Hebrew Concordance, or its equivalent in Greek for the NT), theological word dictionaries; and Bible dictionaries. We turn to commentaries only after we have done our private exploration. On Isaiah 40:1-11 we will want to do research on terms such as "comfort," "reward," "glory of God," and notions such as preparation for royalty, theophany, and shepherding.

Here, for example, is what I found about "comfort." A Hebrew dictionary explains that "comfort" means "to express one's condolence," "to reassure." A concordance puts me in touch with life situations of severe loss followed by efforts to comfort. For example, Jacob, as he sees it, has lost a son, Joseph, to the ravages of wild beasts. "Then all his sons and all his daughters arose to *comfort* him. . ." (Gen. 37:35). I find that the word "comfort" is used in Isaiah 40-66 (to which our text is an introduction), ten times in all. Interestingly, the last chapter's "wrap-up" reference to "comfort" helps supply a very down-to-earth touch: "As one whom his mother comforts, so I will comfort you" (66:13).

Later, when checking a commentary, I learn that had I examined all the references to comfort in Isaiah 40-66, I would have found 1) that the one who comforts is God, 2) that Israel is the one comforted and this by an intervention of God, and 3) that the comfort consists in turning away suffering and helping. [2] Or as another commentator puts it: to comfort is "not to console in trouble, [but] to comfort him out of his trouble into joy." [3] The double use of "comfort" (Isaiah. 40:1) suggests urgency (cf. 51:9; 51:17).

The speaker is the Lord God. The command, in the plural, suggests that an audience, perhaps the heavenly council, is in view. One such scene of God in session with his council is given in 1 Kings 22, during which a messenger— in this case a deceptive spirit–is dispatched. By contrast, here a set of voices (messengers) pass on a message to Jerusalem.

Leaping forward to the final speech by one of the anonymous voices (v. 9), we find ourselves asking, Who is addressed? Grammatically one could read, "Get yourself up on a high mountain *to* Zion." Those who prefer this reading, point to Isaiah 52:7 where a messenger announces a similar message about God's reign *to* Zion. Jerusalem (=Zion) is passive, only a spectator. Against this view it has been noted that the tone is missionary. Many quite rightly read "O Zion." It is Zion that is addressed. The image is one of Jerusalem, itself on a hill, which is to ascend to still higher hills and from these trumpet the message of good news. The poet keeps the hearers in suspense, for while urging that the message be shouted, he does not give its content, until at last with dramatic effect the specifics are disclosed: "Here is your God" (40:9).

The expression signals a theophany, an appearance of the Almighty. In our research concerning theophanies we single out Judges 5:4-5. Deborah's poem exults in God's march from Seir, one which had the mountains quaking. God appeared, and from that moment the fate of Sisera, the enemy, was sealed. Or, to take another instance, Habakkuk, the prophet, found himself in an arid atmosphere. He himself was in anguish about the evil in society and God's failure to take action. He prayed that God would revive his work. And then the theophany! God came. He appeared. Mountains collapsed. The landscape changed and so did everything, including Habakkuk's perspective (Habakkuk 3:16-19). In both these instances the appearance of God clearly made the difference.

God's coming marks a change in circumstances. The prophet in our Isaiah text had complained that all was transient, like grass, and falling apart like wilted flowers. Now there is One who takes charge. Verses 10-11 depict God as Ruler, the strong man with "His arm ruling for him." God the Judge is accompanied by his "reward" or trophy, namely his people who had been delivered from exile. God as Shepherd nurtures his lambs; these feeble and the weak ones receive V. I. P. treatment. Nothing can be quite the same after God comes on the scene!

In the way we have begun to examine "comfort" and "theophany" we could examine other key notions. Before long the passage becomes an index to the rest of Scripture. Research of this nature opens up the nuances of the Scripture text and firmly establishes its meaning.

Step Four: Relate the Parts

The text at this stage lies before us rich with information but still somewhat piecemeal in nature. What is now needed is a sense of the whole. We move from analysis to synthesis and we do so by asking and answering the question: How are the parts related to each other? This step is not merely a matter of rehearsing the contents in serial fashion from beginning to end. Rather, when we look intently at the inter-connections within the text, fresh insights almost certainly will emerge.

It is helpful to use colored pencils to mark repetitions, contrast and continuity. In vv. 9-11, the startling news, "Here is your God", is preceded by piled-up imperatives: "Go up," "Lift up," "Declare" (v. 9). Something momentous is in the offing. The climactic announcement is "Behold your God." The next sentences briefly but powerfully remind us that God is King, Judge, and Shepherd. For God's people this would mean powerful rule, just decisions and tender care. These statements link with the opening imperative "Comfort My People": they emphasize the authority back of that imperative, and also stress, first and last, that God comes to his people with the tenderness of a shepherd who recognizes the weakness of his people.

"It's no use," complains the prophet (part IV, vv. 6b-7c). His comment, "All flesh is as grass" (v. 6), means that nothing is permanent. Everything fades. What is there to get excited about? So someone bursts on the scene with excitement, "Call out!" (v. 6a). The prophet, along with the exiles, is languishing in captivity. For them hope is gone. They are not about to stir, lest their hopes will be dashed once more. Part VI (vv. 9-11) bears on this down-beat mood by stressing the good news ("gospel" in New Testament language) that God is on the scene. Part I (vv. 1-2) also anticipates this despondency by announcing a message of consolation, beginning with forgiveness.

"Call out" is the directive in verses 2, 6 and 9. A voice that is calling is introduced in v. 3. Indeed, the picture that emerges is that of God in his heavenly council issuing an announcement. That announcement is taken up by the first messenger (v. 3), is picked up in relay fashion by still another anonymous messenger (v. 6), and apparently by the prophet himself (after his objections have been met), who shouts the message to the residents of Jerusalem, who in turn, completing the relay of messages, announce to the whole of Judah: "Here is your God." This is fast-moving drama! We hear about the "glory of the Lord" revealed (v. 5), about the "Word of God" being established firmly (v. 8), and climactically, about God himself appearing!

Step Five: Stating the Thrust

By now we can gather up the message of the text in a single sentence. The thrust statement is intended to get to the heart of the text. Keeping in mind the background situation of dismal exile, the climactic news of God's appearance and presence, and the relay set of messengers, we can arrive at the following: *Comfort to a troubled people—a message relayed by messengers—is grounded in God's forgiveness and in His personal appearance.* True, this statement of thrust is decidedly lacklustre when compared to the picturesque, emotionally-laden poetry of Isaiah 40:1-11. Even so, there is value in being precise about what is the "bottom line" of the passage. It is this summary that will become the starting point for sermonizing.

Step Six: Examining the Context of the Message

It is useful to compare our text with antecedents, with subsequent texts in the Old Testament, and with concepts in the New Testament, in order to appreciate its dimensions and nuances. Within the judgment messages of chapters 1-39 stands Isaiah's vision of God's holiness. This vision (Isaiah 6:1-13) is foundational for Isaiah's ministry of announcing judgment. Our text (Isaiah 40:1-11) is foundational for the messages of salvation. Both Isaiah 6 and Isaiah 40:1-11 presuppose a heavenly council (cf. "Who will go for us?" 6:8). Both speak about God's glory. In Isaiah 6 "the whole earth is full of God's glory." In Isaiah 40 "the glory of the Lord shall be revealed, and all flesh will see it together." In the temple vision the prophet acknowledges, "Woe is me. . ." (6:5). In Isaiah 40 the prophet protests, "All flesh is as grass." Additional comparisons show that Isaiah 6:1-13 and Isaiah 40:1-11 are something of a pair.

Subsequent to Isaiah 40, in Ezekiel 37:1-4, the exiles deplore their situation: "Our bones are dried up, and our hope has perished. We are completely cut off" (Ezekiel 37:11, NASB). God's answer through Ezekiel is the vision of the dry bones coming to life, "an exceedingly great army." As in Isaiah 40, the prophet is assigned to announce a word of hope to people in a desperate situation.

The New Testament counterpart to this text is first of all the story of John the Baptist. He identifies himself as a voice in the wilderness calling for people to repent and so remove the obstacles that hinder God's coming to them. Very striking is the sequence in John 1. The author, having alluded in John's testimony to Isaiah 40:3, reports, "Behold the Lamb of God" (John 1:29), thus echoing "Behold your God" (Isaiah 40:9). Now on a grand scale, God has dispatched his word of comfort to the world. Messengers like John the Baptist announce the good news (the evangel) that God has appeared in the person of Jesus. Something new has come.

By looking at the biblical context of the message we have broadened the base, so to speak, and see implications more clearly. It is in the application section of the sermon that these implications will likely be reflected. And that raises the question, How does one get from exegesis to the sermon?

The Transition From Text to Sermon

Specific helps on moving from text to sermon are relatively few in number when compared to commentaries and books on exegesis/homiletics.[4] Three comments may be helpful as guidelines.

First, the starting point for an expositional sermon must be a grasp of the thrust of the text. In Isaiah 40:1-11 that thrust is about God's comfort to a despairing people, a comfort grounded in God's personal appearance as "the strong man," the ruler and shepherd. The sermon, to be aligned with the text, will deal with good news of comfort to the distressed. In fact, the message of the text, crystalized through exegesis, now becomes the sermon's theme sentence. I might recast that statement somewhat, selecting perhaps an aspect for emphasis in the light of the needs of my audience. But the "burden" of the text becomes the "burden" of the sermon. Thus the move from the text to the sermon could be captured in the following theme sentence:*The good news is that God, enroute to meet you in your distress, has arrived and is now on the scene.* The sermon would incorporate 1) the distress of those in the text, 2) the prospect of God's appearance, and 3) the excitement of his immediate presence. The sermon is biblical when the theme of the sermon is the theme of the text.

Woven into the main theme are other themes, of course. The preacher might be fascinated by the crisp comment of a sub-theme, for example, "The Word of our God stands forever" (v. 8), around which a sermon could very profitably be built. By "sub-theme" I do not mean a theme of small importance, but a theme which is noted but not elaborated. However, even a sermon on this sub-theme, unless it is an outright topical sermon (for which v. 8 is a "pre-text" more than a "text"), the preacher will want to take into account the emphasis on God's good news to the despairing. Such a sermon about "The Enduring Word of God" could highlight the great contrast of this enduring Word of God with human transitoriness (vv. 5-6), the permanent validity of the "good news" that "Here is your God" (v. 9), and the joyful urgency of passing this Word on. Even concentrating on a sub-theme--of which there are more than a dozen--one should not drift from the over-riding "burden" or thrust of the text.

Secondly, though the theme sentence must be rooted in the text, its development might, but need not, follow closely the order of the text. The preacher has certain freedoms, one of which is that the preacher can shape a sermon with creativity. He or she may substitute an order of development different from the progression given in the text. Thus, while the text begins with a message of comfort, the sermon might better begin with the mood of the addressee, "What's the use? All flesh is as grass." Or, while the text climaxes with "Here is your God," the sermon could conclude with the exhortation, "Clear the way for the Lord. . ." or "Remove the obstacles!" In the shaping of the sermon texture the preacher enjoys some freedom.

Thirdly, the preacher must be preoccupied, not in moving from Scripture to sermon, but in moving from Scripture to life. How can one cross Lessing's proverbial "ugly ditch" and take a text, such as Isaiah 40, written for a specific moment, and make it applicable for the present? I cannot escape the claim that the Bible is God's word of address to human beings in their differing situations. The word of address becomes a paradigm, a way for me to see God at work. The written word is there as a window that allows me to see how God is at work; in this case, how God comes to a people who are in a difficult situation. Leaning heavily on the principle of analogy, the sermonizer, open to the illuminating Spirit, places the message of that text alongside a comparable and current situation. The procedure has been described technically. The interpreter engages first in distantiation (the text is put at arm's length) in order to discern the message of the text. Next the interpreter collapses the distance between himself and the text by receiving or appropriating the text, thus fusing the horizons of "then" and "now."

One implication of this approach is that there is no *absolute* need to "filter" this text through the New Testament, as though only by being treated antiseptically can it find application for today's believer. Yes, a text must be viewed in its larger context, and that context includes the New Testament. Yet one should keep in mind that the New Testament itself asserts that "all Scripture" (a reference in the first instance to the books which the Christian church called the Old Testament), "is profitable for teaching, for reproof, for correction, for training in righteousness" (2 Tim. 3:16). The Old Testament can stand on its own feet. Of course it is incumbent to listen to the New Testament, just as it is important, if one has a New Testament text, to listen to the Old Testament. Listening to a biblical text is an exercise in stereophonic listening. However, the Old Testament text can be appropriate for today's believer via a direct line, without a detour through the New Testament.

Nor is the gap between "then" and "now" necessarily spanned by a "ladder of abstraction." Walter Kaiser advocates that from the text there be abstracted a universal principle. The interpreter dismisses the particularities of the situation in which the text is found, and mounts the ladder to a point from which he can see what universal principle lies hidden in the text. Then, armed with this principle, the interpreter dismounts the ladder in the direction of the present day and makes application of this universal principle to the current scene. [5] But the assumption--misguided, I think--is that the Bible is a book whose stories are to be decoded into universal principles. We are closer to the Bible if we see these stories and events as windows into how God operates. As we look responsibly, with the help of the Spirit of God, the window becomes a mirror; we recognize ourselves in that story. God is speaking to us.

Bridging from an Old Testament text to the present day is not different from bridging from the New Testament to the current situation. The three observations apply essentially to texts in both Testaments. These comments do not do justice to the problem, but they should assist in preparing a sermon or even in evaluating the following illustrations.

Preaching the Message: Two Sermon Formats

The excavation of the text through exegesis has now produced its treasures. The preacher knows that the treasures are needed by his people. The preacher is then faced with the task of presenting the treasure appropriately. There is no one right way of "packaging" the message-treasure for the audience. Possible formats are those of drama, song, or sermon. In the sermon also there are options, two of which are illustrated below through sermon briefs. [6]

The Point Sermon

One form of casting the sermon is in the point mode. In this well-known format the preacher states a proposition (really the conclusion of his textual investigation), and then with sub-points supports, amplifies, and illustrates the proposition. [7] Of the many preachers who are masters at the point sermon, Dr. David Ewert is certainly one. His sermon on a text similar to Isaiah 40:1-11, prepared for a college chapel illustrates the format. [8]

"God's Call to Redemptive Ministry"

Scripture: Exodus 3:1-12

Theme

God's call to redemptive ministry comes in a definite but unique way.

Purpose

To show God's call to redemptive ministry operative in one person's life and to use this call as a mirror for our life.

Design

Introduction
A family moves to Egypt; threat of genocide; Moses

I. The Time of the Call
   A. In the course of his daily work,
      e.g. Hans Nielsen Hauge
   B. God calls after past failures,
      e.g. Peter, Phillips Brooks
   C. When he did not expect it,
      e.g. John Mackay

II. The Manner of the Call
   A. By giving Moses a new vision of God
      e.g. R. Otto
   B. By opening Moses' eyes for the need of the people (vv. 7-9)
   C. It is a call to personal involvement in the redemptive purposes of God(v. 10). Illustration: French statue of Christ without hands

III. The Response to the Call (vv. 11-12)
   Illustration: The disciples

Among the numerous potential seed thoughts from Isaiah 40:1-11, one centers on the theme of the human condition and the divine provision, as follows:

Human Frailty/Divine Permanence (The Word)

Human Hurt/Divine Comfort (The Shepherd)

Human Loss/Divine Hope (The Advent of God)

What theme sentence and title might be supplied to capture all three? Should that sermon be developed in the "point" mode or are there other options? Or should all three be treated in one sermon? Seizing on a subtheme in the text, Judson Cornwall wrote a booklet under the title *Freeway Under Construction*, with chapter titles such as "Straighten those Curves," "Graded, Gravelled, and Paved," and "Access Assured." No doubt building on G. A. Smith's comments about "four voices to startle," B. A. Copass used the following outline. [9]

I. A Voice of Grace, vv. 1-2

II. A Voice of Providence, vv. 3-5

III. A Voice of Assurance, vv. 6-9

IV. A Voice of Hope, vv. 9-11

From the sermon books comes a full-dress model, by J.H. Morrison, of a "point sermon" on our text. Although preached some fifty years ago, this sermon by J. H. Morrison, is readable and relevant for today. It is built squarely on the thrust of the passage, even though he has singled out verse 1 for his text. In the second paragraph of the full printed sermon the subject-matter is laid out, and in the third, the listener is clued in on the direction the message will take. From there the sermon points follow from the theme which is already announced in the title. The sermon does not, nor should it, incorporate all of the text. One theme is in view. Each of the sermon sections begins, as does Ewert's sermon, with elaboration from the text; it ends with a paragraph or more on the present-day.

"The Gospel of Comfort"

Scripture:Isaiah 40:1 [1-31]

Theme Sentence

The gospel is above all else a message of comfort, a declaration of the kindness and love of God our Savior.

Purpose

To show that ours is indeed the gospel of comfort, to urge that it be embraced, and that it re-echo from us to others.

Design

Introduction

'Comfort,' it should be remembered, does not mean simply to soothe, but, as the word itself signifies, to make strong, to invigorate.

I. The Need of Comfort

-Israel's need: forlorn, yoke of exile, foreign religion
-A universal need: world not full of the proud who need to be broken, but of broken and weak who need to be strengthened
- This generation's need: social unrest, awful fear of war

II. The Message of Comfort, viz. divine deliverance

-God comes in infinite power (valleys to be exalted)
-God comes in infinite tenderness (shepherd)
-Christ is "full of pity joined with power"

III. The Recipients of the Comfort, viz. people of God

-Not a general assurance that all is well for all
-"Omnipotent love is at work for our salvation"[10]

The Move Sermon

The "point" sermon is better-known than the "move" sermon. The move sermon differs from the point sermon in the following ways. The point sermon is deductive; it is upfront with the conclusion. The move sermon is inductive; it works toward a conclusion. The point sermon, like the lecture, is essentially an appeal to the intellect. The move sermon is like a story. The move sermon appeals to the intellect too, but attempts self-consciously to engage the listener more fully by drawing the listener into the conflict or the flow of the story. The point sermon had its origin at a time when people's main channel of communication was listening. The move sermon is in part a response to the current age of television where communication is visual and story-like rather than only oral. The move sermon relies heavily on the imagination and seeks to draw the audience into an experience. [11] One might say, in what is clearly an over-generalization, that the point sermon focuses on the written text; the move sermon tries to capture the event about which the text speaks. The essential material in the two sermons could be much the same, but the packaging is different.

For example, a "move" sermon on the text of Exodus 3:1-11 might take as its title, "The Start of a Redemption-oriented Pilgrimage." The theme sentence and the purpose remain as given in the "point" sermon. The "moves," still to be refined, could be the following:

*In our life, as in Moses' life, there come curious combinations of the
    insignificant (e. g. bush) and the significant (life's vocation).
**Tobe alone is sometimes strangely to be in the presence of the Al-
mighty.
***Wonderfully one is moved, like Moses, from a menial task to an
    exalted redemptive task.

With a little rearrangement, the substance of David Ewert's material could
be incorporated in the above "moves." The "move" sermon, which is plot-
like, is less predictable than a "point" sermon.

In the following example of a move (or mood) sermon on Isaiah 40:1-11,
the preacher begins by noting the "voice" in Isaiah 40, hanging, so to
speak, in the air. The voice is not identified, nor are the listeners. After
setting a mood of wonderment, the focus shifts to the plight of an ancient
group, a group not unlike some moderns. The listener is not informed
from the outset as to what the direction of the sermon will be. It can be
rightly stated that the sermon "grows." But the move sermon does more
than concentrate on mood, for a point sermon can do that as well. The
move sermon is a type of story, weaving the present with the past, not so
much to preach about what was in the past that can be applied for today,
but to preach so that a single word, the word for the present, is heard
throughout.

"Something to Shout About"

Scripture:Isaiah 40:1-11

Theme: There are situations that seem hopeless (*Theme I*)

    All the more urgent to proclaim that God is present (*Theme II*)

Purpose: To show that in disheartening situations the Word from the Lord
    is that He is there, is present

Design:
    I. A Voice is heard calling--who? to whom? (then, now)
    II. It's hard to know what to say in a dull, painful situation "All flesh is as
grass" (exile, today) *Theme I*
    III. True, there are some things one could say, even there *Theme II*
    For example:
        A. The Word of God stands sure (v. 8)
        B. God's Forgiveness (v. 2)
        C. The coming glory of God (v. 5)

IV. Surprise! The Greater News is that God is Here. . . Now! *Theme II*
Illustration: A family waiting for homecoming of college student.
    God Comes!
        A. God is King/Judge (the referee is here
        B. God is Shepherd (the nurturing One is here)

V. Preach it! Act on it!
Illustration:John, the Baptist, wilderness, Here is the Lamb of God!
Illustration:The world mission scene, the anemic church, the ill mother
    (*Theme I: Theme II*)

Which package--point sermon or move sermon--is best? The answer
depends on the nature of the text and the purpose of the preacher. The two
kinds of sermons emerge from quite different assumptions. The point sermon, by its nature at least, is designed to convey information. The move
sermon assumes that the purpose is something of an event, an event in
which the listener participates. It were well that preachers who have only
one style at their disposal would read, learn, and work on an alternate
style. Surely the Bible itself urges us in that direction. In it one can find
point sermons (Jer. 7) and move sermons (Acts 7), and many other communication forms besides.

One issue in preaching, as I have indicated, is the packaging. It is not a
small issue, though its importance can be overplayed. It is in the packaging that the appeal and power of the message, humanly speaking, lies.
Another issue is the bridge from the text to the present-day. But of still
greater importance is the thrust of the text, namely (for Isaiah 40), the
realization that God is immediately present in the hard situation. If you
know who God is, that is wondrous news. Preach it, pastor! Teach it,
teacher! Live by it, believer!

ENDNOTES

1. The method of exegesis is illustrated in my "Psalm 73: A Corrective to a Modern Misunderstanding," *Direction*, Vol. XII (October 1983):15-26. The steps resemble closely those in Douglas Stuart, *Old Testament Exegesis*, (Philadelphia: Westminster, 2nd ed. , 1984).

2. Claus Westermann, *Isaiah 40-66*, (Philadelphia:Westminster Press, 1969), pp. 34, 37.

3. G. A. F. Knight, *Isaiah 40-55*, (Grand Rapids: Wm B. Eerdmans Publishing, 1984), p. 7.

4. See the recent contributions of Walter Kaiser, Jr. , *Toward an Exegetical Theology: Biblical Exegesis for Teaching and Preaching*, (Grand Rapids: Baker Book House, 1981), and the demonstration of his method in *Malachi, God's Unchanging Love*, (Grand Rapids: Baker Book House, 1984).

5. Walter Kaiser, *Toward Discovering the Old Testament*, (Grand Rapids: Zondervan, 1987), pp. 164-166, 174.

6. The form for the "sermon brief" is that used by Ian Pitt-Watson, Professor of Fuller Theological Seminary. His small book, *A Primer for Preachers*, (Grand Rapids: Baker Book House, 1968), is excellent for the novice, and provides good review for the veteran.

7. For a discussion, almost exclusively on the "point sermon," see the widely used text by Haddon Robinson, *Biblical Preaching*, (Grand Rapids: Baker Book House, 1980).

8. David Ewert kindly furnished a manuscript copy and granted permission for use of its abstract as I prepared it.

9. B. A. Copass, *Isaiah: Prince of Old Testament Prophets*, (Nashville: Broadman Press, 1944), pp. 99-100.

10. Edward Hastings, ed. , *The Speaker's Bible. Isaiah*. Vol. II (Aberdeen, Scotland: "The Speaker's Bible" Office, 1935), pp. 3-6.

11. Eugene Lowry, *The Homiletical Plot* , (Nashville: Abingdon, 1980); Don M. Wardlaw, ed. , *Preaching Biblically*, (Philadelphia: Westminster Press, 1983); Ralph Lewis, *Inductive Preaching* ,(Westchester, Ill: Crossway Books, 1983).

PART II

THE CHURCH

"The Church is not a gallery for the exhibition of eminent Christians, but a school for the education of imperfect ones."

Henry Ward Beecher

7

THE CHANGING ROLE OF BIBLICAL/THEOLOGICAL EDUCATION IN THE MENNONITE BRETHREN CHURCH

Abe J. Dueck

During the past four decades we have witnessed very significant changes in higher theological education among Mennonite Brethren in North America. This is true in a general sense, but it is also true for the particular area of biblical scholarship wherein David Ewert was, in many ways, a pioneer , especially so for Canadian Mennonite Brethren. This essay seeks to analyze these developments by providing some historical background in Russia and the earlier period in North America, but focuses particularly on the transitions in Canada since World War II. An attempt is then made to assess the current state of biblical/theological scholarship as it relates to the present identity and self-understanding of the Mennonite Brethren Church. The thesis of this essay is that there has been a significant shift in the last generation which is, in many respects, paralleled by changes in the larger evangelical community in North America, and that this shift has resulted in a number of unresolved tensions in the Mennonite Brethren community as such.

The Anabaptist movement of the sixteenth century, as well as the Mennonite Brethren renewal movement of the nineteenth century, manifested a very special concern for the recovery of the Bible and its authority for the church. Luther's emphasis on *sola scriptura* is often seen as having been applied with greater rigor and consistency by the Anabaptists. In addition, scholars refer to the Anabaptists' concern for the priority of the New Testament, for the enlightenment of the Holy Spirit, and for the role of the faithful community in interpreting the Scriptures. The Anabaptist understanding of the priesthood of all believers is seen as especially related to the role of the faithful community in the interpretation of the Scriptures.

The Mennonite Brethren renewal movement of 1860 was also spawned, to a considerable extent, by the recovery of the Bible. Small groups gathered to study the Scriptures as early as the 1840s and 1850s. Later this emphasis evolved into the regular convening of Bible conferences (*Bibel Besprechungen*). John B. Toews comments as follows concerning these events:

> For each conference--an annual event in every organized church--a book of the Bible or some selected chapters were selected. One of the ministers would present a general introduction to the book. The study that followed assumed the form of a discussion more than a lecture. Teachers, ministers and the people from the pews participated. The process was a verse by verse study. Here and there one of the more gifted teachers would summarize the major truths which emerged from the discussions. Ministers from the congregations would participate in as many Bible conferences of this nature as possible by attending the gatherings in their area and even in distant localities.[1]

The ministry at that time was, of course, a lay ministry, and no specialized training was possible. A further step was the introduction of special minister seminars *(Prediger Kurse)*. This became possible particularly after more and more Mennonites went to Germany and Switzerland to study in a variety of schools there. Toews mentions the following as being frequent resource persons for these seminars: Jakob Reimer, David Duerksen, Herman Neufeld, Peter Koehn, and J.B. Wiens[2]. In America a similar tradition developed.

A final phase toward more extensive theological education in Russia was the institutional phase which never fully matured. The General Conference of Mennonites in Russia had for years attempted to establish a theological seminary but various circumstances always intervened. The Mennonite Brethren, however, finally did establish a school at Tschongraw in the Crimea in 1918, which functioned to some degree until 1925.[3] This school was also referred to as a seminary, although in terms of level of preparation it was clearly more like a Bible school. Its main initial purpose was to train missionaries and, to a lesser extent, to train church workers for the Mennonite congregations in Russia. Several other Bible schools functioned for brief periods of time after the Revolution.

The theological impact of the various schools in Germany and Switzerland, which Mennonite Brethren and other Mennonites attended, was obviously significant. The main schools to which Mennonites went included the Baptist Theological Seminary in Hamburg; Barmen Theological Seminary, Berlin (later Wiedenest);[4] St. Chrischona;[5] Basel Theological Seminary; and the University of Basel. In addition, the influence of the Blankenburg Alliance Conference in Germany, which was founded in 1885, must be recognized as significant especially for Mennonite Brethren, even though it did not take the shape of a traditional theological program.

Overall, however, the level of theological education and the number of people who received it was still relatively very small. N. J. Klassen, in an article entitled, "Mennonite Intelligentsia in Russia," lists a total of eleven Mennonite theologians or ministers who had received a university or seminary degree.[6] At least two in the list were Mennonite Brethren (Jakob Kroeker and Benjamin H. Unruh). Other leaders, like Peter M. Friesen, are listed under the category of teachers. The list is obviously incomplete, but the fact remains that higher theological education was a rarity among Mennonite Brethren in Russia. *Table I* supplies a list of seventeen Mennonite Brethren students who studied theology in European schools, most of them (14) at the Hamburg Baptist Theological Seminary (*Predigerseminar*). Most of these were engaged in missionary preparation and went to India. Training for ministry in the home congregations was evidently not seen as very necessary. In fact, the German Baptists had also begun educational efforts in relationship to missionary training in 1849, and only later did the School develop more broadly into a training school for ministers. Johann Gerhard Oncken, the founder of the German Baptists, had reservations about formal training for church leaders, perhaps because he had no formal training himself.[7]

The curriculum at Hamburg included general courses on education, philosophy, Greek, English language, and theoretical and practical theology.[8] The faculty members had received a respectable theological training, having studied at universities in Berlin and Leipzig, at Rochester Theological Seminary, and at Regents-Park College in London.[9] More work needs to be done on the nature of the curriculum in some of the other schools, but in general the studies probably did not involve serious consideration of some of the findings of more radical biblical scholarship in Europe around the turn of the century.

The two Mennonite Brethren mentioned above, Jakob Kroeker and Benjamin Unruh, made significant theological contributions and had a number of works of biblical scholarship published. Kroeker, who was a graduate of the Baptist Theological Seminary in Hamburg but was also significantly influenced by Baedeker and very active in the Blankenburg conferences, wrote prolifically on the books of the Old and New Testaments.[10] Unruh was more involved in the study of issues pertaining to Mennonite history, but also dealt with more specifically biblical and theological issues.[11] In terms of biblical interpretation, the Blankenburg influence through various channels was probably the greatest for Mennonite Brethren in the long run. Not only did Mennonite Brethren leaders bring back a distinctive (dispensational) system of biblical interpretation from Blankenburg, but a number of non-Mennonite Brethren were also invited to speak at various occasions such as Bible conferences in Russia.

The individual who brought a sense of continuity in theological education from Russia to Canada was the brother of Benjamin H. Unruh, Abraham H. Unruh. Abraham Unruh was one of the leading teachers of the Tschongraw Bible School in the Crimea. Others included missionary Johann Wiens and Heinrich Braun, both of whom had studied at Hamburg, and Gerhard J. Reimer who, however, had received no higher theological education. Unruh himself also had not received any formal theological education. After the 1917 Revolution in Russia brought about a total disruption of life and had forced the closure of the Bible School, three of the teachers (excluding Braun) migrated to Canada and all became involved in a new institution in Winkler, which was called "Mennonite Bible School Peniel." Finally, in 1944, it was Unruh who was again instrumental in the founding of a "higher Bible school," the Mennonite Brethren Bible College in Winnipeg.

In his biography of Abraham H. Unruh, David Ewert comments that "there is probably no man who influenced the Canadian Mennonite brotherhood as profoundly as did A. H. Unruh."[12] He further states that "our American brethren got the impression that the theology of all Canadian Mennonite Brethren was that of Abraham Unruh." Although, as indicated above, Unruh had no formal theological education, he was a man of considerable breadth and depth of learning. He was a great admirer of Charles H. Spurgeon, but made generous use of the writings of prominent European theologians like Emil Brunner and Karl Barth.[13] His lack of competence in the biblical languages was to some extent made up by the extensive use of critical commentaries, such as those by Adolf Schlatter, as well as by the comparison of various translations of particular texts. He never became involved in the fundamentalist-liberal controversy and even though, as Ewert states, he might be called a "dispensationalist," he "didn't become entangled in the intricacies of the end times."[14]

Unruh's concept of higher theological education could be characterized as "liberal" in the sense that he appreciated the need to combine the liberal arts with theology. Theology, he felt, should not be taught in isolation from other disciplines such as philosophy, history, literature, etc. Therefore, the Mennonite Brethren Bible College in Winnipeg had a broadly based curriculum from its very inception.

In a sense the later years in Russia, and the early years after the 1920s migration to Canada, were each characterized by two parallel streams of theological identity. The one was symbolized by Unruh and was more mainstream and moderate in its theological identity. The Tschongraw curriculum had been patterned after the Hamburg Seminary curriculum. The other was symbolized by Jakob Reimer and the dispensationalist hermeneutic of Blankenburg. Both were transplanted from Russia to Canada--both Unruh and Reimer were very active for two or three decades, one in a church-institutional setting and the other in a much less denominationally oriented context. Both were also reinforced by movements already established in North America which were having their impact on Mennonite Brethren who had arrived here earlier. Finally both were transformed, but the inner tensions remained and are still being felt by Mennonite Brethren in ways that prolong the identity problem that seems to have plagued Mennonite Brethren from the beginning of their history.

There have been many recent studies of the origins of fundamentalism in the nineteenth century and the developments that led to the crisis of the fundamentalist-modernist controversy in North America in the 1920s. The various Mennonite groups that already existed in America were affected by it to varying degrees. The Mennonite Brethren of the earlier migration were centered in the United States and had already felt the impact of the North American religious environment in some measure. A number had also begun to move northward into Canada and had established missionary and educational endeavors there.

The theological stream in North America which ultimately reinforced the dispensationalist theological stream that was developing in Russia, and was carried to Canada by leaders like Jacob W. Reimer, was originally mediated to the Canadian Mennonite Brethren constituency primarily by William J. Bestvater. Bestvater had migrated to the United States from Russia in 1894 and, after his conversion, had attended Light and Hope Bible Institute in Cleveland where dispensationalist theology was taught. Later he joined the Mennonite Brethren Church and spent eight years in the Winnipeg City Mission and nine years as instructor at the Herbert Bible School. There can be no doubt that the curriculum was basically patterned after the model of the American Bible School movement which was the product of the dispensationalist-fundamentalist movement.[14]   A dispensationalist hermeneutic was unquestioningly accepted and this became the predominant mode of understanding the Bible. Bestvater was also the author of numerous articles and books which popularized the dispensationalist hermeneutic. Other prominent individuals who advanced a similar hermeneutic included Jakob F. Redekop and Heinrich Regehr, both of whom taught at the Herbert Bible School while Bestvater was there. Very detailed charts of the dispensations of human history were drawn up and used in churches and institutions. A favorite textbook was Clarence Larkin's *Dispensational Truth or God's Plan and Purpose in the Ages* (1918). The differences in orientation between the two hermeneutical or theological streams can readily be discerned. The dispensational teachings undoubtedly also prepared the way for the adoption of other elements of the North American fundamentalist social, political and religious orientation.

Until World War II, the Russian immigrants of the 1920s did not have to grapple seriously with the North American religious environment. True, they had a variety of contacts with the Mennonite Brethren of the earlier migration and also worked together at the institutional level in such places as Tabor College and Herbert Bible School. But by and large they settled in different areas in relatively closed communities and did not master the English language during the first generation. Thus the complex situation which resulted from different, although to some degree parallel experiences in different countries did not become fully evident until the decades after the War.

In the meantime, the religious climate in North America was undergoing further significant change. The general scholarly consensus was that the fundamentalist forces had suffered a serious defeat in the 1920s, although liberalism was also forced to retreat in the face of new theological currents stemming from Europe through individuals like Karl Barth and the movement labelled neo-orthodoxy. A segment of fundamentalism gradually became transformed and before long an identifiable evangelical movement was taking shape. We shall return to this subject later.

In the larger Mennonite world, winds of change were also blowing with a renewed interest in Anabaptist origins in the sixteenth century and the formulation of what came to be called the Anabaptist vision. The name of Harold S. Bender came into increasing prominence, not only in his own denomination, usually referred to as (Old) Mennonite, but increasingly among Mennonites of Dutch/Prussian/Russian origin. The Mennonite Central Committee and the Mennonite World Conference created an increasing awareness among Mennonites of each other, particularly in North America.

As the second generation of English-speaking Mennonite Brethren of the 1920s migration faced the post-World War II North American religious environment, the situation had indeed become complex. The major options included at least the following: 1) Dispensationalist fundamentalism, somewhat moderated by factors such as the Mennonite teaching on nonresistance, 2) Evangelicalism, which was a new and intellectually more respectable movement, and 3) Anabaptism, as redefined by North American Mennonite scholars, most of whom were of Swiss Mennonite background. These options were not mutually exclusive, of course. Some Mennonite Brethren leaders moved in one or other of all these directions and the identity of the institutions which they served was often determined by the strongest personalities within them.

The earliest Mennonite Brethren teachers who taught in the various Bible institutes that were established in many places by the Russian immigrants of the 1920s had received such education as they possessed, in Russia or in the European schools mentioned above. But before long a number began enrolling in a variety of seminaries and universities in Canada and the United States, and the schools in which they enrolled were to have an important bearing on the theological direction which the denomination and its schools would take in the future, particularly in Canada. Among the first leaders of the new immigrants to receive advanced theological education in North America were John B. Toews, Sr., and George W. Peters. The first generation of Canadian Mennonite Brethren educated in North America, and the institutions they attended, are indicated in *Table II*, which includes primarily the graduate record until 1960.

It is noteworthy that, in the main, this generation received their education during what Marsden refers to as the "fourth stage of evangelicalism," namely after 1940.[16] The second stage, which he dates from about 1919 to 1926, was the "dramatic phase" when the anti-modernist crusade peaked and fundamentalism became a clearly identifiable movement. The most sensational event of the period was the Scopes Trial in Tennessee in 1925, which dramatically focused the conflict on the teaching of biological evolution in the schools. This stage of the evangelical movement (i.e., the fundamentalist-modernist controversy) did not directly impact many Canadian Mennonite Brethren because the large migration from Russia, following the Revolution, had just begun and it was a long while before Canadian Mennonite Brethren had fully settled into their North American environment.

The third stage, from 1926 to about 1940, is characterized by Marsden as one of withdrawal and regrouping. Fundamentalism became less mainstream in America and "moved so much in the direction of sectarianism that the doctrine of separation was often a test of fidelity".[17] Dispensationalism also was often considered a tenet of orthodoxy and it frequently worked primarily through independent denominations, Bible institutes, and avenues other than the institutional church, which was often considered to be apostate. No doubt some of these influences were already felt by Canadian Mennonite Bethren, but not primarily as a result of the formal theological education which leaders were receiving in North American schools. Much of the influence came by way of popular speakers who were traveling to various centers in the United States and Canada. Reuben Torrey, for example, addressed Winnipeg audiences on a number of occasions and, no doubt, quite a number of Mennonite Brethren attended, including William Bestvater, during his ministry in Winnipeg.

The fourth period, which commenced in 1940, was the period of more decisive impact of evangelicalism in terms of higher theological training of Canadian Mennonite Brethren. It really marked the division of the original fundamentalist movement into two relatively distinct movements--evangelicalism and separatist fundamentalism. The latter movement continued to be militant and almost exclusively dispensationalist in character. The former was a broad coalition of theologically conservative Protestants and was much more open to dialogue on various issues.[18] The National Association of Evangelicals was formed in 1942, Fuller Theological Seminary was established in 1947, Billy Graham came into international prominence in 1949, and Carl F. H. Henry published his *The Uneasy Conscience of Modern Fundamentalism* in 1947. Other important symbols of the new evangelicalism included Wheaton College and the influential periodical, *Christianity Today*. A variety of denominational seminaries also became broadly identified with this movement.[19] The situation was obviously much more complex than can be outlined here and particularly in recent years it has become necessary to distinguish even more clearly the variety of orientations which have their roots, to some degree, in the earlier evangelical and fundamentalist movements. The noteworthy point is that Canadian Mennonite Brethren in particular were thrust into a dynamic religious situation in the North American environment and that although they felt a significant kinship with North American evangelicalism as a whole, they did not share the particular heritage which gave rise to the various controversies and were therefore left groping, in a somewhat confused manner, in the endeavor to shape an identity within this new context.

According to *Table II,* at least eight leading Canadian Mennonite Brethren received some of their initial theological education at Tabor College in Kansas--most of them in the 1940s. Ranking next in importance are a variety of Baptist schools such as Central Baptist Seminary in Portland, Oregon. Several also attended United College in Winnipeg, no doubt because of the convenience of its location. It is interesting to note that none of the schools could really be characterized as strongly fundamentalist in orientation. None of the schools which Quebedeaux lists under either "separatist" or "open" fundamentalism[20] appears in the academic vitae of prominent Mennonite Brethren prior to 1960. Most would probably belong to his category of "establishment" evangelicalism, with the exception of United College.

A recent study by Mark A. Noll surveys the gradual acquisition of widely recognized academic credentials in biblical studies by evangelicals since World War II.[21] The same trends would no doubt be true with respect to theology in general. Whereas the fundamentalist-modernist controversy of the 1920s tended to drive a wedge between "pious" and "academic study of the Bible," by the 1940s American evangelicals were attending some of the most respected American universities such as Harvard University, and were receiving doctorates in increasing numbers. Wheaton College, for example, had no Bible professors with a university doctorate before 1935, but by 1952, seven of fifteen had university-level doctorates.[22] Noll provides additional interesting information in several other tables. Of thirty Old and New Testament faculty members with doctorates at three prominent evangelical seminaries in the early 1980s, eight had received their degrees at Harvard.[22] Thus, very significant changes have occurred in theological education among evangelicals in North America since the 1940s.

Mennonite Brethren theological education in Canada, as reflected by the educational background of faculty within its institutions, has generally followed the same trends, although there has been a time lag here of a decade or more. Unruh had laid the groundwork for such a development, and the next generation brought about a significant transition. John B. Toews, who became the second president of MBBC after Unruh had served in that capacity for only one year, moved the school more forthrightly into the North American environment. Although Toews had received much of his education before coming to Canada, he continued his education in American schools and thereby also raised the suspicion of some prominent Mennonite Brethren leaders such as Benjamin B. Janz. By the 1950s and 1960s, however, a new generation of American-educated scholars was entering the scene and made a major impact on the Canadian Mennonite Brethren Conference as a whole. The first faculty member with an academic doctorate to teach at a Canadian Mennonite Brethren school was Frank C. Peters, who taught at MBBC from 1957 to 1965; he received his Th.D. from Central Baptist Seminary in Kansas City. But before Peters joined the faculty, David Ewert had already arrived at MBBC (in 1953) and, although he did not receive his doctorate until 1969, was making an impact on biblical interpretation, particularly during the next generation, which would be unsurpassed. Most of his teaching career was spent at MBBC during an era when the majority of Mennonite Brethren leaders were trained at the College. A third individual, whose influence during that generation was exceptional in terms of establishing a Canadian Mennonite Brethren identity, was John A. Toews. He received his Ph.D. in 1964 after completing a dissertation on Sebastian Frank's relationship to the Anabaptists. A variety of other individuals also helped to shape Mennonite Brethren identity during the 1950s and 1960s. Most of them belonged to the first generation of American-educated Mennonite Brethren. The sources of the formation of that identity, however, were primarily the new evangelicalism as it related to the methods of biblical scholarship and the new Anabaptism as it was defined by Harold S. Bender and his colleagues in relation to theology, history and ethics. Both movements had emerged at about the same time and came to relative maturity in the 1950s.

The curriculum at MBBC during the late 1950s and 1960s was significantly influenced by both John A. Toews and David Ewert. Among the scholars whose writings were used extensively, either as textbooks or otherwise, were Merril C. Tenney and V. Raymond Edman of Wheaton College (where David Ewert had attended), George Eldon Ladd of Fuller Theological Seminary, and Harold S. Bender and his colleagues at Goshen College Biblical Seminary. In connection with the new emphasis on the Anabaptist concept of discipleship, the writings of Dietrich Bonhoeffer were also frequently cited. Bonhoeffer's *The Cost of Discipleship* was in fact used as a textbook in a course on ethics. Somewhat less compatible with some of our Anabaptist emphases was the text, *Systematic Theology,* by the Baptist professor at Rochester Theological Seminary, Augustus Hopkins Strong.

All in all, the theological identity at MBBC, which was the primary theological and ministerial training institution for Mennonite Brethren in Canada, was shaped by a wedding of new Anabaptism to new evangelicalism. Both had gained new academic respectability. At the Bible institute level and at the local congregational level these emphases still stood in considerable tension both with the earlier dispensationalism carried over from Russia and increasingly with new fundamentalist influences in North America. The dispensationalist eschatology was often debated at annual ministers' courses at MBBC. But very few academically trained individuals promoted what might be considered a fundamentalist theology in Canada. These influences came primarily at the popular level through the media of radio and television as well as through the popular religious press.

The above analysis may help us to understand the present theological climate among Mennonite Brethren in Canada and to define the tensions which still prevail. As indicated in the introduction, some tensions run parallel to the tensions in the larger evangelical community but are nevertheless unique because of the distinctive historical and cultural forces which were at work. Two themes in particular stand out within the context of these tensions.

The first theme is that of the separation of the pew from the academy. As Noll indicates, this separation has been a serious issue for evangelicals in the United States.[24] He states that the religious culture in the United States has been generally anti-theological as well as individualistic and egalitarian.[25] In a somewhat similar vein, Nathan O. Hatch states that evangelicalism "threw theology open to any serious student of Scripture and they considered the 'common sense' intuition of people at large more reliable, even in the realm of theology, than the musing of an educated few."[26] Hatch concludes that despite the recent emphasis on education, evangelicals have failed to sustain serious intellectual activity.[27]

Mennonite Brethren have also nurtured their own brand of anti-intellectualism. Despite the fact that, according to James Urry,[28] Mennonite Brethren were among the more highly educated Mennonites at the time of their origin (1860), this fact is not to be construed as indicating that they were more open to theological education. Indeed the pietism which influenced them was often very critical of a trained and educated clergy. The early Mennonite Brethren revived a healthy lay emphasis which, however, created new perils. The German Baptist influence was often also one which generated suspicion of higher theological education. These factors, when combined with the individualism of the North American religious culture, often worked against the more desirable elements of a sound theological education. Christianity was ultimately understood as being simple, and the schools rather than being the watch-dogs to safeguard doctrinal purity, were actually seen as the vehicles through which aberrant theology entered the church.

A second area of tension has to do with Mennonite Brethren identification with the ideals of North American society as a whole. Historically, Mennonites and Mennonite Brethren have functioned more like a sect than like a church. Although there were times in the Russian experience when they were a privileged minority, they were still quite separate from the larger Russian environment. In America they also displayed a distinct sect-consciousness during their earlier experience. The early evangelical experience in America, on the other hand, was one of dominance. It was only when fundamentalism developed in the twentieth century that some ambiguity emerged about whether they were a suffering minority or a triumphant majority. For a time both fundamentalism and evangelicalism as a whole functioned more like a sect which was in conflict with the predominant religious culture in the United States. But this once again shifted in the 1970s when evangelicals began to feel that they were the predominant culture and tried to bring their influence to bear in politics, education and other areas.

Mennonite Brethren seem to have attached themselves to the new wave of evangelical popularity which emerged in the 1970s and, in the process, have lost many of their sectarian characteristics.[29] But the basic tensions remain and continue to influence the nature of theological education as well as other dimensions of religious life. Mennonite Brethren in Canada manifest many of the same ambivalent attitudes toward the intellectual aspects of faith and toward education which are prevalent within fundamentalism. The roots of that ambivalence, however, are found in vastly different cultural experiences and therefore aggravate and prolong the theological identity crisis. Mennonite Brethren really don't know who their closest theological kin in America are and will continue to struggle until a more common basis for theological education is established.

TABLE 1

MB THEOLOGICAL STUDENTS IN EUROPE

A. Hamburg Baptist Theological Seminary

Note: A list was originally compiled by Peter J. Klassen from the *Festschrift zur Feier des 50 jaerigen Jubilaeums des Predigerseminars der deutschen Baptisten zu Hamburg-Horn* (o.O., o.D.). Additional information was compiled from various sources.

	Years	*Positions*
Braun, Daniel(1892-?)	1911-1913	?
Braun, Heinrich(1873-1946)	(graduate)	Taught at Tschongraw, 1918-19
Friesen, Abraham(1859-1919)	1885	Miss.-India, 1889-1908
Friesen, Jakob(1863-?)	1889-93	?
Huebert, Abraham(1867-?)	1893-97	Miss.-India, 1898-?
Kroeker, Jakob(1872-1948)	1894-98	Theologian, writer
Penner, Johann(Jakob)(n.d.)	1903-13	Miss.-India, ca 1915-?
Peters, Anna(n.d.)	n.d.	Miss.-India, 1909-?
Reimer, Heinrich(n.d.)	1897-1901	?
Reimer, Katherina(n.d.)	n.d.	Miss.-India
Unruh, Heinrich(1868-1912)	1895-96	Miss.-India, 1899-?
Unruh, Kornelius(n.d.)	Grad., 1903	Miss.-India
Warkentin, Abraham (n.d.)	n.d.	?
Wiens, Johannes G.(1874-1951)	1899-1903	Miss.-India, Tschongraw, Winkler B.S.

B. Other Schools

Neufeld, Kornelius G.(1871-?)	Basel Theol. Sem	Miss.-India
	U. of Basel (1895-97)	
	London, 1905	
Unruh, Benjamin H.(1881-1959)	U. of Basel	Teacher,Writer
	Lic.Theo.Basel Predigerseminar	
Wiens, Franz(n.d.)	Bible School, Berlin	Miss.-India

TABLE 2
SEMINARY AND UNIVERSITY EDUCATION OF
CANADIAN MB LEADERS TO 1960

	Degrees Earned to 1960	*Position to 1960*
Baerg, Henry R	B.A. Tabor(1949 B.D. Tabor(1951) M.A. Wichita(1953)	Pastor MBBC, 1956-62
Baerg, Reuben M.	B.A. Tabor B.D., Th.M., Th.D. N.W. Evangelical Seminary	 Bibl e Institute, 1942-1945 MBBC 1945-49
Ewert, David H.	B.A. UBC (1951) B.D. Central Baptist, Toronto(1953) M.A. Wheaton(1956) M.Th. Luther Theol. Seminary(1961)	Bible Institute, 1944-52 MBBC 1953-72
Huebert, Gerhard D.	B.A., B.D. Tabor(1946) Th.M, Th.D. Northwest Theol. Seminary	Bible Institute MBB C 1948-53 Pastor
Peters, Frank C.	B.A., Th.B. Tabor(1948) M.Sc. Kansas State Teachers College(1948) B.D. U of West. Ontario(1951) M.Th. Victoria, Toronto (1953) Th.D. Central Baptist (1957) Ph.D. U of Kansas (1960)	Tabor Instructor Pastor MBBC 1957-65
Peters, George W.	B.A. Tabor(1943) Ph.D. Hartford Seminary Foundation	Bible Institute
Pries, George D.	Th.B.(1939),B.A.(1956) Tabor M.A. U of Wichita	Bible Institute
Quiring, Jacob H.	B.A. Tabor(1945) B.A. U of Manitoba(1948 B.D. United College, Winnipeg	MBBC, 1945-55 1959-66 Pastor

Redekopp, Henry	B.A. U of Manitoba B.D. United College, Winnipeg	Bible Institute
Redekopp, Isaac W.	Th.B., B.A. Tabor(1946) M.Sc. Kansas State(1948	MBBC Pastor
Toews, Jacob J	Th.B. Western Baptist(1941)	Pastor
	B.A. Willamette(1945) M.A. U of Toronto(1951) B.D. U of West. Ontario (Wat.) (1959)	MBBC, 1959-66
Toews, John A.	Th.B. Tabor(1940) B.A. U of Saskatchewan(1946) B.D. United College(1950) M.A. U of M(1957)	MBBC 1947-67
Toews, John B	B.D. Western Baptist(1939) Th.M. Western Baptist(1941)	Pastor MBBC, 1945-48 Mission s Secretary, 1953-63
Unruh, Abraham A	Th.B. Tabor(1937)	Bible Institute Miss.-India, 1935-67
Unruh, Abraham H.	Th.B. Tabor	MBBC 1944-55

Voth, Abraham J.	Baptist Theol. Seminary
	  Rochester(1926)
	Th.B. Northern Baptist
	  Theol Seminary(1928)
	B.D. Northern Baptist(1935)
		MBBC

Voth, Henry H.	B.A. U of W. Ontario(1951) B.D. Emmanuel College(1958)	High School
Voth, John H.	B.A. Tabor(1918) McPherson College Baptist Theol. Seminary	Miss.-India,1908-42)
Wall, Cornelius	B.A. Tabor(1928) M.A . Winona(1943) B.D. Th.M., Princeton(1948)	MBBC

ENDNOTES

1. John B. Toews, "The Teaching Ministry in the Mennonite Brethren," in *Called to Teach: A Symposium by the Faculty of the Mennonite Brethren Biblical Seminary*, ed. by David Ewert. Perspectives on Mennonite Life and Thought, No. 3 (Fresno, CA: Center of Mennonite Brethren Studies, Mennonite Brethren Biblical Seminary, 1980), p. 182.

2. Ibid., p. 183.

3. See the account in Margaret Reimer, *The Story of the Crimea Bible School Theological Seminary, 1918-1924*, tr. by Edwin Reimer (Kingsville, ON: Issued by the author, 1972).

4. This school was established by Friedrich Wilhelm Baedeker in 1905.

5. This was a Plymouth Brethren school.

6. N. J. Klassen, "Mennonite Intelligentsia in Russia," *Mennonite Life* XXIV (April 1969): 59.

7. William L. Wagner, *New Move Forward in Europe: Growth Pattern of German Speaking Baptists in Europe* (South Pasadena: William Carey Library, 1978), p. 24.

8. Rudolf Donat, *Das Wachsende Werk: Ausbreitung der Deutschen Baptistengemeinden durch Sechzig Jahre (1849-1909)* (Kassel: J.G. Oncken Verlag, 1960), p. 463.

9. Ibid., pp. 466-67.

10. See for example, Jakob Kroeker, *Das Christozentrische Paulusbild* (Wernigerode-am-Harz, Deutschland: Verlag "Licht dem Osten," 1923), and *Das lebendige Wort: Beitraege zur Einfuehrung in die goettlichen Gedankenwege und Lebensprinzipien des Alten Testaments*. Baende I-VIII (Basel: Brunnen Verlag, 1957-61).

11. See for example Benjamin H. Unruh, *Leitfaden fuer den Religionsunterricht: Altes Testament* (Halbstadt, Taurien: Verlagsgesellschaft Raduga, 1913).

12. David H. Ewert, *Stalwart for the Truth: The Life and Legacy of A.H. Unruh* (Winnipeg: Board of Christian Literature, General Conference of MB Churches of North America, 1975), p. 127.

13. Ibid., p. 111.

14. Ibid., p. 135.

15. John A. Toews, *A History of the Mennonite Brethren Church: Pilgrims and Pioneers*, edited by Abram J. Klassen (Fresno: Board of Christian Literature, General Conference of Mennonite Brethren Churches, 1975), p. 260.

16. George Marsden, "From Fundamentalism to Evangelicalism: A Historical Analysis," in *The Evangelicals: What They Believe, Who They Are, Where They are Changing*, ed. by David F. Wells and John D. Woodbridge (Nashville: Abingdon Press, 1975), pp. 128f.

17. Ibid., p. 127.

18. As Quebedeaux states, they reacted to "the obscurantism, anti-intellectualism and bad manners so characteristic of what Fundamentalism had been up until then." Richard Quebedeaux, *The Young Evangelicals: Revolution in Orthodoxy* (New York: Harper and Row, 1974), p. 28.

19. Ibid., pp. 28-30.

20. Ibid., pp. 18-28.

21. Mark A. Noll, "Evangelicals and the Study of the Bible," in *Evangelicalism and Modern America*, ed. by George Marsden (Grand RapidsI: William B. Eerdmans Publishing Company, 1984), pp. 103-121.

22, Ibid. , p. 105.

23. Ibid., p. 106.

24. Ibid., p. 116.

25. Ibid., p. 117.

26. Nathan O. Hatch, "Evangelicalism as a Democratic Movement," in *Evangelicalism in Modern America*, p. 75.

27. Ibid., p. 81.

28. James Urry, "The Closed and the Open: Social and Religious Change Amongst the Mennonites in Russia (1789-1889)," (Unpublished doctoral dissertation, Oxford University, 1978), pp. 569 ff.

29. For a comprehensive analysis see Peter M. Hamm, *Continuity and Change Among Canadian Mennonite Brethren* (Waterloo: Wilfrid Laurier University Press, 1987). Cf. the various essays on the Mennonite Brethren Church Membership Profile, ed. by John B. Toews, Abram G. Konrad, and Alvin Dueck, in *Direction* (Fall, 1985).

8

GIVE ATTENDANCE TO THE PUBLIC READING

Esther Wiens

During the summer of 1987, I participated in a Sunday morning worship service of the All Souls Congregation in London, England. The entire service brought me nearer to God: I had a strong sense of "the church" as I saw the rich variety of nations represented in the congregation. The order of service contained the usual elements of Christian worship -- congregational responses, solos, sermon, as well as the more unusual--a short drama. But the highlight of the worship hour was the public reading of the Scriptures. Nigel Goodwin, a former actor by profession and an associate of Genesis Arts, read the Word in the compelling manner of a human being in the joyful service of his God. As he read a passage from Isaiah 44, a stream of spiritual vitality flowed from reader to listener. When I later contemplated the black, brown and white faces of those who had worshipped with me, I thought of how God's Word had indeed gone out into the world, empowered by the same Spirit that had inspired its writers throughout the ages.

What stands out, as I now recall that service, is the centrality of the Scripture reading. In this service it was not only a fulfilling of an important tradition; it was not a means whereby some neglected church member was given a task to do; it was not even primarily a prelude to the sermon. Rather, it was a distinct part of the service with a life of its own, important enough, apparently, to have prompted/encouraged the reader to careful preparation-- a preparation of mind and heart.

This kind of attention to Scripture reading is rare. Even though we in the the Believers' Church tradition like to be known as people of the book ,our public reading all too often hinders its "going forth." It's not that we lack respect for the Bible, but we appear to lack enthusiasm for it. We allow only a short time for Bible reading in our services, and the reader all too often sounds unprepared. He may use little expression, and give almost no attention to structure, tone or pronunciation of unfamiliar names. Sometimes it appears as if the reader is trying to be neutral-- to avoid interpretation, as though in doing so he or she leaves the Word inviolate. This "objective" approach is often coupled with undue speed. It is interesting to observe how we tend to rush through the words of Scripture, then give ample time and emphasis to our own, whether in the form of announcements or a sermon. Whatever passion we feel about our faith may be expressed in our preaching or singing, but seldom in our reading.

The public reading of the Scriptures has a very long and important tradition. Although not much detail is known about the reading of the Torah in Old Testament times, we do know that there was a practice of reading covenant stipulations. When Israel was in the desert, Moses read to the people from the Book of the Covenant (Exodus 24:7). During the reformation of the Kingdom of Judah, in the period of the Late Monarchy, Josiah read to the people from the "book of the covenant which had been found in the house of the Lord" (I Kings 23:1-3). And during the post-exilic restoration of the nation, Ezra read to the people from "the book of the law of Moses" (Neh. 8:1-8).

In Luke we read that Jesus went to the synagogue and according to the custom of the day "stood up to read" (Luke 4:16). When "the scroll of the prophet Isaiah was handed to him," he apparently read Isaiah 61:1-2 and 58:6 with little commentary. In I Timothy 4:13, the young pastor is counseled to "devote [himself] to the public reading of Scripture", along with preaching and teaching. The Church Fathers gave it priority in their services: in the second century Justin Martyr made quaint reference to this practice and encouraged his flock to read "the memoirs of the apostles and the writings of the prophets as time 'permitted.'[1] And Tertullian carefully explained the significance of such a practice. His words apply well to our own day:

> We meet together to bring to mind the divine writings, if current events make us derive a warning from them or recognize some fulfillment of them. In any case, we nourish our faith with the holy words, lift up our hope, confirm our confidence, and establish our discipline by impressing the precepts.[2]

The practice of Bible reading had prominence in the church until the sixth century when the Divine Office was neglected in favour of telling legends, and Scripture reading in the congregation was reduced to a verse or two. But dissatisfaction with this neglect arose even before the Reformation and was alleviated both during the Reformation and the Counter-Reformation, when all Christendom seems to have developed a hunger for the Bible.[3] In Luther's church the Word was "free to act sacramentally, bringing the worshipper into the presence of God." In his counsel to the church Luther says: "Therefore the Word should be heard and read above all else. It is the vehicle of the Holy Spirit. When the Word is read, the Spirit is present."[4] All the churches of the Reformation laid increased emphasis upon the ministry of the Word, and this not only for edification, but also for worship.

In our own century pastor and theologian Dietrich Bonhoeffer dedicates a portion of his manual for Christian community, *Life Together*, to the importance of communal Scripture reading. He counsels against the practice of reading a verse for the day or "brief verses" and in favor of longer passages; only then, he remarks, will the unity of the Word and the centrality of Christ become evident:

> As a whole the Scriptures are God's revealing Word. Only in the infiniteness of its inner relationships, in the connection of Old and New Testaments, of promise and fulfillment, sacrifice and law, law and gospel, cross and resurrection, faith and obedience, having and hoping, will the full witness of Jesus Christ the Lord be perceived.[5]

Our churches have often encouraged people to read the entire Bible consecutively in their private devotions, but little has been said about the value of consecutive oral/public reading. Bonhoeffer encourages this kind of reading within the context of "family fellowship," by which he apparently means an intentional Christian community, but his advice might well apply to the church family as we generally experience it:

> Consecutive reading of Biblical books forces everyone who wants to put himself, or to allow himself to be found,

where God has acted once and for all for the salvation of men. We become a part of what once took place for our salvation. Forgetting and losing ouselves, we, too, pass through the Red Sea, through the desert, across the Jordan into the promised land. With Israel we fall into doubt and unbelief and through punishment and repentance experience again God's help and faithfulness. All this is not mere reverie but holy, godly reality. We are torn out of our own existence and set down in the midst of the holy history of God on earth. There God dealt with us and there He still deals with us, our needs and our sins, in judgment and grace. It is not that God is the spectator and sharer of our present life, howsoever important that is; but rather that we are the reverent listeners and participants in God's action in the sacred history, the history of the Christ on earth. and only in so far as we are *there*, is God with us today also.[6]

One way in which we might give more attention to the public reading of the Word is to set it apart from the sermon, giving it its own place in the church service. Many churches follow a liturgy which prescribes passages from both Testaments to be read during all worship services. The Anglican liturgy requires daily Bible reading, giving the church the opportunity to hear the entire Bible within a three-year period. It must be said, however, that most of the people attend only Sunday services. The Free Church tradition has set liturgy aside in an effort to follow the Spirit's leading in choosing sermon topics and Scripture passages. But this practice does not preclude more extensive reading of topically coherent passages from both the Old and the New Testaments.

We need to be encouraged to read more of the Bible during the service and also to improve the manner in which it is read, for its oral presentation often minimizes its effectiveness. A major purpose of this paper is to set forth a case for a reading that is energetic and intelligent (informed), authoritative and humble. A reading, which, along with the preaching and singing, might go forth to the glory of God.

Basic to any reading of the Scriptures is the understanding that we are presenting the inspired Word of God to the congregation. But the Bible is also literature, not in the sense of a text whose purpose is primarily aesthetic, but as a text profound in thought and feeling, rich in allusion and diverse in literary form. Wallace Bacon, author of *The Art of Interpretation*, says,

> [Literature] explores relationships between language and
> the lived world. Plays, poems, satires, want, by and large,
> to embody *both* the processes of thought and the proces-
> ses of lived experience--to get the feel of the lived world
> into the process of thought about that world. [7]

The Bible is a repository of life waiting to be released in reading, whether oral or silent. Many scholars whose focus is the oral interpretation of litera- ture emphasize the importance of including the feeling level in oral reading. To be oblivious to it, or to purposely ignore it, is to exclude something es- sential to its meaning.

The Bible portrays the greatest drama of all time--the universal struggle be- tween good and evil. It is the story of God creating and humanity rebelling, of God pursuing, judging, loving, dying for humanity and finally claiming the victory over Satan. It is a book about the profoundest experiences of life, made available to us because "holy men of God . . . spoke as they were *moved*" (II Peter 1:21 [italics mine]).

In his preface to *The Literature of the Bible*, Leland Ryken says, "Christianity is the most literary religion in the world, the one in which the word has a spe- cial sanctity. . . [the Bible] a book in which literary form is of overriding importance."[8] Ryken's catalogue of literary forms is extensive and includes the following: "story of origins, heroic narrative, epic, parody, tragedy, lyric epithalamion, encomium, wisdom literature, proverb, parable, pastoral, satire, prophecy, gospel, epistle, oratory, and apocalypse."[9] This comprehen- sive list is helpful to the biblical scholar, but the typical reader might best be served by the more general categories of story (including history), poetry, oratory and epistle.

Anyone wishing to prepare a passage of Scripture for public reading must approach it with an attitude of humility and receptiveness that allows its own life to emerge. When Milton took upon himself the onerous task of justify- ing the "ways of God to men" in *Paradise Lost* (Book I,ll.25-6), he called on the Holy Spirit to be his muse. So might the reader, conscious of the Word's sacredness, invoke the Holy Spirit.

The next preparatory step is to acquire a basic understanding of the text. Preachers and Bible scholars have an advantage here, but not every public reader needs to be a scholar. The one who reads the Scripture in the con- gregation should determine, through close reading and by an acquaintance with the context, the text's "plain meaning"[10] A Bible dictionary will provide the correct pronunciation of its unfamiliar names. After reading the portion silently, several times, with a listening attitude, the reader should read it aloud several more times in order to get a feeling for its rhythms and its subtle nuances.

Another way of submitting to the text is to pay careful attention to literary form, for it is an essential guide to oral interpretation. The story, which is the most common literary form in the Bible, contains not only a logical sequence of events, but also an emotional shape that cannot be ignored. The opening sentences of most well-made stories identify setting and characters and introduce the conflict--the opposing forces that interact with one another and cause the tension to rise and fall. At the moment of highest tension there is a turning point that resolves the struggle and releases the tension. This is followed by the resolution and concluding statements. For the reader to be oblivious to the increase and decrease of tension in a story, to read it as if every event were of equal emotional content, is to deny what is essential to it; it is to fail the story. For it is close enough to life to enable a reader to feel its movements and become involved in them. An effective story reading calls less for special training than for setting aside inhibition and for submission to the whole of what is there.

There are many wonderful Bible stories that some of us have not heard in their entirety since we were children. At that time we heard them with a child's understanding and appreciation, which is, admittedly, considerable; but they are stories for every season of life and need to be heard over and over again. We need to hear the *whole* story of Abraham in one sitting, of Isaac, Joseph, Esther and Ruth--the heroes of sacred history who followed God beyond reason. Those who left material comfort and social security in obedience to His call. We need to hear and contemplate the epic of the children of Israel in order to enter their world and be moved by God's wonderful ways with his people. A reading (individual or dialogical) of the entire passion and resurrection of Christ narrative offers a unique perspective on its meaning and power. The reading of the story does not take the place of a sermon, although it may fill the spot in a service usually designated for a sermon. Its effect is to bring us into the world where God reveals himself to us as He did to men and women long ago.

Many of these stories lend themselves to a dialogical reading. In a book entitled *Dramatized Bible Readings,* Miriam B. Maddox offers a number of familiar Bible passages in the form of dramatic readings.[11] She uses the King James Version, which version has a certain beauty and dignity, but which also creates a certain distance because of its archaic language. The reader/director, wishing to make the story come alive, would do well to substitute a more contemporary version of the Bible, particulary when children are allowed to participate. And a dialogical reading is a fine way to invite children to enter the world of the story; it also fosters intergenerational participation.

Bonhoeffer says, "The reader should never identify himself with the person who is speaking in the Bible." He should not read as though it is he rather than God "giving consolation" or "admonishing," but with "inmost concern and rapport, as one who knows that he himself is being addressed."[12] This takes us back to the necessity for a listening, hearing attitude. But this does not preclude the use of emotion in reading. Moreover, it must be said, there is at least a minimal identification by virtue of the fact that the words are being read at all. As long as the passage and speaker are clearly identified, neither reader nor listener needs to confuse the human voice with God's voice. Given Bonhoeffer's "rule," one wonders how the Old Testament prophets communicated God's words. Would they have delivered them as though an emotionless deity had spoken them? As God called men and women to be his spokespersons, He surely must have communicated both thought and feeling. Also, it must be said that many passages in the Bible contain only human emotion. To present biblical characters as though they had no feeling is to render them colourless and to misrepresent them.

Bonhoeffer's concern that the reader not become "coercive" and "imperative," drawing the listener's attention to himself, is surely a valid one.[13] The problem can be averted by reading as though one is hearing even while speaking. But the emotion expressed is the same emotion that is heard; else the message will be distorted. It is possible, of course, to serve the ego while giving the appearance of serving God, and no honest defense of this can be made. But this is a problem not limited to Bible reading, as we all know. It may even in some perverse way express itself in a dry reading.

Poetry is another biblical "form" that has great potential for the enhancement of worship. In the Letter to the Ephesians the congregation is exhorted to "speak to one another with Psalms, hymns and spiritual songs"(Eph. 5:19). Some sort of music making may be implied here but the word, "speak," in this case, means to "teach," and may therefore indicate the spoken Word, by individuals or the group, or both.

The Psalms are powerfully proclaimed when they are well spoken by the congregation. Not everyone comes to church ready to voice praise to God. It is generally assumed that the fervor must begin in the heart and move outward through the voice. But speech teachers know that the flow of energy can also take the opposite direction: it can travel from the outside to the inside and move the person at the deepest level of being.[14] The dynamic is, in fact, cyclical: it can begin anywhere and move through the whole person. Thus a member of the congregation, initially indifferent, may be moved to praise in the experience of congregational reading.

Many churches use Psalms in a call to worship, in the manner illustrated here

> LEADER: Sing to the Lord a new song.
> PEOPLE: Sing His praise from the end of the earth.
> LEADER: Sing to the Lord, bless His name.
> PEOPLE: Tell his salvation from day to day.
> LEADER: Declare His glory among the nations.
> PEOPLE: His marvelous works among all the peoples.
> (Psalm 96:1-3)

When people are invited to participate in this kind of dialogue, they cease to be an audience and become a congregation. There is no place for an audience in a worship service!

A Psalm may also be used in response to a sermon, or as a closure to worship. This is a good alternative to the closing hymn.

Athough we do not know many details about the use of Psalms in Israel's worship, we do know that both leader/priest and people participated in speaking them. Not all biblical researchers agree on the amount of participation by the people. Some are of the opinion that "the people would respond by refrains and shouts, leaving the presentation of the texts and the leading of chants to the experts".[15] Others think the people particpated rather extensively. In his analysis of Psalm 44, one probably used in this way, Peter C. Craigie says:

> The language alternates between the first person singular ("I, my, me") and the first person plural ("we,us"), and though the alternation may be merely a literary convention, it is more likely to reflect alternation of speakers.[16]

He reconstructs the pattern of Psalm 44 in the following way

1. God's past acts as basis for currrent confidence (44:2-9)
   a. PEOPLE: God's acts in the past (vv2-4)
   b. KING: the appropriation of the past (v.5)
   c. PEOPLE: the normal grounds of confidence (v6)

    d. KING: declaration of trust (v 7)

    e. PEOPLE: declaration of confidence (vv8-9)

2. The Lament (44:10-23)

    a. PEOPLE: lament of the present crisis (vv10-15)

    b. KING: declaration of shame (vv16-17)

    b. PEOPLE: declaration of innocence (vv18-23)

3. Concluding Prayer (44:24-27)

    KING and PEOPLE pray for deliverance and help. [17]

A lament upon loss in battle may not have a direct parallel in the context of worship, but this reconstruction is helpful in demonstrating how the liturgical Psalms might have been used in Israel's worship. And although the congregation as a whole is unlikely to have spoken the words designated for them, ideally they would have done so. Today, with the printed Word in the hands of a literate congregation, it is possible and well for all to participate.

There are many Psalms suitable for a service of Christian worship. Psalm 24 seems to have been used antiphonally; the following is a possible pattern for reading:

    Psalm 24

    LEADER:The earth is the LORD'S and
       everything in it,
     the world, and all who live in it;
     for he founded it upon the seas
      and established it upon the waters.
    PEOPLE:Who may ascend the hill of the Lord?
     Who may stand in his holy place?
    LEADER: He who has clean hands and a pure heart,
     who does not lift up his soul to an idol
     or swear by what is false.
     He will receive blessing from the LORD
     and vindication from God his Savior.
    PEOPLE: Lift up your heads, O you gates;
     be lifted up, you ancient doors,
     that the King of glory may come in.
    LEADER: Who is this King of glory?
    PEOPLE: the LORD strong and mighty,
     the LORD mighty in battle.
    LEADER: Lift up your heads, O you gates;

> lift them up, you ancient doors,
> that the King of glory may come in.
> PEOPLE: Who is he, this King of glory?
> ALL: The LORD Almighty–
> he is the King of glory. Selah

This attention to units of thought is more conducive to worship than the mere alternation of verses.

It is generally felt that poetry is more difficult to read aloud than prose because it (poetry) is often more compact and more dependent upon rhythm. Also, the tone in poetry may shift or be very subtle. Thus people tend to be afraid of poetry. Leland Roloff, professor of performance studies at Northwestern University, tells his students to allow themselves to "fall into poetry." Instead of trying to control the text, they should approach it with an openness and a relaxation that allows them to sense its feeling (tone) and its rhythmic movements. At all times, but especially in oral reading, one must submit to the poetic text.

Although there are many tone shifts in the Psalms, some of which are radical, the specific kinds of tone are not difficult to identify, because they are clear and uncomplicated. The reader may identify tone in a poem by asking what attitude the speaker is expressing. For tone derives from the speaker's/writer's attitude.[18] Psalm 24, for example, begins with a tone of exultant praise that gives way to a questioning tone, returns to praise and confidence, and ends with a full-bodied praise tone. Interjected into this last section is the question, "Who is he, this King of Glory?", which calls for a rhetorical tone.

Poetry of the Old Testament was originally written in Hebrew and has therefore lost most of its phonetic rhythm in translation.[19] But the English text, with its accented and unaccented syllables, has a rhythm that is close to the rhythm of everyday speech and is therefore easy to read. Rhythm and meaning are, moreover, related: the important words are usually accented. The first line of Psalm 27, for example, scans like this: "The LORD is my light and my salvation," and Psalm 42:2: "My soul thirsts for God, for the living God."

The most important poetic feature of the Psalms is the parallel structure of the lines, a feature sometimes referred to as the rhythm of thought.[20] Parallelism entails a certain amount of repetition which may result in a monotonous tone in the reading, but need not do so. For parallelism is not mere repetition: the lines are intended to play with each other and release meaning in that interplay.[21] Psalm 38:1 is an example of "synonomous parallelism" in which the same meaning is repeated with different vocabulary in the second line: [22]

> O Lord, do not rebuke me in your anger
>> or discipline me in your wrath

A fine lyrical feeling is produced by a plaintive personal tone in which the reader begs for mercy. Any potential monotony is subverted by an emphasis on, "O Lord," and on the two verbs "rebuke" and "discipline," and by allowing the hard sounds of "anger" and "wrath" to emerge.

In "antithetical parallelism" the meaning of the first line is balanced by one directly opposing it: as in Psalm 20:7:

> Some trust in chariots and some in horses,
>> but we trust in the name of the LORD our God

The lines should be read with a confident tone. A slight emphasis needs to be given to "Some" and a more full-bodied emphasis to "we," to indicate antithetical thought.

The most challenging pattern that confronts the reader is "synthetic parallelism" in which a single phrase is repeated two or three times. It is found in the opening paragraph of Psalm 96. But the repeated, "Sing unto the LORD," introduces new thoughts, and herein lies variety. Line two, for example, should give the emphasis to its second half, because here lies the new thought. And line three calls for an increased momentum that allows it to flow over into the praise of line four, thus preparing the listener for the energetic sweep of the last two lines.

> Sing to the LORD a new song;
>> sing to the LORD, all the earth.
> Sing to the LORD, praise his name;
>> proclaim his salvation day after day.
> Declare his glory among the nations,
>> his marvelous deeds among all peoples.

Finally, there is "progressive parallelism" as in Psalm 127:1:

> Unless the LORD builds the house,
>> its builders labor in vain.
> Unless the LORD watches over the city,
>> the watchmen stand guard in vain.

There is a natural contrast between the first and second parts of the sentences which may be communicated through a slight contrast in pitch. The second verse calls for an overall rise in energy. Also, the repeated phrase, "Unless the LORD," should give the emphasis over to the last part of the verse, because it contains a new thought. The meaning of the verse might best be summed up with a slight pause before the final "in vain."

Psalm 136, with its oft-repeated refrain, "His love endures forever," is quite obviously a liturgical Psalm. But while the second half of each verse is repeated, the first half tells a story of God's mighty acts. It can be a powerful vehicle of praise when attention is paid to its structure: 1. Call to Praise, vv 1-3; 2. God's Power in Creation, vv 4-9; 3. God's Victory over Israel's Enemies, vv10-20; 4. God's Loving Care of his People;. vv 21-25; 5. Final Call to Praise, v 25.

The parallelism of the first three verses with all their repetition represent a particular challenge:

> 1. Give thanks to the LORD, for he is good
>   His love endures forever.
> 2. Give thanks to the God of gods.
>   His love endures forever.
> 3. Give thanks to the LORD of lords
>   His love endures forever.

The first line might be read with the natural cadence of an enthusiastic call to worship. The exact parallelism at the beginning of v 2 should give the emphasis over to the last part of the line, because it contains the new thought. The first half of v 3 calls for an emotional curve with "thanks" at its crest, followed by a downward flow that moves into the beginning of the story of creation. The listing of God's mighty acts in the second section should be given a cumulative effect that peaks somewhere around v 7. The story of the defense of Israel may have a similar shape, coming to a climax with the victory over Pharoah. Section four calls for a tone of warm appreciation for all God's love and care. Finally, there is a fervent summary of praise.

The shape of each of the Psalm's five sections should guide the congregation in interpreting the choric line, "His love endures forever." Its tone runs parallel to the story line of the Psalm. Throughout the reading of this and other Psalms, there should be a submission to the inherent rhythm. Thus everyone is "in the Psalm," moving as it moves.

Knowing the form and submitting to the rhythm is important in effective congregational reading. Studying the biblical text and practicing the oral reading of it are essential. But nothing exceeds the importance of God's Spirit in revealing to us the "life" of the Word and in touching the chords within our hearts--chords that can and will respond. When this happens, we will not only read, we will cry from the depths of our hearts, clap our hands and shout for joy in praise of God.

ENDNOTES

I. Stanley L. Greenslade, "Epilogue: The Circulation of the Bible," in *Cambridge History of the Bible: The West from the Reformation to the Present Day*, edited by Stanley L. Greenslade (Cambridge: CambridgeUniversity Press, 1963), p. 479.

2. Ibid., p. 480-1.

3. Martin Luther, "The Word is Alive and not a 'Dead Letter'," in Volume 3 of *What Luther Says*, compiled by Ewald M. Plass (St. Louis:Concordia Publishing House, 1972), p. 1462.

4. Ibid., p. 1462.

5. Dietrich Bonhoeffer, *Life Together* (New York: Harper and Row, 1954), p.51.

6. Ibid., p. 53-54.

7. Wallace Bacon, *The Art of Interpretation*, 3d edition (New York: Holt, Rinehart and Winston, 1979), 7.

8. Leland Ryken, *The Literature of the Bible*, (Grand RapidsI: Zondervon Publishing House, 1974), p. 9.

9. Ibid., p. 15.

10. John E. Toews speaks of a tradition of Bible interpretation in the church that is "prior to and outside of the critical mode." He believes that the Christian community has the ability to read and understand the "plain (most obvious) meaning" of the Bible. ("The Meaning of Meaning," unpublished lecture presented at MBBC, March 5, 1987).

11. Miriam B. Maddox, *Dramatized Bible Readings* (Grand Rapids: Baker Book House, 1986).

12. Bonhoeffer, p. 56.

13. Ibid., p. 56.

14. Speech theorist, Arthur Lessac says, "Vocal life is at the same time both cause and effect: Emotional life and physical life extend into, and are informed by, the fullest capacities of the vocal instrument. . . . The action becomes an interaction, a perpetual 'round dance' among the trinity of emotional-physical-vocal life." *The Use and Training of the Human Voice*. (New York: Drama Book Specialists, 1967), p. 181.

15. Erhard S. Gerstenberger, "The Lyrical Literature," in *The Hebrew Bible and its Modern Interpreters* edited by Douglas A. Knight, (Chico: Scholars Press, 1985), p. 427.

16. Peter C. Craigie, "Psalms 1-50," in Volume 19 of the *Word Biblical Commentary* edited by David A. Hubbard and Glenn W. Barker, (Waco: Word Publishers, 1983), p. 331.

17. Craigie, p. 332.

18. Edgar V. Roberts, *Writing Themes About Literature*, 5d edition (Englewood Cliffs: Prentice-Hall, 1983), p. 138.

19. Pius Drijvers, *The Psalms: Their Structure and Meaning* (Montreal: Palm Publishers, 1964), p. 27.

20. Ibid., p. 26.

21. I am indebted to my colleague, Gordon Matties, for this idea as well as for some of the general information in this paper regarding ancient Hebrew worship.

22. Thomas R. Henn, *The Bible as Literature* (London: Lutterworth Press, 1970), p. 29. Henn distinguishes the various types of parallelism here discussed.

9

PREACH THE WORD

David Ewert

Paul's charge to Timothy, his junior associate, is, "Preach the word" (2 Tim. 4:2). The Greek verb *kerusso* means "to herald" or "to proclaim". The noun form (*kerux*) describes the town crier who in classical times went through the city proclaiming messages. Timothy is to fulfill his calling as a herald of good news.

The message he is to proclaim is "the word". Paul does not need to specify further what that means. It is not *any* spoken utterance, but clearly it is God's word as found written in the Old Testament and in the teachings of Jesus and the apostles. In the following verse (4:3) it is described as "the sound teaching"; in verse four it is called "the truth". These are, however, only a few of the many ways in which "the word" is designated.

This command to preach the word is one from which the church can never escape as long as this day of salvation lasts. It is, therefore, of utmost importance that those who are called to the teaching/preaching ministry of the church be reminded that it is "the word" that builds the church. What Amos predicted many centuries ago, "a famine not of bread, nor a thirst for water, but of hearing the word of the Lord" (Amos 8:11), has indeed come upon us. In spite of Bible institutes, colleges and seminaries, in spite of a staggering amount of Christian literature, in spite of a great amount of sermonizing on radio, TV and in the pulpit, many of God's people go hungry.

In 1979 *Time* magazine carried an article entitled "American Preaching: A Dying Art?"[1] The writer of that article said that "the *chilling of the Word* is a major contributor to the evident malaise in many a large Protestant denomination these days."[2]

Dr. Donald Miller in his book *Fire in My Mouth* tells of a seminary student who called him one Saturday evening, after he had completed the preparation of his sermon for Sunday, to ask his professor if he could suggest a suitable biblical text for his sermon. Miller nearly choked, and he was tempted to say sarcastically, "Take any text, it won't matter; it won't make any difference."[3]

It is this kind of situation that led James Smart in 1960 to write a book entitled *The Strange Silence of the Bible in the Church.* He expresses the fear that the preaching of topical sermons which touch only lightly upon biblical texts, sermons in which there is no room for an exposition of a passage of Scripture, in effect silence the Bible in the church.[4] It does not follow from Smart's comment that topical preaching is not biblical or that expository preaching always is. One can, unfortunately, interpret a biblical text from a worldly standpoint. But there is the danger when passages are not expounded that the biblical texts become only springboards for the development of the preacher's ideas. Smart returned to his criticism of topical sermons in a later volume. "The popularity of topical sermons and the comparative ease with which they can be prepared discourages ministers from undertaking the more difficult task of letting the ancient texts come alive in the modern situation."[5]

As Mennonites we make much of our biblicism. We confess that the Bible is our ultimate authority in all matters of faith and practice. In our theological schools we emphasize "biblical" over against "systematic" theology. And yet in our preaching we often fail to be truly biblical. Spurgeon warned against this failure in his day.

> Some brethren have done with their text as soon as they have read it. Having paid all due honor to that particular passage by announcing it, they feel no necessity further to refer to it. They touch their hats, as it were, to that part of Scripture, and pass on to fresh fields and pastures new.[6]

I know we have a great many pastors who faithfully expound the word from week to week and they will not take this as a criticism but as an encouragement, for they will heartily endorse the point I am trying to make. All of us, however, need to be encouraged by Paul's words to Timothy, "Preach the word," and a little exercise in homiletics may not hurt us. If, then, we are going to preach the word, we must, first of all, recognize the importance of a text or texts of Scripture if our preaching is to be biblical (and that holds for both topical and expository sermons).

I. The Importance of a Text

When a text is read with the purpose of expounding it, the level of expectancy is raised in the listeners. The audience is alerted to the fact that what is to happen in the next thirty or forty minutes is not going to be a discourse in which the wisdom of this age is to be proclaimed, but the word of God. When a text is read, questions arise in the minds of the hearers about the meaning of the text, and so there is an air of expectation, as one waits for the exposition of the text.

Moreover, if one preaches from a text, the sermon has a ring of authority about it. It was the note of authority in the teachings of Jesus that attracted people in his day (Mark 1:22). Obviously we do not speak with the degree of authority with which our Lord and the apostles spoke, but if we interpret and apply correctly the teachings of Jesus we speak with considerable authority. Dr. Donald Coggan, former archbishop of Canterbury and a fine evangelical, once made the observation: "In order to preach, a man must know the authority of being under authority."[7] When the word of God is our authority we can also proclaim it with authority. "It is authority that the world chiefly needs and the preaching of the hour," wrote P.T. Forsyth, "calls for an authoritative Gospel in a humble personality."[8]

There is also great practical value in preaching from a text. It helps to put restrictions and limitations on the preacher. It helps him to focus on one or a few main ideas at a time. There is, to be sure, a place for preaching on themes which can be traced through a book of the Bible, or the Bible as a whole. And if texts which support this theme are expounded, thematic or topical preaching can be quite biblical. However, a congregation does not want to make the journey from Genesis to Revelation every Sunday, and so by limiting our sermons to a specific text, we set certain parameters for ourselves. Dr. A.H. Unruh, founder of our College, who began to preach when he was eighteen, confessed later in life that what had saved the day for him was the fact that although his knowledge of the Bible was very limited in those early years, he always preached from a different text (even if he said more or less the same thing). Dr. Unruh, after a long life of preaching, often expressed the hope that people who had forgotten his sermons would at least remember his texts.

A text builds a bridge between speaker and audience, and, I dare say, that's a better bridge than an opening joke with which some preachers think they must establish rapport with the audience, especially when the joke has no bearing on the sermon. Every congregation is diverse; people have different needs; they come from different walks of life; they have had different experiences in the past week; they have different questions and concerns. But when a text is read, it draws the thinking of the hearers in the same direction; they now have a common platform to stand on. Over a period of time, many passages will be expounded and the church will be anchored in the word of God and become strong.

To facilitate bridge-building between speaker and audience it is helpful if the text of Scripture is read immediately before the sermon. In a recent book on preaching written by Ian Pitt-Watson, who came from Britain to teach at Fuller Theological Seminary, this practice is strongly advocated.[9]

Preaching from texts will also further the minister's own growth and development, for he will have to take the study of the Scriptures more seriously. He will have to discipline himself, keep his eyes open for good commentaries, wrestle with problem texts. Also it will keep him from riding hobby-horses. There was a time when (at least in some church traditions) the minister was the most educated man in the community, and the temptation to instruct the audience in other matters than the biblical faith was never far away. Today, however, with so many people in our churches who are experts in a great variety of disciplines, the minister better not attempt to be an authority on every subject. One area, however, in which a congregation should expect from him some degree of expertise is that of the Scriptures. Constant study and research on biblical texts in preparation for preaching will go a long way in making him conversant with the word of God.

G. Campbell Morgan, a great Bible expositor of London, England, emphasized the necessity of having a text and elucidating it. By contrast, Morgan mentions a certain Dr. Benjamin Jowett, of Oxford, who made bold to say that "it was his habit to write his sermons, and then choose a text as a peg on which to hang them." Morgan adds, a bit sardonically, that the study of his sermons reveals the accuracy of his statement and shows the peril of his method.[10]

If, then, it is so important that we preach from biblical texts, how shall we choose them? I am, of course, aware of the practice in certain church traditions that preachers follow lectionaries, in which the text for each Sunday is prescribed, but most of our Mennonite churches do not observe this practice.

II. The Choice of a Text

In choosing a text the needs of the congregation must be kept in mind. There are, obviously, some needs which are present all the time. The need to instruct, to encourage, to comfort, to exhort is present in all those who come to hear the word of God. However, from time to time special needs make themselves known in a given congregation, and a text may be chosen with that in mind.

Every preacher has his favorite passages or his preferred books of the Bible; and even though we may claim that the Bible is God's word from cover to cover, we all tend to be selective. And, I suppose, some selectivity is appropriate. It would be strange, I think, if Christian preachers spoke more often on Old Testament than on New Testament texts. However, if we preach mainly from the Epistles, or the Gospels, or the Revelation, we will not be good stewards of the mysteries of God. Paul claimed before the Ephesian elders that he had preached "the whole counsel of God" (Acts 20:27). It should, therefore, be our fixed resolve, as Charles Simeon of Cambridge put it, never to run after certain themes, and never to avoid them either. Certain events in the life of the church, such as a tragedy or a very joyous experience, will call for sermons on appropriate texts.

The seasons of the year, especially the church year, provide an excellent occasion for proclaiming the great truths of God's word. Most Christians observe at least three major Christian festivals annually--Christmas, Easter and Pentecost. It is a pity when one passes up these great events to preach on the fundamental doctrines of the Christian faith. But there are also other seasons of the year that provide occasions for preaching on topics such as spring (creation), harvest, the new year, and even winter (Dr. Clarence McCartney, a great Presbyterian minister, preached a powerful sermon, now available in print, on the topic "Come Before Winter" (2 Tim. 4:9)).

A preacher who constantly studies the Scriptures will have no difficulty in finding a text. James Stewart of Scotland writes: "Here let me add that it is only as we live in the Bible—devotionally, and as students of the sacred Word–that we can hope to find the manna falling regularly for our people's needs. Again and again in the reading of the Bible, texts will come out from the page begging us: 'Won't you preach on me?'"[11]

When a preacher chooses to preach through a book of the Bible from Sunday to Sunday, he is of course spared the dilemma of having to choose a text, although he will still need to decide how big a slice he wants to take on a given Sunday. Working one's way through a book certainly helps to give the church a good foundation in biblical teaching. If the book is long, say a Gospel or Acts or Romans, one may have to do it in sections and allow for other sermons to intervene, especially during special seasons of the year or when unforeseen events in the life of the church or the community occur.

Besides book studies, one may also do a series from time to time. Some pastors have done series on the doctrinal teachings of the Mennonite Brethren Church as these are set forth in our Confession of Faith. It is very important for members of the church to know what, in fact, their denomination believes. Such series can also be expository as one expounds the texts on which these doctrines are based. Then one can also do biographical series on biblical personalities, either from the Old Testament or New Testament. Also, one might do a series of sermons in which ethical issues are addressed. Although the Bible does not speak directly to some of the modern ethical issues, it remains amazingly relevant.

But, having chosen a text, where does one begin to prepare the sermon?

III. The Analysis of the Text

First of all, one must seek to understand the language of the text. The key words of the passage need to be examined. A great deal of rich sermon material can come from the study of the words of the text. Also, one must inquire into the literary genre. Are we dealing with historical, poetic, prophetic, Gospel, epistolary or apocalyptic material? One cannot expound a Psalm in the same way as a letter of Peter.

Also, one must study carefully the syntax of the passage. Are there important conjunctions, prepositions, and the like? What about the tenses of the verbs? Theology is, finally, subject to grammar, or, as Luther put it, "Grammar is the handmaiden of Theology." And if one does not work with the original languages, one must make sure that several versions in English are consulted or that appropriate helps to get at the meaning of the original Hebrew or Greek are at hand.

One will also want to examine the passage to identify idioms and figures of speech. Metaphors and similes, personification and hyperbole, euphemisms and symbolism, must be identified, if the text is to be understood correctly.

Out of the study of the text there will emerge a theme which represents the major thrust of the passage. And, as the text is analyzed further, the different aspects of the passage will have to be related to this central thrust. It should be noted, however, that the same text can be discussed from different angles and under different themes, as long as one remains true to the fundamental meaning of the passage.

It is easy enough to do a "running commentary" on a text, and there may, in fact, be a place for that in Bible study groups. But a sermon without a theme or topic can hardly be called a sermon. People should be able to sum up a sermon in a sentence or two. If someone should ask us later what the preacher spoke on, we should be able to put the essential content of the sermon in a sentence.

However, simply to go round and round on the theme can be very confusing. One must seek to relate the salient emphases of the passage to the main theme. A sermon needs structure, if people are to follow easily and if they are to remember its content. A sermon can be without form and still not be utterly void, but, as Dr. William Sangster once put it: "How much more powerful it would have been had that sincerity and passion glowed at the heart of a well-structured sermon, and how certain it is that the blessing of God would have crowned it."[12] Sangster is convinced that "the strength of a sermon is so often in its structure."[13] Dr. Luccock, onetime professor of preaching at Yale, wrote:

> A sermon is more like a highroad, well-posted with legible signs indicating, 'This is where we are now; the next place will be so and so.' A panorama without a pattern is a distraction to the mind, no matter how bright the occasional vistas. . . . Stages of movement, definitely announced, clarify the mental trip as helpfully as do the announcements of the railroad conductor when he calls out, 'This station is Utica; the next stop is Syracuse.' That may be stooping to a lowly service, but it does serve the traveler in a way that no eloquence alone could match.[14]

The outline of a sermon has often been compared to the bones of a skeleton, and people are obviously not particularly edified by looking at a skeleton. However, a jellyfish, that has flesh but no bones, is not a very good symbol for a sermon either. The outline should not protrude too much and certainly it should not be artificial, but it will help the listeners immensely when the great truths emerging from the biblical text are ordered in such a way that they are easy to follow. The feeling that the preacher knows where he is going is already a great help in retaining the attention of the audience.

Once an outline has emerged from our study of the text, our great concern must be to put flesh on this skeleton. Much information will already be available to us from the study of the words and syntax of the passage. Another important source of information is the context of the passage. One can, for example, take note of who the writer of the words of the text is and under what circumstances the lines were penned or the times in which he lived. Quite obviously one will make liberal use of good Bible commentaries when studying the text. Sometimes it is illuminating if one draws upon parallel passages. Also, one can glean important information from sermons that others have preached on our text. Wide reading in such areas as history and biography, as the late Dr. Martin Loyd-Jones has suggested, are very helpful in sermon preparation. Some years ago, when Dr. John R. Stott spoke in a chapel service at Eastern Mennonite Seminary, he suggested to the seminarians that they should hold the Bible in one hand and the newspaper in the other. Half a century ago C.H. Spurgeon published a booklet entitled *The Bible and the Newspaper.* It was, of course, a symbolic way of saying that we must be familiar not only with the world of the Bible, but also with the world in which we live. And that leads us to what is perhaps the most crucial aspect of preaching: the interpretation and the application of the text.

IV. The Interpretation of the Text

Every preacher preparing to preach a sermon is confronted by two worlds: the world of the Bible and the world of today. It is highly instructive to notice that John Stott has entitled his recently published book on preaching *Between Two Worlds.*[15] Expository preaching takes both of these worlds seriously.

Occasionally one meets someone who says with great feeling, "The Bible doesn't have to be interpreted; all one needs to do is to read it and do what it says." Sometimes this sentiment comes through as a layperson's way of protesting against the complicated interpretations given by some scholars, interpretations which at times actually remove the Bible from ordinary men and women. And we must agree that the Bible was written to be understood by rather ordinary people. It was, indeed, out of this conviction, the perspicuity, i.e. clarity of Scripture, that translators have dared to translate the Bible into the mother tongue of hundreds of peoples. And, as a general rule, an interpretation that flows naturally from the text and makes good sense is probably correct. Abstruse interpretations, more often than not, do not reflect accurately the author's intent.

But, scholar or not, everyone who reads the Bible also interprets it, whether he thinks so or not. In fact, to read the Bible in English is to read an interpretation given to the Bible by the translator. All translation from one language into another is to a certain degree interpretation. Expository preaching, however, demands not only an interpretation of the passage under consideration; it also calls for a transfer of the meaning of that passage into the twentieth century.

James Smart in his book, *The Strange Silence of the Bible in the Church,* focuses this twofold challenge for us: "The preacher faces each week the problem of bringing together the world that meets him in the Bible and the world in which he is living, of finding his way from an ancient text to a restatement of the meaning of that text in terms that will make sense and have significance for his congregation and community."[16] To put the question differently: "What did the text mean originally, and what does the text mean for us today?"

Preachers can fall into the temptation of remaining in the thought-world of the Bible without making any attempt to bring biblical principles to bear on the life of the congregation. This can, in fact, become a form of escapism. And to argue that it is the Holy Spirit's task to apply the truths of the Scriptures to the hearts of the hearers, while perfectly true, does not absolve the preacher from the arduous task of making the transfer from the first to the twentieth century.

Some preachers at times do little more than restate the biblical passage which they have read, or retell the biblical story. And whereas we do not doubt for a moment that God's word is powerful, we should not think that by repeating the phrase "Jesus is Lord" a dozen times we have truly proclaimed the lordship of Christ. Most of our listeners believe that Jesus is Lord, but they want to know what that means when they go to work, when they buy and sell, when they go on vacations and when they choose careers.

Anthony Thistleton observes that "a literalistic repetition of the text cannot *guarantee* that it will 'speak' to the modern hearer. He may understand all of its individual words, and yet fail to understand what is being said."[17]

By contrast, there are preachers who are very much at home in the crosscurrents of modern thinking. They avidly read the newspapers, watch a lot of TV, read the latest novels, see films; in other words, they are thoroughly up to date. Often, however, they lack a good understanding of the thought-world of the Bible. If one had to choose between Bible exegetes and preachers who are caught up in the relevance-syndrome, we would probably choose the former. However, if we are to preach the word faithfully, we have to try to build a bridge over the chasm that lies between the world of the prophets and apostles and our modern, technological society.

John R. Stott is right when he insists that

> We should be praying that God will raise up a new generation of Christian communicators who are determined to bridge the chasm; who struggle to relate God's unchanging Word to our ever-changing world; who refuse to sacrifice truth to relevance or relevance to truth; but who resolve instead in equal measure to be faithful to Scripture and pertinent to today.[18]

As we undertake the responsibility of interpreting an ancient truth for a modern audience, we soon discover that this is no easy task. Just as we can err in our understanding of what the biblical text meant originally, so we can also make grievous mistakes in applying the message of the text to the current situation, as James Smart rightly affirms:

> The road from an ancient text to the present meaning, has on it many pitfalls that can obstruct, distort, and falsify the words of the original witnesses. There is no simple easy route either back into the ancient situations where the words were first spoken or written, or forward from there into our own situations in the world of today, where they must be translated, that they have their original enlightening and transforming power.[19]

We must, then, make sure that we have understood the words of the original witnesses first, before we attempt to apply them to our situation. A crass illustration of what can happen when one doesn't understand the biblical text correctly is the following: A husband, whose heart had been causing him some problems, came joyously from his devotional Bible reading to announce to his wife that God had healed his heart. When his wife asked him how he knew that, he explained that he had just read it in a Psalm: "My heart is fixed, Lord, my heart is fixed." Now, whether God in fact healed his heart is not for me to say, but I do know that the Psalm he quoted had nothing to do with the repair of that rather important organ in the man's breast. The application of the biblical text was perverse, because the text had been misunderstood.

However, it is possible, also, to have a perfectly correct understanding of the biblical text, but to make a wrong application. The words of Jesus to the rich young ruler are clear: "Sell all that you have and give to the poor." But when we begin to apply that text, what does it mean? Since riches kept this young man from the kingdom, he had to make a choice between the two. However, that cannot be the word of Jesus to everyone--Paul knows of members of the church who are well to do (1 Tim. 6:17). Although there is an important and permanent truth in the story of Jesus' encounter with the rich young ruler, the words of Jesus cannot be absolutized and transferred to every Christian in the literal sense.

The transfer from the first to the twentieth century becomes even more challenging when a biblical text is culture-bound. How, for example, do we apply the instructions Paul gave to slaves and their masters? Since our society is not based on slavery, as was the Roman world of the first century, it is too simple to transfer the New Testament passages concerning slaves and masters to modern employers and employees. That is not to say that there is nothing permanent about Paul's instructions, but a straight carry-over could be disastrous.

This holds true, also, for such matters as footwashing, exchanging the holy kiss, eating idol food, or Paul's instructions to Corinthian women to wear the headcovering to church. Surely Paul did not intend Christian women everywhere and for all generations to wear a kerchief to church! Is 1 Corinthians 11, then, of no permanent significance? Of course it is; but Paul is arguing from a divinely-established order of creation (which is unchanging) to a local practice (which is relative, not absolute). What might be some permanent and universal applications of this passage? As I see it, it teaches us to respect local customs in the matters of dress--Christians should be careful not to shock the public sense of decency by the way they dress (that there are also indecent customs hardly needs to be mentioned). Also, 1 Corinthians 11 suggests that the differences between the sexes, differences rooted in creation and expressed by differences in dress and hairstyle, should be upheld. Moreover, the passage also teaches that propriety in worship should be observed. And certainly the passage underscores for all times the dignity of womanhood and, in contrast to synagogue custom, assigns to her a meaningful place in the life of the congregation. No doubt there are other permanent teachings in this passage, but I think enough has been said at this point.

Obviously when such applications are made on the basis of a passage that speaks to a temporal and local situation, we must be somewhat more tentative in the application than in the exegesis of the passage. And if someone should wonder whether such a handling of a passage does not open the door to a completely arbitrary handling of Scripture, our response would be: No, this is the way we keep Scripture alive and relevant. For if we do not make serious efforts to bridge the gulf between the Bible and our current situation, it can happen that the words of Scripture become a dead letter.

John R. Stott, in his book *Understanding the Bible*, writes:

> Since God's revelation was given in particular historical and geographical situations, this means that it had a particular cultural setting as well. And the social customs which form the background of some Biblical instruction are entirely foreign to those of our day. Are we then to reject the teaching because it is culturally dated? Or are we to go the other extreme and try to invest both teaching and setting with some permanent validity? Neither of these seems the right way to escape the dilemma. The third and better way is to accept the Biblical instruction itself as permanently binding, but to translate it into contemporary cultural terms. . . . Let it be clear that the purpose of such a cultural transposition is not to avoid obedience, but rather to ensure it.[20]

After we have chosen our text, have carefully analyzed and structured it, after we have come to grips with its meaning and have seen some of its implications for the life of the church, we must write out the sermon in a style that our audience can easily comprehend. The manner in which we deliver the sermon will vary from person to person, but without prayer and the help of the Holy Spirit even our best efforts in the study and in the pulpit are in vain. It is true, as Dr. Ronald Ward puts it, "We cannot explain the operation of the Holy Spirit which charges a bare verbal cable with high-voltage spiritual power. But we can ask what are the constituents of a good 'cable'."[21] This chapter has been an attempt to do just that. Those who take seriously Paul's exhortation to "preach the word" are always looking for ways and means of improving "the cable".

ENDNOTES

1"American Preaching: A Dying Art," *Time*, (Dec. 31, 1974), pp. 64-7.

2. Ibid., italics mine.

3.Donald Miller *Fire in My Mouth* (Nashville: Broadman Press, 1954), p. 38.

4. James Smart *The Strange Silence of the Bible in the Church* (Philadelphia: Westminster Press, 1970), p. 22.

5. James Smart, *The Cultural Subversion of the Biblical Faith* (Philadelphia: Westminster Press, 1977), p. 126.

6. Helmut Thielicke, *Encounter With Spurgeon* (Philadelphia: Fortress Press, 1963), p. 190.

7. Donald Coggan, *Convictions* (Grand Rapids:Wm. B. Eerdmans Publishing Company, 1975), p. 160.

8. Peter T. Forsyth, *Positive Preaching and the Modern Mind* (London: Independent Press, 1957), p. 136.

9. Ian Pitt-Watson, *A Primer for Preachers* (Grand Rapids: Baker Book House, 1986), p. 89.

10. Cited in John R.W. Stott, *Between Two Worlds* (Grand Rapids: Wm B. Eerdmans Publishing Company, 1982), p. 130.

11. James S. Stewart, *Heralds of God* (Grand Rapids: Baker Book House, 1972), p. 154.

12. William E. Sangster, *The Craft of Sermon Construction* (Grand Rapids: Baker Book House, 1972), p. 62.

13. Ibid.

14. Robert E. Luccock, *Halford Luccock Treasury* (Nashville:Abingdon Press, 1963), p. 173.

15. See Note 10 above.

16. Smart, *The Strange Silence of the Bible in the Church*, p. 33.

17. Anthony Thistleton, "The New Hermeneutic," in I. Howard Marshall, ed., *New Testament Interpretation* (Grand Rapids:Wm. B. Eerdmans Publishing Company, 1977), p. 309.

18. Stott, p. 144.

19. Smart, *The Cultural Subversion of the Biblical Faith*, p. 126.

20. John R.W. Stott, *Understanding the Bible* (London: Scripture Union, 1972), p. 228.

21. Ronald Ward, Commentary on I and II Thessalonians (Waco:Word Books, 1976), p. 34.

10

PREACHING THAT DELIGHTS

John Regehr

Immediately you will think that this article is about humor in preaching. But it is not. And yet humor is of interest to the serious preacher. A preacher who never has a twinkle in his eye, and cannot ignite one in his hearers, will have to work harder than necessary to get a hearing.

Before I proceed I want to get another matter out of the way. It has to do with the language I will use. When speaking of the hearers, I will generally use the plural, and thereby I will have easily, if not cleverly, avoided exclusive sexist language. In speaking of the preacher, I will use the masculine exclusively. I delight in good sermons whether they are delivered by men or by women. And I am quite convinced that the gift of preaching in the church is given to men and women alike. At least the New Testament indicates no limitation. I will use the masculine pronouns for practical reasons. Yes, I have devised a method of using inclusive pronouns, but that method is still very new even to me, and I have not had sufficient opportunity to test it with colleagues and students, so I shall overcome the temptation to use it here.

Though good humor may add significantly to the delight which a sermon causes, delight in preaching has to do with much more than prompting chuckle and laughter. Delight has reference to the more general enjoyment of the hearer. The delight I want to talk about is more akin to the enjoyment we experience when we drink a zesty punch, or eat a superb casserole, or smell a fragrant rose.

Early in our training in homiletics we heard the ancient wisdom that every sermon ought to delight, inform, and activate. Though any one portion of the sermon may accomplish any one of these functions more deliberately than do the others, the three really want to be interwoven throughout the entire sermon. Delight makes instruction more interesting. Delight is a better motivator than is guilt. Delight wants to be interwoven throughout.

The delighting should happen early in the sermon, already in the first sentence. Actually it should happen even before that. Some of you will remember our brother and teacher J. B. Toews. If you do, you will remember with delight his unique procession to the pulpit. He held his soft leather-bound Bible by its bottom right hand corner, the thumb of his right hand opposing the force of the two first fingers. The Bible arked downward, leading the way into the pulpit, with brother Toews following about fourteen inches behind. He walked slowly, with a sombre religious mixture of assurance and awe, into the place from which he would preach. Though in time this highly symbolic procession came to be quite predictable, it never failed to heighten our expectation. Our delight had been kindled before ever he spoke a word.

The element of delight ought to be sustained throughout the entire sermon. When it sags during the delivery, the hearers find it more and more difficult to sustain their eagerness to listen. If the level of delight in the delivery is to be maintained, the preacher must himself have a good measure of delight in what he is saying, and a generous measure of delight in the people to whom he is saying it. Boredom is deadly.

Before I go any further, I want 'to make assurance doubly sure' that your understanding of the word delight is not too thin. I am not speaking of the widened eyes that see a sprig of parsley atop the dish of potato salad, nor of the ripple of chuckles that follows from a clown's silliness. Members of the congregation of which I am a part helped me understand the deeper kind of delight which this article is about. In preparation for the writing, I asked in my congregation for volunteers to write in one sentence or so what it was that delighted them about a sermon. Almost without exception the responses had to do with the content of the sermon and the manner of the preaching, and not with the frills and frolics of the presentation. The delight of which I want to speak, then, is the delight of prime rib roast and mashed potatoes.

It is the delight that results when a knotted muscle is massaged to rest, or when intense thirst is quenched by pure, clear, cool water.

Such wholesome, thoroughgoing delight derives from a number of sources. It comes from the way the preacher connects with the hearer, and from the way in which the preacher approaches the text, and the topic, and life. It comes not so much from the condiments which are provided, but from the way staple food is offered. I would like now to deal with these sources of delight.

I. Delight Through the Immediate Connectedness of the Preacher and the Hearers

I am thinking of immediate connectedness in the first few seconds of the preaching event. The first quarter minute can either raise expectations or dampen them. If we try to create delight in some unnatural and artificial way, we may create a kind of expectation that gets in the way of the hearers when we want the Word to be taken seriously. The sermon is not a circus act. The expectation which we wish to elicit is more like that which the waiter evokes when he approaches your table at Victor's Restaurant. The bow tie, the towel draped over his arm, the slight respectful bow, the invitation to order,--all these, even though they are predictable, create in us a sense of expectation, a delight. But it is not the expectation of the frivolous. You are in for a good meal, and that expectation prompts delight.

The sermon is not a circus act, to be sure. And yet we ought not utterly to stifle the Old Testament prophet in us. Sometimes the symbolic garb, the strange item we carry with us, and the surprising action, are effective means of stirring interest and building delight. If such things are more weird than purposeful, and the interest they evoke is more distracting than focused, then the very enjoyment becomes a hurdle to be overcome if the sermon is to recover its effectiveness. But if such things are tastefully and purposefully done, then the delight which they engender grows from the connectedness of the preacher with the hearers, and his message with the realities of their lives. That connectedness produces delight.

The way we use our voice can delight. A voice that grates gets in the way of the message. The hearers will be annoyed, and then angered, and then dis-interested. A voice that lulls the senses, may drive the hearers to disinterest even more quickly. Resentment and sleep are equally effective in making hearers into non-hearers. The voice itself can connect or disconnect preacher and hearers.

The very timbre of the voice can arouse interest. I envy Mary's warmth of tone. I envy the brother who has a deep resonant instrument which conveys strength and compassion simultaneously. I envy the one who can increase the intensity of the voice without losing its compelling magnetism. But even the more ordinary among us have a range and spectrum which we don't use fully. We, too, can make melody, call up a storm, subdue rage to a calm, and climb to fever pitch. To use our instrument with a measure of artistry, will create delight. We must remember, however, that true art does not draw attention to the instrument itself. Amazement about the strangeness of what we are doing is not to be equated with wholesome delight. The hearers are to be connected to us through our voice, not mesmerized by the instrument itself.

I recall the black preacher at a Martin Luther King Memorial Service in Pasadena. He was alive with emotion from the outset, yet he was subdued and disciplined too, like an oat-fed horse in harness. In making the final ascent, he lifted the tone and pitch of his voice to an urgency, soared to a crescendo of emotion, and climbed to the summit while his whole being throbbed in the grandeur of the moment. Then he stopped, stood still, looked long at the horizon of the call of God, and let our own feelings tumble for a moment until we, too, felt the hallelujahs trembling in our souls.

The preacher's face is important in making an immediate connection with the hearers. It needs to be an 'open face', as one senior sister put it. And the openness must remain throughout the preaching event. Always and consistently the hearers want to be assured that the preacher is more interested in the people to whom he speaks than in the pages from which he is getting his material. Perhaps it is difficult to define what an open face is. It is certainly not one with a ceramic smile, so rigid that the seven-year-old boy in the second row finds himself massaging his cheek muscles in order to relax them. Nor is it a glued-on graciousness. The open face is one that says in feature what is true in disposition, namely that this preacher will let you look through the window of his face to his soul, and this preacher will invite you into his inner space where you will find acceptance and refuge. The invitation which the open face extends, the invitation to look through this window into the soul, and the invitation to walk through this door into the safety of warm hospitality, creates delight in the hearer even before the first words are spoken. That is the immediate connectedness of unspoken but genuine hospitality.

The next connection with the hearers is made with the first words the preacher speaks. Those first words are to corroborate the impression which the open face has already made, and are to give assurances for the journey ahead in the next twenty-five minutes or so. If there is corroboration, the delight which the open face created will continue. If the assurances are present in the words as well as in the face, the delight will be strengthened. The journey promises to be a good one. Excessive humility in the first sentences will snuff out any delight which the open face engendered. So will weak apology, which conveys the message that the preacher thinks that he really has no business being here, and that he is immensely grateful that anyone would have 'come out' to hear him. Neither will arrogance sustain the delight, nor create it, if there was not an open face to engender it. Which one of us has not heard the interminable recounting of stories of all the places where this preacher has been, how large the gatherings were at each of the important places where he was invited, and how impressive were the results of his 'ministry'?

What connects quickly with the hearers, and creates expectation in them, is the preacher's respect for them. If the preacher is afraid of them, or is disinterested in them, or disdains them, they will not find an expectation building through the first words and sentences of the preacher's sermon. Respect connects, and then builds delight.

The delight of expectancy which the preacher has been able to achieve through the immediate connectedness with the hearers, is now to be maintained through the preaching event. It can be lost rapidly if the preacher will allow his manuscript to get between him and his hearers. The pages can become a paper veil that hides the open face. The distancing that happens, however, does not come from the fact that he is using a full manuscript, unless the hearers are so prejudiced against his use of it that they turn him off even when the preacher himself has not crawled behind the pages. The distancing results rather from a poor use of the manuscript. The hearers will know quickly whether the preacher is using his notes as a help so that he can talk to them, or whether he is merely reading stuff from a page which lies between them. And if he is not actually reading from the pages, but has rehearsed and memorized his material so that he is now reading it off the screen in the back of his head, the hearers will know that too. Both the paper page and the memorized page can get between the preacher and the hearers. Both can snuff out the initial delight of expectancy. The preacher who cares deeply about the hearers, will see to it that neither paper nor memory will distance him from them.

II. Delight Through the Preacher's Choice of Text
and Approach to it

It was at Winona Lake that I heard a man introduce his text by telling us that since other persons during that week of special presentations had chosen difficult and way-out passages, he would do the same. And then he proceeded to expound the first eight verses of the sixth chapter of Genesis. He told us what he thought about the 'sons of God' coming to the 'daughters of men', and how from that union giants were born, and how these giants, already strong physically, were also strong of intellect, and could therefore make evil more evil. I am amazed today that I actually stayed to hear the brother out. The delight which I had felt earlier when I saw the announcement that this was a Moody Bible Institute series, and that formidable figures were to preach, was all but turned to dust when I heard the man announce his text and tell us why he had chosen it. And the sermon itself blew away even the dust of what had been anticipatory delight.

Since Christian hearers for the most part already have a respect for the Scriptures, and are expectant about having the text address them, the preacher does not have to whip up enthusiasm and delight about the Scriptures themselves. But the choice of the text can either deflate or enhance the delight. The text itself must connect with the hearers, or at least they must be very quickly assured that it will connect. Believers who love and trust the Word, want to hear a text that is significantly long and able to stand on its own, making an impact simply in the reading because it addresses them where they are in life. If the text is too minute, or is obscure, or fragmentary, or irrelevant, then the anticipatory delight is aborted. The hearers feel cheated because they sense that the very resource which they have come to trust is not being honored. They know that they will have to depend largely on the insights and ingenuity of the preacher for the food that delights. They will worry early in the sermon that the preacher may well be reading thoughts into the text rather than listening to the text on their behalf. If the whole exercise is more a human enterprise than an occasion in which the Word becomes flesh, then the delight will dissipate. Or at least the delight will be derived from frills and frolic rather than from substance.

If delight is already ignited in the pious hearers by the announcement of the text and the preacher's approach to it, it is fanned to flame by the good reading of it. One who trusts the Word wants to hear it read in a way that suggests that the reader trusts it too. When we read it well, we attribute worth to it. The care with which we read it is a measure of the degree to which we value it. The believing hearers catch that, and are lifted up and carried by it. We honor the Word when we read the Scriptures with a clear voice, clean articulation, and an alert mind. When we read in thoughts rather than in sentence fragments, in phrases rather than in isolated words, then the hearers will listen with understanding and be able to enter into the text's meanings with us already in the reading. This understanding heightens delight.

When the preacher reads the text in a perfunctory way, indicating that this part of the proceedings is something to be gotten over as quickly as one can so that one can get to the really important stuff, then the believers who trust and love the Word will find their spirits slump. Delight is diminished. If, on the other hand, the Scriptures are read with strength and confidence, accompanied by humility, and are read so as to suggest that the reader stands with the hearers under the text rather than in mastery over it, then the delight of the saints will be increased.

The preacher's approach to the text will show very early in the sermon. Does he see this text as something that the hearers need to hear and respond to, or is it something which has addressed him and his own life prior to this hour? Has he submitted his life, his thinking, his attitudes, to this text, and is he willing to come before the hearers with an 'open face' to let them know that the text has done its work with him? If the preacher has immersed himself in the truth of the text, and has received the text into himself and incorporated it into his life, then the expectation of the hearers will grow. They will come under the text expecting that the truth of it will be workable for them too. That strong expectancy is itself the delight.

The hearer's delight in the sermon will be sustained by a pervasive spiritual quality in the preacher, the sense of his being in touch with God while giving himself fully to the preaching. It will probably not be possible for the hearers to come to their own sense of being close to God if the preacher himself does not have that sense and does not communicate it. The preacher's sense of being in touch with God will be perceived by his clear expectation that he and the congregation will encounter God in the text. When he does have that expectation, the sermon has the potential of becoming an event, a spiritual happening in which the hearers actually come face to face with God. When that sense of being in the presence of God and being addressed by God is sustained throughout the sermon, then the delight which characterized the initial moments will be sustained and enhanced throughout the event.

From this sense of being in touch with God it is a small step to that deep awareness that the Word in the sermon is doing what the Spirit himself wants to do. There is that strong sense of congruity, The Word and the Spirit, together with the preacher and the hearers, are all together the context in which God is doing his work of grace. The delight which the hearers experience now is derived from being nurtured, fashioned, built up into God's own design in Jesus. The enjoyment becomes much like the enjoyment of 'Mrs. Hamm's borscht',- the delight of having a perceived need met. And when the needs are not of the strident kind, it is more like the delight of a child who already feels deeply loved, but jumps up on grandfather's lap anyway and rejoices again in the affection.

The delight may be more focused. I remember with wonder still the repeated times when during my university years I would find questions arising in my mind throughout the week. They were troublesome questions, questions which unsettled and unnerved me. And I would regularly ask God to provide some helpful answers for me from the preaching on Sunday. The answers came. Again and again I would sit in rapt amazement, listening from the heart to the sermons of A. H. Unruh, H. H. Janzen, and others. I had once more heard what I needed to hear in answer to my quite specific confusion, and my delight was mixed with awe.

Nor is the delight any less potent when the need which the Word addresses has to do with something which must be eradicated. It is no less delightful to have a faulty attitude challenged and changed than to have a right attitude affirmed and commended. Of course, the delight of surgery may be associated with some pain, but it is no less a genuine delight. Squeezing out a boil may hurt some, but it feels good nonetheless. Having a knotted muscle massaged may cause a brief moment of sharp pain, but the pain holds a promise, and so it too is a delight. If the massaging continues past that moment of acute hurt to the place of the release of destructive tension, then follows the rest, the relaxation, the easing of the agony. A sermon can delight even while it disinfects, and even when the disinfection stings.

III. Delight in the Way the Preacher Approaches, Shapes, and Expresses the Sermon Material

A preacher who will be heard often by the same congregation does well to vary the way he introduces his material. Sometimes a sharp, short, pithy statement will arouse interest and heighten expectation. Generally speaking, a preacher ought to be able to state the entire sermon in one comprehensive but concise sentence. If he cannot do that, he probably has not thought sufficiently about what he wants to say in the sermon and what he wants to accomplish through it. That capsule sentence is the more compelling if it is stated in an arresting way, without any attempt at cuteness. It must encapsulate without being pretentious. The delight which the genuine seeker after truth brings to the preaching event will not long survive a preacher's ostentation and pretention.

Though the preacher ought to have worked through the text sufficiently, and ought to have thought through his ideas so carefully that he can state his sermon in one terse sentence, he ought always to reckon with the reality that this sentence is not the last word on the subject. The preacher ought not to try too hard to make his formulation the incontrovertible, conclusive and exhaustive articulation of the truth. If the hearers catch such a sentiment in the preacher, they will in all likelihood build some resistance. The delight will diminish. If the preacher introduces his subject and theme with a series of superlatives, the astute hearers will probably become suspicious. The preacher who begins by stating that what he proposes to say is the most important thing they have ever heard, will overawe some hearers, but these will probably be the more naive ones. If on the following Sunday the same preacher, speaking to the same hearers, begins his message by declaring that what he is going to call them to is the most important thing which they will ever decide to do, a few more will become suspicious. After the sixth such superlative introduction, most of the hearers will not be expecting the preacher to deliver on that promise. The delight will have been dulled to the point where new superlatives cannot fan it even to glowing.

The shape of the sermon can also either delight or deaden. Here again a couple of options are open to the preacher. He can let the hearers know from the start what shape the sermon has, so that when he gets to each succeeding point, they have some assurance that the roadmap they were given does in fact indicate the road they are traveling. This gives the hearer some sense of assurance, and assurance does have a delight component. It feels good to know where you are driving, even when you are sitting in the passenger seat. On the other hand, the preacher may choose to keep the shape a secret. The delight on such a journey comes more from the surprises that one experiences along the way. These surprises, however, ought not to come on the heels of prolonged anxiety. They are surprises that burst in on us on a road we travel in confidence and hope. We need to know that the preacher knows where he is going. Even when the travelers are not given a roadmap, they want to travel with assurance. Nor ought fine surprises to be the sole source of that assurance. The preacher himself must communicate certainly, even while he is keeping secrets.

Aimlessness and predictability are both equally capable of snuffing out delight. Aimlessness breeds confusion, and confusion breeds disinterest at best, and in the end disdain. Predictability breeds boredom. I remember thirteen year old boys speaking a preacher's prayer a half beat ahead of him. And so I listened to my own prayers, and discovered to my dismay that they are pitifully predictable. Certitude and creativity combine beautifully to produce delight.

Language itself can create delight. Here too we can try too hard. Contrived parallelisms, forced alliteration, fabricated rhyming suffixes and serial prefixes, these may all have some merit in aiding memory and jogging initial interest. But what is forced, is probably not forceful. What is cute and clever seldom cuts to the core.

And yet beautiful words and gripping metaphor have a power which adds thrust to the truth which the Spirit wishes us to take to heart. Poetic turns of imagery, paintings in words, colors and smells and sounds, all lend their dynamic to stir the emotions of the hearers and move them to open their windows and doors to let the light and the Presence in. In the turn of words new color can be given to what had become trite, and old ideas can be turned inside out to reveal depths we had forgotten.

IV. Delight in the Content Itself

I indicated at the outset that I had learned from members of my home congregation that they expect delight to come from the solid food of the sermon, not from the condiments. The hamburger patty is what we really enjoy, not chiefly the relish. Some of you will recall, no doubt, those days when we did not know better. I do remember, though I do so with some chagrin. I had gone to join my Dad in Vancouver in early April. He had just resigned from teaching at the Herbert Bible School, and had gone on ahead to prepare the way for the family to join him in July. The School gave me grade ten standing at Easter and allowed me to leave early to join Dad. So I got a job, and bought a lunch bucket, and went to the store for stuff with which to make lunch. There it was in a little jar. Sandwich spread, so the label said. So we used it as sandwich filling. A decade later I learned that this was the relish which was to make the real stuff more tasty. I thought it was the real thing. If I today have little taste for a sandwich made of relish only, then I have an aversion for sermons which seek to sell themselves on their condiments. Delight comes from the living, weighty, central stuff of the sermon. It is the large truth, the redemptive reality, the wonder of God in Jesus that the Spirit uses to ground and build the saints. If we cannot preach large truth in a way that delights, then we had best not try to repair the deficiency by winsome entertainment. Don't load on mustard when you have not taken the time to make the meatloaf.

But even the great material disclosed in the pages of the Book will not delight the hearers unless it speaks to their own life situations. The sermon must be as down to earth as the Scriptures are, as down to earth as the Incarnation in Jesus was. If the sermon does not deal with the stuff of life, if it does not meet the hearers in the midst of life, it is not central to life. Rather it is out on a tangent somewhere, irrelevant, remote, obscure. If the hearers are to be touched by the Word, they must be touched where they are living life, and feeling its hurts, and celebrating its joys, and carrying its responsibilities.

If the sermon connects more to what the preacher has read than to what the hearers are living, then any delight which the hearers may experience will be of the academic variety. Facts about obscure people and places are interesting, sometimes even fascinating, but if they remain data at a distance, the delight will be but shallow. Perhaps it is here that a lecture differentiates from a sermon. Lectures, at least as we have come to think about them, may be of interest even if they do not change life's values toward those of the Kingdom. Sermons bring the mind of God quite deliberately into the sphere of our living.

The great truths of the Scripture do not, however, always translate easily into life. At times there are two truths which tug for preference, and the preacher has to make choices. He needs to be so deeply in touch with the people and their situation, and so in tune with the Spirit, that he has some sense of which truth wants to be spoken in this particular situation. Sometimes we need to hear that God is close at hand and ready to intervene. At other times we need to hear that God is beyond us, unreachable, unfathomable, high and lifted up, holy and inaccessible. At one point we need to hear that our freedom has done us in and the mess we are in is the result of our foolish pride, and at other times we need to hear that God can make good come even out of our dumbest mistakes. The preacher walks the tightrope between paradoxical truths, and speaks the one and the other as the Spirit gives him light. The delight for the hearers comes in the inner conviction that the Word which they have heard is indeed the Word they needed to hear at this moment.

There is another kind of tightrope and its accompanying delight for the hearers. The preacher uses both familiar and unfamiliar language and ideas. There can be the delight of comfort in hearing what we expect to hear, and to have the familiar truth sustain and encourage us. And yet not all of our ideas should be on the bottom shelf. There is also the delight of being stretched by hearing words and ideas that are unfamiliar. Of course, these don't do much good if they are unintelligible. We probably will not stretch for that which is quite obviously out of reach, just as the outfielder will not stretch to attempt a catch when the ball is clearly fifteen feet beyond his jump. We do want our hearers to stretch a little, but if we speak in ways that render us incomprehensible, then our presentation stops being a sermon. God ceases to address people with this text because we have screened him out with our words. Even lofty ideas should be said simply. And they can be. If we are not understood, it is likely because we are obscure, not because we are so profound.

Delight comes, then, when the sermon addresses the people in their life situation and gives them something practical which they can apply to life and its demands. The sermon has something to say to us about ourselves, and about our struggles. It offers God's solution to a problem which is a real problem. When it does that, the hearer will find delight in what we say.

Conclusion

Resistance is possible at various levels in the preaching of a sermon. There can be resistance to the hearing itself; the person simply refuses to listen. There can be resistance to opening one's life to the Word; the person refuses to submit the 'everyday of life' to the authority of God. There can also be resistance to putting into action that which the Spirit calls to in the sermon. The person refuses to translate into action and living what he has agreed to in principle while hearing and being open to the Word.

Delight is designed to overcome resistance at any of these levels. The preacher who can delight, can thereby open the ears of the indifferent. The preacher who has learned the art of delighting can more effectively invite people to risk the opening of their inner lives and their way of living to God's Word, and to resolve to act upon what the Spirit has prompted.

So help us God!

11

EVANGELICAL PREACHING AND PASTORAL CARE

Frank C. Peters

Evangelicals have generally placed great emphasis on preaching, and have pointed to the ministry of Jesus for justification. Against a background in Judaism where preaching played only a minor role, Jesus "came preaching." Our Lord bequeathed this task to his disciples who continued with this emphasis. The Book of Acts gives us some cherished excerpts of apostolic preaching.

This article does not focus on preaching as such but seeks to relate preaching to pastoral care. Some critics of preaching see little relationship between preaching and pastoral care except, perhaps, that some preaching increases the need for pastoral care! I personally believe that good preaching often reduces the need for pastoral care in that it helps the listeners to apply biblical principles to their own personal needs.

Preaching in order to aid pastoral care need not necessarily zero in on specific problems of adjustment. There is a danger that preaching becomes mere "psychologizing" from the pulpit. Biblical preaching re-enacts the story of God's personal approach to humanity, and as such demands faith and surrender. The central concern of biblical preaching is so to rehearse the story of God's redeeming acts in Christ that this becomes a living reality in the act of preaching.

The evangelical preacher is completely unapologetic about basing the proclamation, not on mere human insight, but upon divine revelation. The preacher knows that the message did not originate with the person of the preacher. Preaching, as Donald G. Miller reminds us, is an event and Christ was God's event. Pulpit discourse is not simply "a body of ideas, not a way of looking at life, not merely a philosophy of meaning and certainly not a technique for successful or happy living."[1] It is the story of what God has done for human beings in Christ.

A Necessary Relationship

Philipps Brooks, lecturing at Yale University in 1877, suggested that the work of the preacher and the pastor really belonged together and should not be separated. Speaking from his own experience as an expert pulpiteer, he said:

> The work of the preacher and the pastor really belongs together, and ought not to be separated. I believe that very strongly. . . . When you find that you can never sit down to study and write without the faces of the people, who you know need your care, looking at you from the paper; and yet you can never go out among your people without hearing your forsaken study reproaching you, and calling you home, you may come to believe that it would be good indeed if you could be one or other of two things and not both; either a preacher or a pastor, but not the two together. But I assure you, you are wrong. The two things are not two, but one. . . . The preacher needs to be a pastor, that he may preach to real men. The pastor must be a preacher, that he may keep the dignity of his work alive. . . . Be both; for you cannot really be one unless you are also the other.[2]

Young, enthusiastic pastors under the lingering influence of a great seminary teacher whose specialty was either counseling or preaching may develop an "either-or" attitude toward pastoral roles. Even though they might make allowances for both functions, they might see themselves as specializing in one or the other. This, I believe is unfortunate. David A. McLennan, many years ago, advised students wisely in this regard:

> The preaching office and that of pastoral counseling are one and indivisible. Notwithstanding opinions of some

seminarians and working pastors to the contrary, the issue is not 'either-or'–either major emphasis in the pulpit or major attention on the personal interview–but 'both-and', both preaching and pastoral counseling as two indispensable 'offices' of one vocational task.[3]

Actually, the goals of the pastor in preaching and pastoral care are the same. In both cases the attempt is made to reach the individual person. The approach and the technique may be different but the objective is the same. Some human needs are best met in group relationships, as with preaching, while others are best met in close person-to-person relationships as in pastoral care. But the sensitive preacher will soon discover that the individual and group approaches are different aspects of one central task.

There is a danger of emphasizing one ministry over against the other. Pastors who have been influenced by the pastoral counseling movement, and especially by the client-centered approach of Carl R. Rogers, have criticized preaching on several counts. They find that preaching tends to be very directive. Students who in one class learn the value of being non-directive must be confused when in another class they are counseled "to preach for a verdict."

Preaching, at least so it seems to the observer trained in counseling, deals with people wholesale. Judging from the modern emphasis on numbers, the more the better. Is it really possible for one individual to address several hundreds of people in such a way that each feels personally addressed? Since all preaching seems to generalize, pastors whose emphasis is upon individuality sometimes feel that preaching does run counter to their basic premises.

Perhaps the greatest jar which pastors trained in modern therapeutic theories receive from evangelical preaching is the superlative nature of the biblical injunctions. If truth is consistently preached in absolutes, is the preacher not cast into the role of a judge? Such a role would seem to limit effectiveness in pastoral care.

The task of the evangelical preacher is to clarify the meaning of the Christian faith, faith being understood as man's affirmative response to the revelation of God. Such preaching also makes intelligible the response which God requires of people. Pastoral care helps to remove the roadblocks which hinder the human response.

Preaching for Involvement

Evangelical preaching, if it is to be effectively allied with pastoral care, must become a communication which involves the mind and not only the emotions. If evangelical preaching is ever to lead people to an application of the biblical message to those areas of life where they need to experience the transforming power of the gospel, it must move beyond evangelical cliches and trite illustrations. The preacher must preach for intellectual involvement.

By using the word "involvement" I hope I have steered clear of mere intellectualism. In the preaching event the hearer becomes deeply involved with a truth. However, feelings follow quickly in the wake of a truth; feelings are anchored to something with which the hearer can come to grips. The feeling will eventually subside but the idea will remain.

Fiery sermons without intellectual content are psychologically dangerous. They arouse without giving direction. An aroused person must act and since no directed course of action has been suggested, the person is thrown into a state of anxiety. However, where the biblical premise was carefully expounded and a course of action suggested from this premise, the hearer has the option of reviewing the matter personally, and thus of internalizing the message. The action which follows will now be viewed as his own since it grew on the soil of thought and meditation.

Involvement seems to have been the method which Jesus used in his preaching. We have only fragments of his sermons, but it is obvious that his listeners were deeply involved. Edgar Jackson says in his book *A Psychology for Preaching* that "Jesus spent little time sawing sawdust. He ripped into the real problems of people and his age. He generated real participation and response."[4]

The preacher who is an able exponent of thought will, of course, understand the people to whom he speaks. Evangelical preachers generally fall into three groups. Some have a natural warmth and feeling for people and that quality dominates their ministry whether they are highly trained or not. Others have serious personality defects that make it easier for them to reject people than to accept them. Finally, the great majority of evangelical preachers are normal, healthy, individuals who are anxious to improve their techniques of relating themselves and their message to people. These are the ones who would gladly accept the insights of the behavioral sciences in order to sharpen their intellectual tools so that they can work more effectively.

To preach for involvement also demands a certain amount of intellectual daring on the part of preachers. If preaching is an event, then it remains to be said that some events can backfire. Preachers in search of safety seldom find themselves involved with people in search of truth. They may take recourse to trite cliches and pious platitudes. They will side with issues which others have already fought out and settled. When the smoke of battle clears away, they are found raising ancient battle cries and fighting straw men without considering their greater danger of creating a lop-sided faith in people which emphasizes only certain aspects, but which never faces the issues of the day. Such people are ill-equipped to face the battle of the hour. They have been denied the experience of honest intellectual combat and growth. This does not call for a contemporaneity which jumps on every passing bandwagon or joins in with every passing fanfare. However, preachers must think through basic issues facing their congregations and do this honestly and boldly. To fail in this is to fail as a leader. Leaders cannot rely on quotations; they must often quote themselves and take the consequences. This is preaching from conviction.

Pastoral care has a way of conditioning a preacher to preach for involvement. A real interest in pastoral work and skill in it does much to save preaching from an ever-present danger--the danger of merely verbalizing. This interest in pastoral care makes it possible for a preacher to go on preaching month after month, year after year, in the same place without tiresome repetition. The congregation will continue to find his sermons challenging because the sermons have found them where they live and have their problems. Preachers who are in touch with life and who seek to minister to life will find that there is a freshness in their preaching.

Preaching for involvement will bring about the same response which was made to the first Christian sermon at Pentecost: "What shall we do?" Such preaching reaches the secret places of the heart and mind where the springs of life are coiled. It has the same relation to mere general oratory that a personal letter has to a mailbox full of circulars.

Person-Centered Preaching
A number of writers have attempted to define preaching which relates to pastoral care. Charles F. Kemp called it "life-situation" preaching. Henry Sloan Coffin called it "pastoral" preaching but admitted it was a clumsy title. Those in the counseling movement speak of "therapeutic" preaching but I believe the term is too restrictive in its connotation.

There is, I believe, a danger inherent in "life-situation" and "therapeutic" preaching as defined by some of the proponents of these approaches. Such preaching can become too problem-centered. It is possible to preach on life situations in such a way that the preacher raises more problems than he can solve. He may make his parishioners so conscious of adjustment problems that they are almost crushed by the weight of the ills of this world. Perhaps this could be compared to the ads on television and radio which discuss so many symptoms that people come to think they have something which they really do not have.

I have chosen the term "person-centered" because I believe that the best preaching is done when the preacher has the person in mind. Preaching is more than the presentation of a subject. It is a relationship between pastor and person. For this reason a study of preaching can never be merely a study of sermons. A sermon is effective not merely because it is well written and well delivered but because the people in the pew know the person in the pulpit. This one has helped them as individuals. People who know the preacher as a pastor will give a different kind of attention when they hear the sermon.

Preachers cannot engage in person-centered preaching when they do not know the people well. They cannot know what people's needs are until they have spent time with them. This simply means that such preaching grows out of pastoral work. Pastoral work that is neglected or done poorly weakens preaching. If the preacher constantly speaks to humankind in general, the message will have little appeal to particular people.

The preacher who draws his sermons from books and does not have a vital relationship with people, who never gives them an opportunity to share their lives with him, may perfect the academic art of preaching but will fail as a preacher. Perhaps this kind of preacher could be compared to the physician who has mastered the science of anatomy from the study of cadavers but has never studied disease in living bodies.

Much of Jesus' preaching grew directly out of his experience with people. The parables he told of particular kinds of people illustrate this point well. Some of his most profound statements were made to meet the life problems of people like Nicodemus or the woman at the well.

I have found it extremely helpful to concentrate on individuals in my sermon preparation. I cannot visualize the needs of one thousand people but I am always aware of the acute problems which certain parishioners face. A surgeon operates on individuals, one person at a time. A preacher must get away from the myth of the *Massenmensch*. Such a person is always fictitious; only individual people are really alive. If a preacher has no individual in mind when he prepares or delivers his sermons, the sermons will come to people like custard pie. The pie will cover a large area but will hit nothing very hard.

A person-centered sermon should have a basic proposition. It should have a point. No matter how brilliantly or intelligently it has been conceived, it can be nothing more than a harmless essay. If the sermon is not aimed at people in the particulars of life it is useless. When Jesus preached, his hearers, at least some of them, "perceived that he had told the parable against them."

Preachers who are involved in pastoral care need not preach pointless sermons. With deliberate and definite intent, preachers address themselves to people they know. Their object–the helping of some specific person–is always before them as they prepare the sermon. As a pile driver lifts and drops the hammer, so the person-centered preacher lifts a great biblical truth and drops it precisely where it will do some individual the most good.

Preaching and Mental Health

The Christian gospel which the minister preaches and teaches is, according to Paul, "the power of God for salvation." We have been reminded by New Testament exegetes that there is a relationship between our English word "dynamite" and the Greek word translated "power." It would seem that religion is like dynamite; it can be as dangerous as it is useful.

The power of preaching to hurt rather than to heal is something to which every psychiatrist and clinical psychologist can give evidence. However, the answer is certainly not one of scrapping preaching in the interest of mental health but rather one of examining evangelical preaching carefully in order to detect those elements which are not productive of spiritual or emotional health.

There is a strong suspicion on the part of many people in this day of relativism that whatever appears to disturb and upset human beings is either not true or has not been presented properly. This false assumption has produced a very negative attitude toward evangelistic preaching and the expressions of guilt and repentance which it produces.

On the other hand, the preacher must ask the questions: how can I proclaim the gospel in such a way that broken lives are healed rather than mutilated even more? How can I preach so that people become whole once more? The intent in these kinds of questions indicates that the preacher's goals overlap considerably with those of the psycho-therapist. However, the preacher should go much further than the therapist does. The gospel is more than sanctified psychology designed to make people serene and happy.

Positive preaching will not violate a sense of reality. One criterion of the soundness of a pastoral proclamation is the extent to which it aids the believer in dealing effectively with real life. The Master's approach never violated a sense of reality for he did not demand the unrealistic. Nor did his words counsel people to escape life. However, the realism of the pulpit must include the realism of divine revelation, the activity of God's Spirit as well as the realism of life on earth.

It is of significance that Jesus took his illustrations (parables) directly from life. Fables and distortions, though found in the Old Testament, are strangely absent in his preaching. I believe that many of the illustrations used by preachers today are more destructive than they are helpful. Some apocryphal illustrations imply unrealistic goals and, if taken seriously, produce unnecessary guilt. Stories of saints awakened in the night to be directed on mysterious errands may be true but they form normal experiences for so few people that I believe they are best deleted.

Some unrealistic preaching leads people to expect the impossible of God. Now before you tell me that with God all things are possible, permit me to say that God cannot make a thing square and round at the same time. Some preachers lead people to expect God to heal all diseases without exception, give perfect and infallible impressions of divine leadership, remove all anxiety at once, and keep it out, and prevent us who are his from ever having serious crosses.

Illustrating a truth effectively is indeed an art and a necessary one. Each illustration is a vehicle designed to carry a cargo. However, some vehicles are so faulty that they just do not deliver the goods which the preacher wishes to communicate. We must be on guard against "neurotic illustrations." Such a warning, though, should not detract from the necessity of illuminating the sermon properly for this necessity is found in the mental attitude of our people. Whether preachers like it or not, they are preaching to the "moving picture mind" which is accustomed to images, pictures, scenes moving rapidly. The average mind is not accustomed to deep thinking or long sustained argument. As preachers we may not approve of the daily fare of our people, and we may regret their inability to pursue abstract logic, but we will have to recognize that most of our audience can only be reached through truth properly illustrated from real life. I remind readers of the observation made by Henry Ward Beecher when he said, "There are few men who can follow a close argument from beginning to end: and those who can are trained to do it, though of course some minds are more apt for it than others."[5] A more recent source puts it this way: "Most people, even educated people, do not listen analytically but are affected by the pattern of imagery in an utterance."[6]

Rather than decrying the necessity of using illustrations, the person-centered preacher welcomes this. It gives him a wonderful opportunity to dip into the crucible of the daily experience of his people in order to have the gospel speak to these real life situations. The evangelical preacher is also strengthened by A.M. Hunter's recent observation that the parabolic element in Luke's gospel amounts to 52% of the total. Thus more than half of one of the evangelical memoirs is pictorial in form and of the whole of the recorded teaching of our Lord the ratio is much higher--something like 75%. Surely a most impressive proportion!

The truth of the gospel properly illustrated from real life which the hearer recognizes as reflecting his own condition has within it health-producing qualities which are invaluable therapeutic resources. Parishioners who hear their pastor talk about the "abundant life" in a manner which is realistic and hopeful will be helped toward better mental health.

Preaching becomes a resource for mental health when, rather than abandoning the gospel, it recovers those elements within it which in modern times have been neglected or submerged under rigid authoritarianism or moral perfectionism.

Preaching which promotes mental health cannot be divorced from the attitudes and responses of the preacher. Unfortunately, some preachers are not aware of conflicting attitudes and responses in themselves and therefore continue to foster similar deficiencies in their parishioners. There are three factors which control the preacher's responses. The first is his attitude toward persons and their problems. This may range from complete understanding and acceptance to scorn and rejection. It would be determined by the ways in which the preacher has dealt with problems arising out of personal experience. But a person-centered preacher who has worked through a problem to a successful solution will probably be understanding of another who has a similar problem. If the preacher has failed to work through it or feels anxious and guilty about it, he will communicate these feelings to the people. Here the principle of removing the beam from one's own eye could be emphasized.

Many pastors who have taken specialized training in counseling have been subjected to a process of analysis. In this way they become aware of their own mental processes in relation to those of others with whom they deal and they learn how to handle their own feelings in a pastoral situation.

The second factor which controls the responses of preachers is their interpretation of humanity. The understanding that the human family is inherently sinful does not necessitate a negative attitude toward others. On the other hand, an intellectual position that humankind is basically good does not assure an accepting attitude on the part of the counselor. However, where humanity's basic need and condition is understood in the full light of the gospel of redemption and where such understanding is deeply colored by a redemptive attitude, the responses of the pastor will certainly be curative.

The third factor which controls the responses of the pastor or preacher is related to the pastor's self-concept and role as a minister. The role of the minister is very frequently defined in theological symbols but these symbols must be translated into terms of process and structures of life experience. The preacher is truly "a servant of God's servants" and Peter's admonition to "shepherd the flock" must be taken seriously (1 Peter 5:1-4).

(Dr. Peters added here that he intended to give the typist a concluding paragraph to include here. It was, however, not received since he went to be with his Lord shortly thereafter.)

END NOTES

1. Donald G. Miller, *The Way to Biblical Preaching* (New York: Abingdon Press, 1957), p. 13.

2. Phillips Brooks, *Lectures on Preaching* (Grand Rapids: Zondervan Publishing House, n.d.), pp. 75-7.

3. David A. MacLennan, "Preaching and Pastoral Counseling are One Task", *Pastoral Counseling* 3 (March, 1952).

4. Edgar Jackson, *A Psychology for Preaching* (Great Neck: Channel Press, 1961), p. 30.

5. Quoted by I. MacPherson, *The Art of Illustrating Sermons* (New York: Abingdon Press, 1964), p. 56.

6. Editor's note: Dr. Peters was taken home before he edited this article. The source referred to was not available to us prior to publication.

12

BIBLICAL REALISM AND URBAN EVANGELISM

Myron S. Augsburger

"I am made all things to all that I might by all means save some."
(I Cor. 9:22)

The Christian church must repeatedly ask the questions: 1) How do we read the Bible? and 2) How do we share its message with our society? The care with which we work at answering these questions determines the life and growth of any fellowship or congregation. And the two questions are inter-related: for we do not read the Bible realistically unless we read it not only in the context in which it was written, but also in the context in which it is to be heard. Further, we do not truly share its message until we have heard it with a clarity that is free of acculturization and/or synergism.

It must then be said that the Biblical evangelist is both scholar and communicator. If only the latter, as in the case of Apollos, there needs to be an Aquila and Priscilla who explain the Word of God more fully. If only the scholar, there needs to be a vision of responsibility as an ambassador of Christ that will send one out like Saul of Tarsus rather than let him be content only to study at the feet of Gamaliel.

Something is radically amiss when the church has an over supply of bureaucrats and an under supply of evangelists. We are also amiss if our theological work is focused on the "in-group", without due consideration to contextualizing and communicating the gospel. The exercise of theological reflection came into the early church primarily in response to evangelism, the need to interpret the Christian faith in the dialogue of evangelistic ministry. Secondly, it served to enhance the catechism to instruct members of the church for their own stability in the faith as they lived among nonbelievers. Similarly, the Anabaptists did their theology in dialogue with the opposition, seeking to clarify the truth of Scripture, doing theology as a witness to their faith and as a challenge to the faith of their hearers. A good example is the Frankenthal disputations which involved seventy sessions.

It is frequently said that the Anabaptists were not theologians. However, such a judgment is made more from the fact that few, if any, lived long enough in those first years to write and leave a theological tome with us. In actuality, they were some of the best theological communicators of the time, interpreting the Scripture and contextualizing its message for both scholar and peasant, converting royalty and commoner to become disciples of Christ. Within the first five years of the movement, beginning with a little band of sixteen who baptized each other in a prayer meeting in Zurich, January 21, 1525, I estimate that 25,000 members were soon sharing their faith across Switzerland, Bavaria, Austria and down the Rhine to the Netherlands. In the next twenty years that figure appears to have more than tripled, with somewhere between 5,000 and 10,000 martyrs.

As one reads their witness to faith and their doctrinal interpretations in sources like *Martyr's Mirror, The Chronicle of The Hutterian Brethren* and *The Sources of The Swiss Anabaptists*, it becomes evident that they were thinking theologically. And I am saying this in full awareness that their straightforward use of Scripture was very contextualized. However, as Koyama has said, "It is better to become a neighbor with a Samaritan theology. . . than to desert the beaten victim with Jewish theology. . . ." What the Anabaptists rejected was the intellectualization of Christianity; for as Anabaptists, we *live* theology, we do not simply write it. And so it must be in the urban context. We live our faith in relation to one another. It is here that we must, with Paul, "be made all things to all people that we may win some" (I Cor. 9:22).

Today we find ourselves at a radically different place in history, and today the opponents to discipleship are less militant but more subtle. This is shown in the excellent work by Lesslie Newbigin, *Foolishness To The Greeks*, in which he shows that the impact of the Enlightenment and of the scientific approach has led to an acculturization of the gospel to an Americanism that is far removed from the New Testament message. I propose that the answer is not a return to primitivism, but to a Biblical Realism that enables us to interpret discipleship of Christ with the integrity of faith in a secular society. And for those of us in the Mennonite community, this means transcending our ethnocentricity so that the truth of discipleship, of reconciliation, of peace, is not "contained" by our ethnic community--but shared in a style in which a theology of reconciliation impacts society evangelistically. As we confront issues, we are above all bringing people to Christ. Augustine prayed, "For it is better for them to find you and leave the question unanswered than to find the answer without finding you."

Biblical Realism calls us to go where the people are and to meet them at the point of their need. The world we know today is radically different from previous periods. To describe our world, we now use such terms as East and West, Third World, Fourth World, North and South, Global Village, Super Powers, et al. But one of the most radical changes is urbanization, as people have moved to the cities and as life has taken on an urban culture. By the year 2000, the world population is variously estimated to reach 6 - 10 billion. Of that number 85 percent will live in urban settings--half of them in "slum" conditions. The move to urban settings is a global change. Half of Chile lives in Santiago; one third of Peru lives in Lima; Mexico City is now the largest city in the world, and may reach 30 million by the end of the century.

According to a World Vision article, 50 percent of the Third World population will never see a clinic and 80 percent never see a doctor. The problem of exploitation of the powerless by the powerful in many countries will continue to breed revolt. The gap between the "haves" and the "have-nots" will widen rather than close. Our mission to be a presence for Christ in areas of need, calls us to where the people are--in the cities. The strengths of our more rural orientation, initiative, ingenuity, creativity, individual security, facility at creating small communities within the larger social structure, and above all, the integrity of our commitment to follow Jesus--are all qualifications to urban mission. With Paul, we can be weak with the weak, "free from all men yet servant to all that we might win the more" (I Cor. 9:22,19).

Biblical Realism calls for a strategy of presence in world cities. Jesus sent out thirty-five teams into every city he planned to go (Luke 10:1-11). Paul went to the cities and population centers with the gospel, so we need to go where the concentration of people are to be found. Today we have over 2500 cities with population over 100,000 and over 250 cities with a million or more. By the year 2000, there will be over 500 "million-plus" cities. Three of the five largest cities are just south of us: Mexico City, Sao Paulo and Rio de Janeiro. The growth of the church in Africa may bring a change as to the center of Christian activity, for by the end of the century it will no doubt be the continent with the highest percentage of Christians, and we will be their brothers and sisters. A Biblical Realist takes Christ's Commission seriously and begins a strategy of presence in as many of these cities as possible.

Financially, this is overwhelming if we think of absorbing the total costs of travel, housing and living expenses for all the families who will be expatriots. However, if we can train persons to serve at the point of need in another culture, to be accepted into the job-market because their skills are desired, and their goal is to enable others, we can begin a new wave of tent-maker evangelists--who may be school teachers, music teachers, legal advisors, engineers, computer technicians, et al, and who at the same time are witnesses for Christ and developers of the Church.

With patterns of shared leadership, the expatriot can support the native person rather than become the bureaucrat who runs the church. And by letting the native person administer the baptisms, the Lord's Supper, the small group activities, the church then becomes contextualized and effective. We need to rediscover Paul's strategy, patterns in which he performed very few baptisms (I Cor. 1:14-17), he ordained local leaders and, when it was necessary, defended this contextualization before the Jerusalem council (Acts 15).

Biblical Realism calls for compassionate identification with people in the city. With twenty-five years of city-wide evangelistic missions, I was still a visitor to the inner city until the spring of 1981, when Esther and I moved to Washington, D.C. After six years in a row house on 9th Street, NE, we feel "at home." These are our people, black and white. And we came without denying the privileges of our background, culture, education, management, property, travel, etc. With no pseudo-identification of being ghetto people, we simply let it be known that we are here because we care. And this caring is the one thing that builds bridges in a very complex society called "the city."

Amid the many voices in the city, my voice is just one more, except when I exegete the Word! The pastor becomes the prophetic voice, speaking from God, applying God's Word to the lifestyle of the inner city, addressing the issues of motive and relationships, of ethics and community, of work and management, of singleness and family, of discipline and choices. And this is not the presentation of an agenda packaged from outside the inner city context, but shaped and expressed by inner city understandings.

The Biblical Realist is actually a proponent of the "Third Way," the way of the Kingdom of Christ. Being neither rightist conservative nor leftist humanist, we are able to relate to both and to select from both by the criteria of the Kingdom of Christ. While this means being non-partisan, it is more than that--for it is neither being neutral nor is it walking a middle line. The Third Way means being free to critique, to select, to judge and/or to support on the basis of Kingdom discernment. Such a position can keep one from civil religion, from idolatrous aspects of nationalism, from perversions of materialism and from worldly ambition or slavery to power. The Third Way takes seriously Jesus' call to active servant roles, refusing to manipulate people or to use them for one's personal advantage.

This approach can build the trust level between people and can create community as a spirit of relationship within the social community. Actually, the development of a community of the reconciled is an essential aspect of Anabaptist Biblicism, an expression that the people of God are the Church visible in society, living as members of the Kingdom of heaven (Phil. 3:20). And this visibility is the act of faith, the daring to keep on saying "yes" to Jesus even with continuing ambiguity. We are not seeking "proofs" that contain the Kingdom or master a religious position, but are practicing faith as a life pattern of walking with Jesus.

Biblical Realism also means that we engage a society at the median level and reach both ways. We do not come to the inner city "reaching down to help those poor, benighted souls," but we identify without being classed at either end of the spectrum. In being "all things to all people," we are engaged in the most demanding social aspect of evangelism. We are called to work for justice, equity, human rights in an urban setting where 10 percent are the powerful, 40 percent are the power brokers and 50 percent are the powerless. This is far more demanding than a social work program in which one of privilege helps the one with the problem. In this approach, we live and share in both the problems and the privileges, modeling in each the lifestyle of disciple.

Too often our 'city missions' have had a mentality of 'reaching down' to help the needy, and we've helped them up and *out*. In a wholistic community of various cultural levels, the person who is helped 'up' has other peers with whom to share at a new level. We need to create new, wholistic communities which cut across class lines and call persons to discipleship in their setting, enriching their social setting. The current Yuppie lifestyle needs to be penetrated with Biblical understandings of discipleship and stewardship, a mission as vitally important as helping the street people. The new people of God which the Spirit keeps creating, is not a people of particular culture or religion. There is no class that people are to achieve, only a commitment to follow Jesus in life.

Biblical Realism regards worship as the resourcing center for all of life. Beyond our doctrinal understandings is the desire to worship, to honor God. And this is true whether personal or communal, individual or corporate. We do not pit the private and the social against each other, for all of us are participants in each aspect of life. Worship renews our private lives so that we bring a better person to the community; it also renews our corporate lives as we participate together in the demands of life. The wholism of worship will not permit such a false dichotomy as to separate the evangelistic and social dimensions of the gospel! If it is the New Testament Gospel, it is the Evangel, the Good News that in Jesus Christ we become children of God; and, it is social in that none of us is a child of God without interrelation with God's other children, in fact with all whom God would have to hear the Good News and to share the new life (II Cor. 5:19-20). Every area of life needs to be penetrated with the love and grace of Christ, calling people to step out of their social securities to become disciples of Christ.

Biblical Realism is committed in the love of Christ to the reality of reconciliation. We are called to share in the Shalom of God. "He is our peace, who has made both one (Jew and Gentile) and has broken down the wall of partition between us. . . to make in himself of two one new humanity, so making peace" (Eph. 2:14-15). One cannot be a part of the body of Christ without participating in the mission of Christ to bring all people together in his peace. In the context of class distinctions and racial preferences, we need to work together at reconciliation.

In the setting of our work on Capitol Hill, there is the promotion of "regentrification," a restoration of buildings and lifestyle which carries racial and social class overtones. This we must transcend by a practice of equity that helps all persons in the area toward quality living. At the other end of the spectrum are the sections of the city in which "red lining" occurs; that is, the refusal by banks and real estate agents to arrange loans for purchase or improvements, thereby allowing a section of the city to die so that it can be destroyed and redeveloped--and this often without concern for the persons who are hurt in the process. The inner city church has a ministry to help such people, and it's usually a ministry focused on families while also helping the "street people," who are more transient.

Biblical Realism also calls for flexibility in the structures of the congregation and its polity. The New Testament appears to recognize a variety of administrative and polity patterns among the churches, depending upon the cultural setting. In Washington, D.C., we have had the liberty to seek the Spirit's creative guidance in a structure that seems to fit our context. Our commitment at Washington Community Fellowship is to make Worship the center of the resourcing experience for the congregation. We have developed a free, varied yet well-structured service that runs about 1 1/2 hours in length. This pattern provides for more extensive participation by the congregation. We take 'community' seriously and have developed covenant groups for spiritual sharing on a weekly basis. Covenant groups also function to hold each other accountable as disciples of Christ. We have also opened our Fellowship to inter-denominational composition with all members committed to our Membership Covenant, while they may, at the same time, continue their own denominational identification. We have made other adjustments, including the practice of various modes of baptism, the observance of the Lord's Supper the first Sunday of each month along with a Mutual Aid offering, the practice of foot washing on Maundy Thursday evening in a very open, simple style, development of a periodic prayer altar on a Sunday evening where persons share problems, and others come and sit by the petitioner and lead the group in prayer for the person. We have developed mission programs by the congregation plus several others in cooperation with other churches in the area. We support members who work with other churches in the city as well as giving partial support to persons in overseas missions. Our mission commitment is currently 40 percent of our budget, with 50 percent as our goal.

Our realism, as we look to the twenty-first century, is that congregations will need to transcend their denominational ties while remaining true to them so that we can impact the larger society with the gospel of Christ. In no way do we repudiate our denominational name or relationship; rather we open our arms and minds to reach beyond denominational roles. We want to serve in the freedom of the gospel and avoid possessiveness. Contextualization is a profound and broad task of accommodating the gospel to the total life of a people, and we need to discover how to do that in the urban context. With this task, our Biblical Realism is the one corrective to over-contextualizing the gospel lest it become subservient to particular cultural interests.

Biblical Realism calls us to life in the Spirit for daily living. The word of Scripture is that Jesus is risen and that he gives us his Holy Spirit. To be a Christian realist is to acknowledge the Spirit's presence, to walk in the power of the resurrection and to seek his guidance in occupational choices and in the quality of our work. We know that God is sovereign and that we serve him in the power of the Spirit. We do not use him for our advantage. This life in the Spirit means being available to the Spirit and avoiding the pursuits of self-interest that minimize his authority. His power is the power to love, to rejoice even in adversity, to reconcile and enjoy community, to be patient with those who are at a different place, to be gentle in relationships, to have a lifestyle of goodness, to walk by faith in each daily experience, to be meek in enabling others and to practice self-control in life's disciplines. These expressions, called by Paul the fruit of the Spirit (Gal. 5:22) are the extension of power of the Spirit through us.

Biblical Realism sees evangelism as a ministry of reconciliation that is based on our relationship with Christ. Contrary to most systems of theology where evangelism is brought in as a limited application of mission, Biblical Realism places evangelism in direct relationship with Christology. Jesus said, "As the Father has sent me, so send I you" (John 20:21). And Paul wrote, "God was in Christ reconciling the world unto Himself. . . and has committed unto us the word of reconciliation. Now then, we are ambassadors for Christ, as though God did beseech you by us, we pray you in Christ's stead, be ye reconciled to God" (I Cor. 5:19-20). Such a work of reconciliation is a function of the Spirit, of relationship, of presence; not just a function of words. Significantly, Paul holds the word *and* the work of reconciliation together. The work authenticates the word, and the word articulates the meaning; also, the work demonstrates the word, and the word interprets the work. With this awareness, we can say that evangelism is everything that makes faith in Christ an option or a possibility for a person. And in the urban context we need a realism that will develop a network of faith across the city, a network that relates us to other churches that are a part of Christ's team.

Biblical Realism holds a high view of inspiration but focuses more on the authority of Scripture. And in emphasizing its authority, we focus on the role of interpretation. What we believe is what we understand the Scripture to say. In our understanding, it is the one authority for the knowledge of God, of creation, of human sinfulness, of Christ, of redemption, of the Christian Church, of Christian ethics, of mission, of eschatology, of human destiny. . . Our interpretation is with a realism that applies the principles taught in Scripture to the issues of our involvements in a given time and culture. We do not function in a simplistic proof-texting pattern, nor handle the Scriptures as though they make up a "flat-book" with no inner developments in which the Bible interprets itself. Instead we see the unfolding nature of God's disclosure, through the Old Testament and into the New--first hearing his word in a more limited form (example: Judges or Ecclesiastes), and then in its full disclosure in Christ (as in Gospels or Colossians).

This realism calls us to a careful, scholarly exegesis of the text of the Scriptures, as well as a compassionate and sensitive expression of the significance of Scripture in our communications. We are handling the word of God, and his Spirit enables us to do so with integrity. This realism calls us to free the message from sacramentalism even while we worship in the Sacraments, from emotionalism while we engage the emotions in joy and love, from pietism while we promote and share a meaningful piety, from mysticism while at the same time we bow before the mystery of the One who is wholly Other, from nationalism while we seek to be responsible citizens calling our nation to be strong, just, a good neighbor in the global village. Basically Biblical Realism seeks answers as to how we can be a people of God, a family of Jesus in a given society.

Biblical Realism calls us to take the Way of the suffering servant, to live under the cross. This means a rejection of cheap grace, the perversion of Christianity into a success-religion, as is too often the case in America. The church in South Africa, for example, cannot be a church of "success thinking" but one of suffering presence to expose evil. Similarly, the church in China has been one of suffering presence without a success mentality, with the resultant "surprise by joy" in finding that there are variously from 50 to 100 million Christians reported in China.

We need to free the Christian faith from the acculturization of our materialistic society and rediscover the deeper life of death to self, and a resurrection joy in the Will of Christ. We in the North American church must free ourselves from the power mentality and hear again Christ's call to serve. It is as we serve him (by serving others) that we extend his transforming grace into the market place. The church that witnesses to the cross must itself bear the marks of the cross. In ever increasing ways, the true qualities of Christian discipleship are being sorted out amidst the world's idolatries. More and more we need to hear the closing comment of Saint John in his epistle, "Little children, keep yourselves from idols. Amen" (I John 5:21).

In summation I want to apply this realism to ourselves specifically as Mennonite denominations. The church is something like the giant ice-pack arranged by the artist Oldeberg in the art museum of Minneapolis, Minnesota. This giant ice-pack sags without meaning until lifted from above, under which upward lift it takes on its shape. We need the upward lift of a God-given vision.

In reflecting on such a vision for the church, my mind turns to Paul's words recorded in Acts 28. In verse 23 we read that Paul, under house arrest in Rome, spoke with his Jewish guests in his lodging and talked with them of "the kingdom of God, persuading them of Jesus." Again in the concluding verses of the book of Acts, we read that "Paul dwelt two years in his own hired house, and received all that came in unto him; preaching the kingdom of God and teaching those things which concerned our Lord Jesus Christ, with all confidence, no man forbidding him" (28:30-31). This is the focus for the church! We are heralds of the rule of God known in Christ Jesus; heralds of his kingdom.

The church is in need of a renewal of this vision; a revival of the Spirit which will glorify Christ among us and through us. In our various roles in society, in business and professional life, we must discover anew the priorities of Christ and his Kingdom. This calls for willingness to be changed into the image of Christ, to be directed by the Kingdom of the Spirit rather than by the *status quo* of any party or system (Romans 14:17).

We should move beyond defensiveness to creative action. As a small denomination, we are disproportionately defensive, ready to critique each thing or action from the standpoint of our preferences. We easily move from a sense of ownership in programs as an expression of responsibility to a possessiveness which becomes bureaucratic in manner. Consequently we fail to seek and to see the fresh, creative actions of the Spirit who is seeking to confront an ever-changing world order with the Kingdom of Christ. A retreat to defensiveness is a denial of the dynamic, penetrating, converting, healing, discipling, transforming power of the gospel of Jesus Christ.

We should move beyond historical definition to interpretation. The Anabaptists are an example in history of what happens when people take Jesus Christ with utmost seriousness. However, we do not experience the power of the new life by copying them but in the realism of coming to Christ as honestly as they did. Our heritage has many doctrinal and cultural values, as an expression of the fellowship we share in Christ, but all around us are others who have met Christ and who walk with him, conditioned by *their* heritage and culture. Our task is to meet each other around his Word and interpret together the meaning of Scripture in our time and context.

We should move beyond discussion to action. Talk is not enough; our deeds must authenticate and demonstrate the word. In many of our intense conversations it would appear that we are often engaged in getting others to say things in the same way we say them. Actually, when our semantic exercises have concluded, the real work is yet to be done--sharing with others in the Spirit of Christ. Jesus was not an armchair theologian. And to his followers he says, "In as much as you have done it unto one of the least of these, my brethren, you have done it unto me" (Matt. 25:40).

We should move beyond preservation to extension. The greater way in which to preserve a value is to propagate it. Love is to be given away. Light is to punch a hole into the darkness. The gospel is to impact society. It has social and political consequences without becoming involved in the political process. The gospel is prophetic because it holds people accountable to Jesus the Christ. The church is not to be represented to society as a council of perfection, but as a dynamic happening in which sinners are alike being called, converted and created into the church or body of Christ. This is true for all of us, ethnic and non-ethnic alike. Rather than preserving some inherent goodness, we are "becoming" in grace.

We should move beyond exclusiveness to diversity. It is the very diversity of our thought and cultural patterns which will keep our focus on Christ. Symbols are only symbols, communicants of meaning. When the meaning is better communicated by a change of symbols, we are responsible to change. Symbols were made for humanity and not humanity for symbols. To avoid idolizing symbols, we must constantly seek the most effective communication of the meanings to which the symbols witness. Variety can enhance the discussion of meaning, and it can release people to enter the interchange, who would otherwise be excluded by an insistence on sameness. Oneness is not our being "dittos" of one another, but in our being devoted to Christ.

We should move beyond quest for status to incentives of service. As a people move up the socioeconomic scale there is the accompanying communication of class consciousness. Others not moving in the same spiral of success are soon made to feel second-class. Even in the church a psychologized gospel or a materialistic humanism presents the "King's Kid" as flamboyantly successful. We minimize the teachings of Jesus on humble service and reject his call to be agents of his love and peace. The answer is not in rejecting the benefits of education, management, business or professional success, but in exercising these privileges in the Spirit of Christ. With Mother Teresa, it is not that the people to whom she ministers will turn the world upside down, but rather that her service speaks to the world of the value of persons whom Christ calls us to serve.

We should move beyond the idea of "changing the world," to being salt and light in the world. The language many secular people hear coming from the church is not the love and grace of the gospel of Christ, but the powerful language of wanting to be dominant. At a luncheon Dr. Richard Halverson shifted the focus away from this urge to be dominant. Referring to several programs which claim that we should be changing the world he asked, "What ever happened to the awareness that Christ is calling his people out of the world, a people for himself, strangers and pilgrims in the world?" The focus is not on our prestige but on the integrity of the new people of God in each time and culture.

Obviously the faith in which we stand has implications for our life together as God's people in the cultural, material, social and political dimensions. As Christians we are to be ambassadors of Christ in society, and to be in meaningful conversation with its members in the social, political, professional and ecclesiastical roles in which they are serving. As leaders, we must not hear only ourselves, as people who have a one-sided view of the issues. As in the old parable on limited vision, we must not be like the frogs in the well looking at their one small view of the sky as if it were the whole.

As Christians in society, we are not seeking to take over society. We are seeking to relate with respect and fairness to all persons, just as our Father is kind to the just and the unjust. We must accept the challenge of working with the world in the manner in which God works--revealing the quality of his truth and righteousness so that persons may choose his life and fellowship. This is the greater strength, to be in the world but not of the world because there is always another way--His Way.

God calls us, above all, to be his people; a new people of grace in a secular world. The issues of separation between the people of God and secular society may not be as distinct or simplistic as in the first century. The words, "Render unto Caesar the things that are Caesar's and to God the things that are God's" could be understood then in the immediate context of the Roman Caesar; however, we are called to be equally realistic about Biblical authority in our time, and find the meaning and the way of declaring by word and deed that Jesus is Lord.

It is a pleasure to contribute to this *Festschrift* for Dr. David Ewert because he exhibits the scholarship in Biblical studies which we are promoting. His excellence in Biblical scholarship, coupled with his commitment to mission, support the emphasis I have sought to share. My own associations with David Ewert over the past twenty years, in various settings of his service in Winnipeg, at Eastern Mennonite Seminary in Virginia, at the Mennonite Brethren Biblical Seminary in Fresno and again at the Mennonite Brethren Bible College in Winnipeg--have provided occasions for fellowship in the heritage of faith which we share. I have also benefited from special opportunities to be enriched by his work as an exegete, through his books and his lectures. Listening to him lecture in German with great fluency at the Bienenburg Bible Institute, Liestal, Switzerland, I have seen his ability to contextualize the ministry. I thank God for the gift of David Ewert to the church, a servant in the Word, a brother in the community of faith, and pray that his future service among us be a constant walk in the Spirit.

BIBLIOGRAPHY

Bakke, Raymond J. *The Gospel and Urbanization: Urban Evangelism: A Contemporary Perspective.* (Ventnor: Overseas Ministries Study Center, 1985).

Bosch, David J. "An Emerging Paradigm for Mission." *Missiology: An International Review.* Vol. XI, No. 4, (October, 1983): 485-510

Claerbaut, David. *Urban Ministry.* (Grand Rapids: Zondervan Publishing House, 1983).

Colson, Charles W. "A Call to Rescue The Yuppies," Christianity Today, 29. (May 17, 1985): 17-20.

Newbigin, Lesslie. *Foolishness to the Greeks.* (Grand Rapids:Wm B. Eerdmans Publishing Company, 1986).

Tillapaugh, Frank R. *Unleashing the Church.* (Glendale:Regal Books, 1982).

Walker, Alan. *The Whole Gospel For the Whole World.*(Nashville: Abingdon, 1977).

13

THE CHURCH'S MISSION AND ESCHATOLOGY

Victor Adrian

Hope is one of the great theological virtues of the believer; because our God is a God of hope we are "to overflow with hope by the power of the Holy Spirit" (Rom. 15:13). From the beginning God encouraged man to look forward to His acts and deeds in history, and preeminently to the Kingdom of God. The general quest for the meaning and goal of human existence would find its fulfillment in Christ and His Kingdom.

To pray as Jesus taught us, "Thy kingdom come, Thy will be done on earth as it is in heaven" is to pray for the manifestation of God's power and authority in this world. It means to long for the culminating defeat of all who oppose Him and for the establishment of a new heaven and a new earth in which only righteousness dwell (II Pet. 3:13).

C. S. Lewis reminds us that a believer's constant focus on God's future does not mean neglecting responsibilities in this world:

> If you read history, you will find that the Christians who
> did most for the present world were just those who thought
> most of the next. . . . It is since Christians have largely

ceased to think of the other world that they have become
so ineffective in this.[1]

A preoccupation with eschatology--the doctrine of last things--with its
central focus on Christ and His kingdom, not only creates powerful motiva-
tions for action, but also sustains courage in the midst of the great challenges in the world. Being convinced that Christ the Lord will come again to
bring to final completion His Kingdom on earth enables us to work joyfully
and hopefully, thus hastening His coming.

It is indeed the coming of Christ which has during the last few centuries sustained the missionary impulse in the world. It played an enormous role in
the thinking of Zinzendorf, Hudson Taylor, and many of those associated
with the Student Volunteer Movement. The prospect of the coming of Christ
rendered the church's missionary task urgent!

Oscar Cullmann, a New Testament scholar, maintains that in New Testament
times there was a very close relation between Christian action and the expectations of Christ's coming:

> The genuine primitive Christian hope does not paralyze
> Christian action in the world. On the contrary, the
> proclamation of the Christian gospel in the missionary
> enterprise is a characteristic form of such action, since it
> expresses the belief that missions are an essential element
> in the eschatalogical plan of salvation. The missionary
> work of the church is the eschatalogical foretaste of the
> kingdom of God, and the biblical hope of "the end" con-
> stitutes the keenest incentive for action.[2]

Jesus, in His farewell discourse to His disciples, initiates His description of
their mission in the world with a reference to the promises of His return (John
14-17). Paul's commendation of the visibly active Thessalonian church is
summed up in the words--"You turned from idols to serve the living God and
to wait for His Son from heaven" (I Thess. 1:9-10). There can be no doubt
that the great destiny that Christ has for His believers associated with the
second coming, is to serve as a motivation and constant encouragement as
believers complete the mission of the church in the world.

Believers need always to be reminded that God will triumph in history!
There will be a mighty manifestation of God's power and righteousness sup-
pressing all evil and cleansing and purifying the earth of all unrighteousness.
Biblical eschatology, therefore, guards the church in mission from despair
and discouragement. It also guards it against an optimistic triumphalism—a

triumphalism which places hope primarily in human initiative, direction and strategizing. The believer is to be reminded that the mission of the church will succeed under the Lord's direction, in His power and through His Spirit. Biblical eschatology forms a corrective to the altogether too obvious powerful forces of modernity which seek to sidetrack the church from its central mission to go into all the world and make disciples of all the nations.

In this paper biblical eschatology is viewed in a broader context than simply the clustering of future events around Christ's second coming. The Old Testament hopes and the New Testament fulfillments suggest that biblical eschatology incorporates the great redemptive events associated with the coming of Christ, with the creation of the church through His Spirit, and with the mission of the church in the world. We want to do justice to the many references in the New Testament that the last days are now and to the truth that God has injected spiritual forces into the world with Christ's first coming which will find their culmination in the second coming. The church spans the period between the first and the second coming. It fulfills a distinct role in the economy of God. During these last days it fulfills the glorious mission of our Lord as promised in the words, "And this gospel of the kingdom will be preached in all the world as a testimony to all the nations, and then the end will come" (Matt. 24:14).

The missionary activity of the church is therefore not only an eschatological event of tremendous import in the divine economy but also a sign pointing to the coming end, to the coming of Christ. This fact raises the question whether the church through its mission activity hastens the coming of Christ --an exhilarating thought; or whether through neglect of its mission it delays Christ's coming--a sobering thought.

I. The Mission of the Church Must be Seen as an Eschatological Event

The mission of the church can be understood only in the light of the eschatological realities which initiated it. The church and its mission are profoundly rooted in the first coming of Christ, the inauguration of the Kingdom of God, the death, resurrection and ascension of our Lord, and the pouring out of the Holy Spirit at Pentecost.

The central thrust of the New Testament is that with the coming of Jesus the Kingdom has come, not yet in its fulness, but its powers have invaded this age in an unprecedented way. The Old Testament shadows and the Old Testament promises have become a new reality in the world.

The New Testament therefore speaks of the last days as having come upon us. In Christ eschatology has invaded history.

The author of Hebrews sees in Christ the prophet *par excellence* who speaks more clearly, more fully, and more authoritatively than any preceding prophet. This note of fulfillment and heightening of God's self-revelation is expressed in the words:

> In the past God spoke to our forefathers through the prophets at many times and in various ways, but in these last days He has spoken to us by His Son whom He appointed heir of all things and through whom He made the universe (Heb. 1:1-2).

The author of Hebrews goes on to compare and contrast this new revelation in His Son and the enactment of a new and greater covenant through His death. This occurred *in the last days* and *at the end of the ages* (Heb. 9:26). God dealt conclusively with sin at the time of the "consummation of the ages." Paul likewise associates the coming of Christ as an event among mankind--"on whom the fulfillment of the ages has come" (I Cor. 10:11; cf. Gal. 4:4). Peter also speaks of Christ as revealed "in this last time" or "in the end of times" (I Peter 1:20). The New Testament therefore looks at the first coming of Christ and His redemptive work as that of history reaching a new fulfillment, a climax.[3]

There is a new and intense indication of God's presence among men expressed in our Lord's words that the Kingdom is near, or that it is in our midst, or that they are born into the Kingdom through the Spirit of God, or that believers are being transformed from the kingdom of darkness to the Kingdom of His Son.

This Kingdom (rule) liberates from spiritual bondage. Union with Christ and His death and resurrection results in a new life in a broader sense than that of personal experience. Things have become new in this world.[4] Christ, in virtue of His faithfulness as the messianic servant, was resurrected by the power of God and placed above all principalities and powers in this age and the age to come (Eph. 1). As Lord on the right hand of God, He poured out the Spirit of God upon men.

Pentecost is one of those momentous events of the New Testament which marks a new impulse of the mission of the church. The Great Commission had been given; the disciples were to see themselves as those sent by God; but they were first to await the spiritual endowment from on high.

The pouring out of His Spirit promised in the Old Testament, and anticipated during our Lord's earthly ministry, was unquestionably another major eschatological act of God launching the church into missionary action. Peter recognized the worldwide implication of the day of Pentecost when he regarded it as the fulfillment of God's promises for the last days:

> No, this is what was spoken by the prophet Joel: in the last days, God says, I will pour out my spirit on all people. Your sons and daughters will prophecy, the young men see visions, your old men will dream dreams. Even on my servants, both men and women, I will pour out my spirit in those days and they will prophesy (Acts 2:17-18).

The note of universalism, in the sense that men and women everywhere will experience the power of the Spirit, shines through the passage. In a new way the Holy Spirit had become an agent of eschatology.[5] All of humanity could enter the new covenant. The new creation of one man would remove the middle wall between the Jew and the Gentile (Eph. 2).

In focusing on the gifts and the fruits of the Spirit in the individual's life and the life of the church, fundamental as this is, the eschatological dimensions of Pentecost have not been sufficiently recognized! The Holy Spirit became a pledge (Gk. *arrabón*), a deposit guaranteeing much greater participation in the Spirit in the future (II Cor. 1:22). The first fruits of the Spirit would be enjoyed in Christ, with the hope of more to come (Rom. 8:23). At Pentecost the Spirit came to indwell the church, creating a new society which constantly points to the coming fulness in the future.

Pentecost had cosmic historic dimensions, creating the church with its worldwide mission between the comings of Christ. The mission of the church is an essential element in God's plan for the world today. That mission brings to this age its primary meaning and purpose.[6] The ultimate meaning of history is therefore today found in bringing the gospel to the nations. The privilege and opportunity of participating in that ministry is well stated by Ladd: "From the perspective of eternity, the mission of the church is more important than the march of armies or the actions of the world's capitals, because it is in the accomplishment of this mission that the divine purpose for human history is accomplished. No less than this is our mission."[7]

One of the important and influential essays bringing attention to the eschatological significance of the mission of the church was written by Oscar Cullmann. He points out that the presence of the Holy Spirit makes the mission of the church eschatological, and then adds the following comments:

> The Church itself is an eschatological phenomenon. It is in the center of the present lordship of Christ. It was constituted by the Holy Spirit at Pentecost. That is why the task of the church consists in the proclamation of the gospel to the whole world. This is the very essence of the Holy Spirit's work, and the meaning of the miracle of Pentecost, when quite suddenly, all present understood one another. Precisely in the period to which we belong - between the resurrection and the return of Christ - it is the duty of the Church to go out "into all the world, and preach the gospel to every creature," looking toward the end.[8]

The Holy Spirit and the church in mission--these are the signs of the final phase of this age which will lead to the culmination of history and the establishment of the final Kingdom of God. In between the "already" (the presence of the Kingdom and the Spirit), and the "not yet" (the ultimate Kingdom and the greater enjoyment of the Holy Spirit), the world missionary task of the church plays a key role!

Harry Boer, in his significant publication *Mission and Pentecost*, followed similar lines of thought with particular emphasis on the absolute significance of Pentecost for mission. While the Great Commission played a powerful role in the missionary witness of the early church, it derived its meaning and power wholly from the Pentecost event! The Holy Spirit led in the expansion of the early church, and it is the power of the Holy Spirit which can bring enablement for the completion of the missionary task to the contemporary church.[9]

A student of Cullmann, David Bosch, in *Witness to the World*, follows the same strand of thought. He argues that viewing the mission of the church as an eschatological event and as a sign of the coming end does not develop a "ghetto" mentality with its fear of being swallowed up in the world. It stimulates and encourages the church to a broader vision of penetrating the world with the hope of the gospel and the anticipation of the divine fulfillment of the Kingdom. He sums up the meaning of this perspective in the words: "Mission, eschatologically understood, wishes on the contrary to place the Church's calling and responsibility in the widest context imaginable: to the ends of the earth and the end of time. The mission of the Church replaces Apocalyptic self-preservation in view of the end."[10]

II. The Mission of the Church as an Eschatological Event Must be
Completed Before the Coming of Christ

There is a general agreement that the Bible teaches that the mission activity of the church in the world prepares the way for the coming of Christ and the end. In many of the New Testament passages that treat the second coming or the coming of the Kingdom and the end of history, there is reference to the prior urgency of proclaiming the gospel to all the nations.

> A. *Matthew 24:14:* "And this gospel of the Kingdom will be preached in all the whole world as a testimony to all nations, and then the end will come."

Jesus answers the question posed by the apostles about the destruction of Jerusalem, the sign of His coming, and the end of this age. The answer incorporates two main emphases. The church would encounter a troublesome situation including false christs and prophets, wars, famines and earthquakes, persecution and apostasy. But these things did not constitute or determine the end! What would take place, according to Jesus, before the end would come is summed up in the marvelous promise: "And this gospel of the Kingdom will be preached in the whole world as a testimony to all the nations, and then the end will come."

This passage presents a clear mandate to the church. The Lord has entrusted to the church the mission of bearing witness to Him among all the nations. This is His divine plan for the world today and before that task is done the end will not come. This places the mission of the church in the world at the center of God's redemptive purposes in history. It is part of the *Missio dei*. Our stance in the world cannot be one of self-preservation in the fear of being overwhelmed. To the contrary, the divine purpose of history is accomplished through the church's faithful testimony to Christ, the Son of the living God!

> B. *Matthew 28:19:* "Therefore go and make disciples of all nations, baptizing them in the name of the Father and of the Son and of the Holy Spirit."

The Great Commission calls the church to a worldwide discipling mission to all the nations under the authority of Christ, the Sovereign Lord.

The promise of Christ, to be with the church in its mission, assumes its relentless endeavors until the very end of the age. The end follows after the penetration of the gospel among the peoples of all the nations. It is indeed the presence of Christ which guarantees the completion of the task.

> C. *II Peter 3:9:* "The Lord is not slow in keeping his promise, as some understand slowness. He is patient with

you, not wanting anyone to perish, but everyone to come
to repentance."

The promise of the Lord, to which this passage in II Peter refers, is the
promise of His coming. To the questions raised by scoffers who are skepti-
cal of that coming, the writer asserts the certainty of Christ's coming and the
reason for the Lord's delay.

Christ has not yet come because of the very patience of God! The coming
of Christ brings both blessing and judgment; blessings to the believers, who
will participate in the new heavens and the new earth in which only righteousness dwells; and judgment and destruction upon the ungodly. Because God
does not want any to perish but all to turn to Him, He is delaying the end.
His patience with human beings results in salvation (3:15). God is waiting
for the gospel to be brought to humanity everywhere so that people from all
nations might come to repentance. The completion of the mission of the
church, therefore, is closely related to the coming of the Lord.

> *D. Acts 1:6-8:* "So when they met together, they asked
> him, 'Lord, are you at this time going to restore the
> kingdom to Israel?' He said to them: 'It is not for you to
> know the times or dates the Father has set by his own
> authority. But you will receive power when the Holy
> Spirit comes on you; and you will be my witnesses in
> Jerusalem, and in all Judea and Samaria, and to the ends
> of the earth'."

The disciples were interested in the restoration of the Kingdom. The
Kingdom of God was a favorite subject of our Lord. It had come with His
presence and it would come in fulfillment with His return. The disciples had
been taught to pray for the coming of the Kingdom on earth--"Thy Kingdom
come, thy will be done on earth as it is in heaven." When would that Kingdom
come? When would Christ come in His glory and power?

The answer of our Lord was not an attempt to remove from their hearts the
desire to see the Kingdom come. There are consistent emphases in the Scripture encouraging the Christian to await eagerly the coming of the Son and
the coming of the Kingdom. Our Lord's response was rather a suggestion
that the time of that coming was not for them to know. This was in the Lord's
hand. However, that coming and that restoration related to the carrying out
of their mission! Christ's central concern was that they receive the power of
the Holy Spirit, and by that power witness to Him to the ends of the earth.
Through these efforts the rule of Christ in the hearts of men and women in

the world would be expanded until the culmination of that rule at His second coming. Our Lord placed the mission of the church at the center of the *Missio dei,* the dominating purpose of God. The Spirit of power and the worldwide mission of the church are therefore signs of the coming end.

III. The Mission of the Church Hastens the Coming of Christ

It would appear that the Bible teaches that the reason why Christ has not yet come is that the mission of the church is not yet finished; "the gospel must first be preached to all nations" says our Lord in Mark (13:10), before the end will come. It is God's will that all nations have the possibility of hearing the gospel. Christ wants to gather the church from all nations!

This missionary motif is evident in much of Pauline thought. The movement toward the end of history is to be preceded by preaching the gospel to the Gentiles and seeing their fulness come in (Rom. 11:25). Paul is anxious to present the gospel where it has not yet been preached. Oscar Cullmann makes an interesting point in interpreting the "restraint" and the "restrainer" of II Thessalonians 2:6ff as related to the worldwide proclamation of the gospel. The final events of the end, such as the rise of the antichrist and the coming of Christ, are presently held off by God. What hinders them? The mission of the church must first be fulfilled. When that restraint is removed or when that task is completed, then the rush of the end events occur.[11]

If the gospel must first be preached among all the nations before Christ comes, and if this proclamation is the last sign of the coming of the Kingdom of God - can the church then hasten that coming through an intensification of her activity? Can the church delay or speed up the coming of Christ?

In the context of answering scoffers who suggest that God is delaying the *parousia* of Christ, the coming day of the Lord, II Peter gives us an answer. Not only is there the certainty that the day of the Lord will come, but we are to look forward with eagerness to the day of God and speed its coming (II Pet. 3:12). The date of the *parousia* is therefore dependent on world mission.

It is clear from II Peter 3 that divine forbearance determines the delay of the coming: "God is patient not desiring that any should perish but all come to repentance" (II Pet. 3:9). God is holding back His judgment, giving opportunity for people to be saved. This would suggest that in His sovereignty He determines when to bring in the end.

On the other hand, since world evangelization must precede the end, the church's God-given mission and its accomplishment is an important factor in determining the coming of Christ. Not only is the church to anticipate and wait with eager anticipation for the Lord's coming; it is to hasten it, to strive for it. This "speeding up" of His coming must occur through bringing people to repentance as Christ is made known in the world. This mission activity is closely related to the Christian's lifestyle (blameless and godly), to prayer (Thy kingdom come, Thy will be done), and to the proclamation of the Word.

There has been considerable debate on this matter of whether the completion of the missionary task of the church is indeed a prerequisite to the return of Christ. Wiedermann traces the development of thought of theologians generally from the Edinburgh conferences of 1910 through to David Bosch. Two emphases are placed side by side in dialectical relationship. On the one hand, the church's missionary task is considered a pre-condition of the coming of Christ. On the other hand, divine sovereignty determines when the end shall come. There is the believer's side and there is God's side.[12] David Bosch, for example, in his deep concern for the *Missio dei* strongly rejects the view that the church hastens the end through her missionary fervor.[13] This suggests to him too much self-importance or self-regard, as though the church could interfere in God's timetable for the world.

We need, therefore, to take seriously the admonition in II Peter referred to above. Green maintains that Christian listlessness, disobedience and lovelessness are delaying the coming of our Lord. God would draw us into active cooperation with Him in the redemption of humanity through evangelism, prayer and Christian behavior; these are the ways of hastening His coming.[14] Maranatha!

ENDNOTES

1. Clive S. Lewis, *Mere Christianity*, (London: Collins Fontana Books, 1955), p.116.

2. Oscar Cullmann, "Eschatology in Mission in the New Testament" in *The Theology of the Christian Mission*, edited by Gerald H. Anderson (Nashville: Abingdon Press, 1961), pp. 42-3.

3. Frederick F. Bruce, *The Epistle to the Hebrews*, (Grand Rapids: Wm. B. Eerdmans Publishing Co., 1964), pp. 221-2.

4. Lewis B. Smedes, *All Things Made New*, (Grand Rapids: Wm. B. Eerdmans Publishing Co., 1970), p. 106.

5. René Padella, *Mission Between the Times*, (Grand Rapids: Wm. B. Eerdmans Publishing Co., 1985), p. 191.

6. Anthony A. Hoekema, *The Bible in the Future*, (Grand Rapids: Wm. B. Eerdmans Publishing Co., 1979), p. 138.

7. George E. Ladd, "The Gospel of the Kingdom" in *Perspectives on the World Christian Movement Reader*, edited by Ralph D. Winter, (Pasadena: William Carey Library, 1981), p. 65.

8. Oscar Cullmann, p. 46.

9. Harry Boer, *Mission and Pentecost*, (Grand Rapids: Wm. B. Eerdmans Publishing Co., 1961), p. 205.

10. David Bosch, *Witness to the World*, (Atlanta: John Knox Press, 1980), p. 236.

11. Ibid., p. 53.

12. Ludwig Wiedermann, *Mission und Eschatologie*, (Paderborn, W. Deutschland: Druck Bonifacius-Druckerei, 1965), p. 129.

13. David Bosch, p. 129.

14. Michael Green, *The Second Epistle General of Peter and the General Epistle of Jude*, Tyndale New Testament Commentaries (Grand Rapids: Wm. B. Eerdmans Publishing Co., 1968), p. 140.

14

TRANSLATING GOD'S WORD AS MISSION TO THE WORLD:
A Missiological Survey

Hans Kasdorf

Introduction

Those who have sat under the teaching and preaching of Dr. David Ewert, and have read his writings,[1] will agree that his primary concern has always been to make the original text of the Word of God come alive for people in their contemporary context. This is a concern which he shares with countless Bible translators, commentators, and communicators throughout the ages and across the globe. His demonstration has inspired emulation. It is only fitting, therefore, that this contribution in his honor should be devoted to the role which Scripture translations have played as a missionizing action in the world.

This essay is based on the presupposition that the Bible is a missionary book in which the missionarily active God has unfolded his plan of salvation to the world. Its message is a call to repentance with a promise of forgiveness, reconciliation, and transformation. This assumes that God's people must translate God's Word into human languages and transmit it in ways that permit all peoples to hear it in their own tongue and understand it in their own culture.

The story of translating the Scriptures, if we were to trace it to its beginnings, goes back at least some 2,500 years. My essay, however, offers a missiological survey of only the more recent phases of this rather lengthy story (from the first printed Bible in 1456 to the present), under three main headings, and a few concluding observations.

Translation Process Through Scientific Progress

The first era to be considered in this survey of the translation of the Bible spans roughly 350 years--from the first printed Bible in 1456 to the first Bible society in 1804.

Advancing Through Inventions

Johannes Gutenberg (c. 1398-1468) is generally given credit for the invention of the printing press in Europe. With the discovery of movable type in 1452 he broke through a barrier that had heretofore held back God's Word from reaching all the world. Hogg calls this "the second revolution" in Bible translating, the first being the invention of the codex toward the end of the first Christian century.[2] Indeed, printing revolutionized translation, duplication, and dissemination of the Bible in multiple languages across the globe.

The Latin Vulgate was the first Bible ever to be printed. It appeared as the Gutenberg Bible in 1456 and was sold for the exorbitant price of 20 Gulden which is 5,000 DM or about $2,800 per copy.[3] Albert Pfister sought to remedy the problem when he published the *Deutsche Armenbibel* in 1464. Thus the first printed German Bible was printed for the poor. After that other translations and versions appeared in rapid succession. The *Mentel Bibel* (also German) was published in 1466, an Italian translation came out in 1471, a Dutch version appeared in 1477, a Spanish Bible was produced in 1478, and a French edition in 1500. By the time the Reformation was underway, 70,000 copies of the entire Bible--100,000 of the New Testament, and 120,000 of the Psalms--had already been printed and distributed in central European languages alone.[4]

The impact was enormous. "The ready availability, nationally and internationally, of thousands of copies of the same work changed irrevocably the pattern of life on earth," asserts Hogg. And that through "the technological revolution of printing and book making."[5] What was missing, however, was a vision for world mission. With the exception of the Anabaptists who also translated the Bible for evangelistic purposes, neither the printers nor the bookmakers of this time had a vision for mission.[6] But they did contribute to the mission of the church in later times by laying the basis for quantity production and mass distribution of the Bible in whatever language translators were able to prepare it.

Discovery of Scientific Principles

Philologists began to point out that there were obvious vowel shifts within each language and changes in word order from one language to another. Therefore, they concluded, a word-for-word translation can only result in confusion in terms of both structure and meaning. This discovery was revolutionary for Bible translators. For one thing, they realized that the popular Vulgate was itself only a translation and that they must return to the Old Testament in Hebrew and the New Testament in Greek for the best sources. Furthermore, they realized that they needed to give more consideration to the target language of the common people if the translation was to convey a meaningful message to them. This meant the application of new linguistic principles rather than adherence to the traditional principles of rhetoric inherited from the medieval past.[7]

These factors motivated philologists, grammarians, and lexicographers to produce Hebrew and Greek texts in the best readings possible; they also challenged translators to work just as laboriously to render these texts into as many common speech forms as possible.

Martin Luther (1483-1546) became a translation champion. Once he had discovered the meaning of the Bible for himself, he was anxious that all people should be able to read it for themselves. "The Bible," he said in 1521, "is no longer a book reserved for only a certain social class, it is there for everyone. All have a right to possess it."[8] He argued that the Bible had originally been given in intelligible speech forms fully understood by the people who received it, and that a translation must be just as intelligible and make sense to every person who reads or hears it today. This conviction motivated him in 1530 to write his epoch-making book, *On Translating: An Open Letter.*[9]

According to the renowned linguist, Eugene A. Nida, Luther was guided by distinct translation principles that are important to this day: (a) The shift of word order in a sentence; (b) the use of modal auxiliaries wherever needed, even when they are not in the original; (c) the employment of conjunctions when required; (d) the transliteration of Hebrew, Greek or Latin terms which have no appropriate equivalent in the target language; (e) the introduction of phrases when needed to translate single words in the original; (f) the exchange of metaphors for nonmetaphors and vice versa; and (g) the exercise of utmost care in the use of textual variants to insure exegetical and theological accuracy.[10]

Luther created a common German language of such genuine native earthiness that the people who read his translation heard "Moses [speak] so German that no one would suspect he was a Jew."[11] This came from his willingness, as he put it, "to let the literal words go and try to learn how the German says that which the Hebrew expresses" in a given context.[12] "Whoever would speak German," he wrote in his Defense of the Translation of the Psalms, "must not use Hebrew style. Rather he must see to it, once he understands the Hebrew author, that he concentrates on the sense of the text, asking himself, 'Pray tell, what do the Germans say in such a situation?' Once he has the German words to serve the purpose, let him drop the Hebrew words and express the meaning freely in the best German he knows."[13]

Philologists and linguists since Luther have made giant advances in translation techniques. But that is a subject beyond the scope of this essay.

Widening the Base Through Geographical Exploration

When the Europeans discovered for themselves the "highway of the seven seas" beyond the Mediterranean world, they had nowhere to go but outward and forward. And forward they went until they reached every island, continent, and land with countless tribes and peoples of exotic tongues and customs. Even if the majority of explorers and conquistadors had no evangelistic motive whatsoever, they opened the way for others to bring the gospel to the literal "ends of the earth". No one could have guessed at that time what implications such exploration would have for world mission in general, and for Bible translating in particular. Soon hundreds--and then thousands--of men and women were involved in both. Our sovereign God works in wondrous ways his mission to perform.

Several notable achievements with regard to Bible translating during this era of geographic expansion must be highlighted. Each of these achievements is distinctly missional in nature, though some may not have been entirely free from missio-political motives. The Jesuits deserve credit for translating the New Testament into Japanese and for publishing the first Oriental translation in 1613 for missionary purposes. Inspired by the Catholic example, the Dutch East India Company sponsored a Malayan translation for "Christianizing" purposes. The Gospel of Matthew was published in 1629, the other Gospels in 1646, and the New Testament in 1668. This was the first Bible translation in any Southeast Asian language.[14]

When the Congregationalist John Eliot (1604-90) became pastor of Roxbury, Massachusetts in 1632, he almost immediately began learning the languages of native Americans and translating the Scriptures into some of them. While the annals of history record his fame for establishing the "Praying Towns" among the Natick people, his greatest contribution was the translation of the Bible into the Moheecan tongue. He completed Genesis and Matthew in 1655. The entire New Testament was published in 1661, and the Old Testament appeared in 1663. This was the first missionary translation of the entire Bible during this period. But there is a shadow of great tragedy hanging over this achievement. "Long before his death," notes Neill, "John Eliot had seen his work almost completely destroyed by the war between the Indians and the English. Whole tribes have died out; it is a sad fact that today there is no one living who can read Eliot's 'Moheecan' Bible."[15]

Another great accomplishment of missionary labor was the Tamil Bible, translated by Bartholomaeus Ziegenbalg (1682-1719). He and his colleague Heinrich Pluetschau (1677-1747) were the first Protestant missionaries ever to cross the ocean and, in this sense, were the true fathers of modern mission. Sponsored by the royal Danish-Halle Mission, they arrived in Tranquebar, Southeast India, in 1706. The first two of their five mission principles relate directly to Bible translating: (a) Christians must be able to read the Word of God; therefore, they must be educated. (b) Christians must have the Word of God in their own language; therefore, the Bible must be translated. Being a linguistic genius, Ziegenbalg became a master of Tamil. Although he conceded that Tamil was very difficult, he wrote fourteen schoolbooks in that language during his first two years in India and began translating the Bible during the same time. By 1714 he had completed the New Testament and before he died in 1719 he had finished the Old Testament up to the book of Ruth. His successor, Benjamin Schultze, completed the Tamil Bible and a New Testament in Urdu by 1728.[16]

The Bible into Sinhalese (Ceylonese) translation must also be noted. Sinhali belongs to the Indian branch of the Aryan family of languages and is spoken by many millions, especially in Ceylon. The Gospels were translated by the Dutch minister W. Konjun and published in Colombo in 1739. In 1776 the New Testament appeared in print, and in 1823 the entire Bible. Unfortunately, the Sinhalese became embroiled in the colonial conflicts between Portugal and the Netherlands and between the latter and Great Britain. Because of this fact, the Bible has never had a significant impact on their lives beyond that which they saw in the behavior of the Europeans who had originally brought the Book to them, but had themselves failed to live by its precepts.[17]

The greatest translation achievements at the threshold of the nineteenth century was the phenomenal work of the Serampore Trio, consisting of William Carey (1761-1834), the cobbler; Joshua Marshman (1768-1837), the schoolmaster; and William Ward (1769-1823), the printer. Emulating the principles of the Danish-Halle missionaries of Tranquebar, Carey built the operational structure for the Serampore Trio on a similar foundation: (a) widespread teaching and preaching of the Gospel by every possible means; and (b) preaching and distributing the Bible in the language of the people.

Each person of the Trio was dedicated to the primary task of translating the Bible, a fact that overshadows many of their other achievements. In thirty-six years they completed six translations of the whole Bible, produced twenty-three complete New Testaments, and rendered portions in ten additional languages. This means that the Serampore Trio translated the entire Bible or parts thereof into some thirty-seven languages. Carey alone was responsible for the entire Bible in Bengali, Sanskrit, and Marathi.[18] Such achievements are unthinkable without much prayer and the aid of the Holy Spirit.

Vision for Translating in the Context of Mission
The dominant period of Bible translating in the missional context runs parallel to the colonial era, covering some 140 years--from the founding of the first Bible society in 1804 to the organization of the United Bible Societies in 1946.

A Concept in the Making

The founding of Protestant mission societies gave rise to the idea of Bible societies. The seed-thought, however, was planted much sooner, but the germination process was long in the making. As I have pointed out earlier, Pamphilus of Caesarea operated a one-man Bible society as early as 300 A.D., and Albert Pfister printed and distributed the Armenbibel from 1464 onward. Duke Ernest the Pious of Saxony-Weimar made a similar attempt in the seventeenth century. "People are starving for the Holy Book," he said,"because they cannot afford to buy it." His vision was to produce a Bible which they could afford. He recruited thirty theologians and charged them with the editorial task. Then he contracted with a publisher in Nuernberg to print a Bible at the lowest price possible. This *Kurfuerstenbibel* went through many editions and experienced phenomenal distribution. Again, it was the work of one person in terms of philosophy, yet in terms of success it can be likened to that of a societal organization.[19]

The German Pietist movement also played a significant role in the development of Bible societies. August Hermann Francke (1663-1727), co-founder of the Danish-Halle Mission, established a printing press to publish inexpensive Bibles in Halle. His printer, Elers, invented the stereotype-plates, a breakthrough in producing mass quantities of printed materials. Baron von Canstein financed printing and distribution endeavors. History calls this venture the *Canstein'sche Bibelgesellschaft*, recognizing it as a Bible Society. Between 1712 and 1722 this Society printed and distributed 100,000 Bibles and New Testaments. In the years immediately following it sent over three million Bibles and Bible portions into all parts of the world for the incredibly low cost of two to nine Groschen (pennies) each.[20] In these ways the Pietists had demonstrated the potential of the Bible societies that emerged a century later.

From Vision to Realization

The missionary vision born in Pietistic circles and Puritan congregations of Protestant Christianity burst through the horizons of Western confinement. Every frontier--be it geographic or linguistic--that came within the focus of the expanding vision of the Occident was perceived as a challenge to be crossed in order to take God's Word to the hopeless and lost on the other side of those frontiers of the Orient.

Behind the move from theory to practice is the story of Mary Jones of Wales and Pastor Charles of Bala. At a meeting of the Religious Tract Society held in London in 1802, Charles told the moving story how young Mary Jones of a weaver family in Wales had walked forty kilometers to see him in Bala, hoping to acquire a Bible from him. He concluded the account with these words: "We must find ways and means to print Bibles for the poor people of Wales." A Baptist preacher named Hughes responded. "Why only for Wales? Why not for the kingdom? Why not for the whole world?"[21] God used this incident to translate theory into practice and the philosophy of a vision into the reality of action by creating the British and Foreign Bible Society (BFBS) in 1804.

Expansion and Concentration

"The Bible for the whole world" became the motto for this new movement throughout Europe. Scores of Bible societies emerged during the first two decades of the century. The Basel Bible Society was established simultaneously with the BFBS in 1804. These were followed by similar organizations founded in Regensburg (Catholic), 1805; in Philadelphia, 1808; in

Stuttgart and Glasgow, 1812; in Moscow, 1813; in Berlin and Amsterdam, 1814; and in New York, 1815.

Initially, the Bible societies engaged primarily in printing and distributing already existing translations in European languages. But soon they worked hand in hand with mission societies and produced Bibles in other languages in many parts of the world. The BFBS, for example, undertook major translation programs during the first years of operation: (a) It continued translation work begun by the faculty of Forst William College in Calcutta when the school closed its department of Bible translating in 1806; (b) it provided generous assistance to the Serampore Trio to translate the Bible or portions of it into more than thirty languages; (c) it published Henry Martyn's translation of the New Testament in Urdu in 1812; (d) four years later it printed the Gospel of Matthew in Bullom for a missionized tribe in Sierra Leone.

Such pioneering ventures have meanwhile increased to some 500 translations in African languages, alone, for which missionaries have created writing systems. The American Bible Society (ABS) and the National Bible Society of Scotland (NBSS) have undertaken comparable tasks for peoples in Africa, America, and Asia by endeavoring to place more Bibles into the hands of more peoples.

In retrospect, one can only marvel at the vision of the Bible societies and their representatives. Yet even their noble vision was not untarnished by cultural and religious blind spots. Delegates at the Ecumenical Missionary Conference, held in New York, April 21 to May 1, 1900, praised the translation work of the Bible societies. Eugene Stock of the Church Missionary Society observed that the BFBS, together "with its Scottish and American sisters, has shown that the Word of God can be translated into all sorts of languages, ancient and modern, cultivated and barbarous, and can prove itself the word of life to all nations, and kindreds, and people, and tongues."[22] Similarly, one detects a sense of pride when a Costa Rican delegate of the BFBS speaks of the Spanish, Portuguese, and English languages which already prevailed in large parts of the continental regions. But he laments that large segments of the population "still speak their aboriginal dialects" and others "are absolute strangers to the rich Castilian, speaking nothing but their own primitive tongue."[23]

Contemporary missiologists may not agree with the judgmental language in talking about the "rich Castilian" over against "barbarous" and "primitive tongues." Yet they must not forget that these persons were children of their time as we are of ours. We, too, possess no 20/20 vision unblurred by social prejudice and ethnocentricity. The uniqueness and dynamic of the Bible society movement lay in its missionary character and evangelistic intention.

As can be gleaned from the figures given in Table 1, the Scriptures were translated into eighty-six new languages between 1800 and 1830. That exceeds by fifteen the number of translations produced during the first 1800 years of the Christian era. Between their beginning in 1804 and the restructuring in 1946, the Bible societies were either directly responsible for or assisted in translating, producing, and distributing 1,250,000,000 copies of the Bible-- in whole or in part--in more than one thousand languages of the world. Most of the translating was done by missionaries, but nearly all printing was handled by the Bible societies. The significance of such team efforts is that the Bible has become available in their mother tongue to more than ninety percent of the world's people.[24] But translating and distributing the Bible was for the Bible societies and missionaries never an end in itself; it was always a means to an end: the evangelization of humankind. Only the eye of faith can here discern what God has wrought through human instrumentality in translation history.

Global Aspirations Toward Final Translations
This last period embraces the decades from the formation of the Wycliffe Bible Translators and the United Bible Societies to the present.

Table 1

Scriptures Published in World Languages
Since the Printing Press in 1452

Year	Gospels/ Portions	New Testaments	Whole Bibles	No. of Languages
1450	0	0	0	0
1456	1	1	1	1
1520	8	2	5	15
1600	-	-	-	40
1700	-	-	-	52
1804	16	15	40	71
1830	50	55	52	157
1850	-	-	-	223
1900	200	91	111	404
1937	617	212	179	1008
1951	650	246	191	1034
1965	716	297	237	1250
1968	830	320	242	1392
1975	930	386	261	1577
1977	945	420	266	1631
1983	930(?)	572	28	1785

Source: Compiled from W. Richey Hogg, "The Scriptures in the Christian World Mission: Three Historical Considerations," *Missiology* 12 (October 1984): 400; Harold K. Moulton, "Bible Translations and Versions," *Concise Dictionary of the Christian World Mission*, ed. Stephen Neill, Gerald H. Anderson, John Goodwin (Nashville, TN: Abingdon Press, 1971), pp. 58-59; Guenther S. Wegener, *6000 Jahre und ein Buch* (Kassel: J.G. Oncken Verlag, 1959), pp. 179-81.

The Historical Context

Missiologists look at World War II as the great divide of modern history for both the world of nations and the world of mission. The demise of Western colonialism gave rise to Third World nationalism and the retreat of the Occident to the ascent of the Orient. The postcolonial era has brought to the Church of Jesus Christ awareness of its own worldwide reality and thereby reduced the geographical, psychological, and spiritual distance between church and mission. What once was a mission church has itself become a missionizing church in some 220 nations of the world.

This development has affected Bible translating in no small measure. Its base has been widened and its force enlarged. Translating the Bible is no longer a burden of the Western church alone, but a shared task of highly skilled multinational teams with global aspirations to hasten the day when the final translation will be completed and every people group, great or small, will have the Scriptures in its own tongue.

Demographic research, linguistic skills, computer technology, and a wealth of other resources are on their side. They know which peoples have the Bible or a portion of it in their own language and which do not. One feels a sense of compelling urgency that the task be completed soon.

Wycliffe Bible Translators

The Wycliffe Bible Translators (WBT) and the Summer Institute of Linguistics (SIL) were formally organized by William Cameron Townsend and L.L. Legters, together with their wives in 1942. Both organizations were an outgrowth of Camp Wycliffe founded by the same persons in 1934. Legters' vision was to "reach the unreached tribes with the Word *in this generation*,"[25] with Townsend vigorously pursuing the idea to develop academic standards for missionaries to learn unwritten languages the world over. Their goal was to train potential Bible translators in the discipline of descriptive linguistics. The time coincided with "an awakening interest in the study of linguistics and of North American Indian languages."[26] It was the time when Franz Boaz (1858-1942), the father of Anglo-American anthropology, and Leonard Bloomfield (1887-1949) and Edward Sapier (1884-1939), the brilliant American pioneers in the study of linguistics, were pursuing new paths of investigation that differed radically from the classic discipline of philology used to study Hebrew, Greek, and Latin. Legters and Townsend were convinced that they were operating within the realm of God's providence, and that a "movement was being born that should go forward until every tribe on the face of the earth has received God's Word in its own language."[27]

During the course of time WBT and SIL have recruited and produced some of the world's greatest linguists and translation experts. With a working force of over 5,000 persons from many countries, they now work in about eight hundred minority language groups in some forty nations. Their primary task is to reduce spoken languages to writing, translate and print the New Testament, and teach people to read the Scriptures. It is their aspiration to cross every linguistic barrier that still isolates over 300 million people from access to the Good News. They firmly believe "that providing God's Word for every person in his [or her] own tongue is an essential element in fulfilling the Great Commission."[28]

The United Bible Societies

The United Bible Societies (UBS) were organized in 1946, incorporating over sixty national Bible societies from all over the world. Both Roman Catholics and Protestants currently cooperate in this gigantic venture, especially since the Second Vatican II Council encouraged Catholic people to acquire and read the Bible in their own language.

When the organization was established, it set for itself important goals: (a) To encourage coordination and cooperation among Bible societies; (b) to facilitate exchange of information among the Bible societies, in policies as well as in technical problems; (c) to render to societies helps and services; (d) to collect and diffuse information on world trends and the use of the Bible in the churches; (e) to represent the Bible societies among international Christian organizations; and (f) to arrange for emergency service needed on specific occasions.[29]

While the WBT are chiefly concerned with translating the Bible for smaller tribes and language groups in isolated and restricted-access regions of the world, the UBS perceive a different calling for themselves. Their program is bigger in scope and more ecumenical in theology. It embraces such primary languages as Hindi, Chinese, and Arabic, spoken by hundreds of millions of people. Only in exceptional cases do the typical translators of the UBS work as pioneer missionaries in primitive circumstances with one or two national helpers. Very often they translate into a language which already has a Bible. But the translation may have been the work of foreigners, too literal in language, and not as clear and idiomatic as it could be. If it needs improvement or updating, the UBS will do it.[30]

World Languages and the Scriptures

A question often asked is how many languages in the past five hundred years missionaries have reduced to writing to provide their speakers with the Scriptures. Between Gutenberg (c. 1450) and Carey (c. 1800) only three or four were reduced to writing for the purpose of translating the Bible. The rest have been done since then. That is the phenomenal missionary achievement.

There is lack of consensus in current missiological research as to the number of world languages. Eugene Nida of the ABS estimates that there are approximately 3,400 languages, Barbara Grimes of the WBT lists 5,445, and David B. Barrett gives 7,010 as the figure for existing languages. Whatever their number, experts like Nida classify all languages into four categories, helping us to understand how the Bible is made available to over 90 percent of the world's people.

Firstly, the Bible has been translated into all seventy-five of the world's primary languages, representing the speech forms of about 80 percent of the world's people. They include English, French, Spanish, Russian, German, Portuguese, Arabic, Urdu, Chinese, Japanese, and Hindi. These languages have a long literary history, are used at varying levels of higher education, technology, and science, and have great influence on other languages of the world.

Secondly, about 13 percent of the world's people speak some 450 secondary languages, such as Swahili, Zulu, Hausa, Pidgin, Philipino, and many others. Over six hundred million people within this category have access to the Bible in their own tongue.

The third category are tertiary or tribal languages, numbering at least 850; probably more than that. But they embrace only about 5 percent of the world's people.

Finally, there may be as many as two thousand quaternary languages--about 750 in eastern New Guinea alone--"spoken by a total population of only about two and a half million people."[31]

What does all this mean in terms of Scripture availability and accessibility? The Bible as a whole or in part has now been translated into nearly 2,000 languages (see Table 1). That means that there are still a minimum of approximately 1,500 to a maximum of about 5,000 languages into which not even a portion of the Bible has been translated. But there is a brighter side to it. Thanks to the Christian world mission, the Scriptures have become available in the form of at least one Gospel to about 97 percent and the whole Bible to approximately 90 percent of the world's five billion people.

That is not to say, however, that the Bible is actually accessible to 90 percent or 97 percent of these people. There are areas in the world where for different reasons people neither have the Bible in their possession nor have access to it, even if it is available in their language. In some instances governments forbid or restrict the printing and importation of Bibles; in other cases, people are too poor to afford them. In still other settings political/religious leaders prohibit their subjects from owning or reading the Bible. Then there are also multitudes of peoples, particularly the adherents of the world's great religions, who do not even know that there is such a book as the Bible in which they might come to know the only true God and Jesus Christ whom he has sent to give abundant life now and for eternity (cf. John 17:2-3).

The figures of Bible distribution reach astronomical heights. The combined circulation numbers of the Bible societies for the year 1975, for instance, are as follows: whole Bibles 6,230,607; New Testaments 10,738,146; portions/Gospels 27,301,781; selections such as the Lord's Prayer or Christmas and Easter stories 259,146,773. All of these amount to a total of 303,467,307 Scriptures distributed to people around the world, excluding disbursements through commercial sales and other profit-making channels.[32] An overview of a decade is even more impressive (Table 2). It shows what translators, publishers, and distributors have accomplished each year through the worldwide Christian mission to reach the people with the gospel in their own tongue and how the work increases from year to year.

Table 2
A Decade of Bible Distribution

Year	Bibles	NewTestaments	Portions	Selection	Totals
1965	4,457,355	4,241,847	31,888,066	36,366,101	76,953,369
1966	5,125,710	5,397,673	35,860,011	48,912,122	93,277,527
1967	4,927,693	13,081,435	31,729,512	55,067,167	104,805,807
1968	4,801,653	9,227,854	32,785,242	63,693,141	110,507,890
1969	5,018,715	11,568,925	36,609,484	92,137,968	145,335,092
1970	5,159,032	11,717,092	32,835,300	123,692,991	173,404,415
1971	5,509,738	11,748,583	31,047,327	122,071,130	170,376,778
1972	5,619,909	14,255,700	31,483,432	167,070,554	218,429,595
1973	5,903,807	13,960,707	44,766,263	184,521,314	249,152,091
1974	6,141,156	12,234,025	33,093,701	202,668,824	254,138,606

Source: Adapted from Klaus Wegenast, "Bibel V," *TRE*, vol. 6, p. 104.

The major nonprofit organizations which place the Scriptures into the hands of people are the WBT, the UBS, the Roman Catholic Bible Federation, Gideons International, The World Home Bible League, and the Ken Taylor Foundation, to say nothing about the many private agencies working toward the same goal. Some of these agencies are from the West, others from countries of the Two-Thirds-World.

There are also other agencies, institutions, publishers, and individuals translating and disseminating the Bible for profit-making or academic purposes. They usually concern themselves with target audiences which already have at least one version of the Bible in their own tongue. David Ewert lists 109 "Twentieth-Century English Translations," of which at least sixty-five appeared between 1942 and 1982.[33]

Historically, the most successful method of distribution has been through colportage. Colporteurs have been for the most part dedicated and simple-hearted, hard-working persons, usually leading a simple life style of constant travel under poor and primitive conditions involving frequent dangers from forces of nature and persecution. The peak period of colportage was the decade before World War I. The BFBS alone employed 1,200 colporteurs who, in fifty-five countries, sold five million Scriptures in 1912, 50 percent of the Society's total circulation that year. The ABS used them mainly in Latin America and the Middle East; the NBSS had its colporteurs largely in Far Eastern countries. In more recent decades, the BFBS reports that nearly half (49 percent) of its distribution, is done through the combined efforts of Bible houses, Bible vans, and Bible colporteurs, 33 percent through religious and secular bookshops, 11 percent through churches and mission agencies, and 7 percent in various other ways.[34] The overarching goal in all of this is to make the Bible available to every person in the world in his or her own tongue so that all can respond to God's salvation plan for the whole world.

Concluding Observations

Regrettably, in this essay I could not deal with the Bible's missionary force and transforming influence in the world, or with the more technical aspects of literary, idiomatic, and common translations. The focus has been that of a survey, showing that translating God's Word is in itself a missionary action amid, and for the benefit of humankind. Here are a few concluding observations.

1. God's people have always been aware that the Bible is the message of God's salvation plan for all people. Therefore, it must be translated into all languages spoken by men, women, and children so that they can understand what God is saying to them.

2. Bible translators concerned with transmitting God's word in understandable speech forms have always believed that an idiomatic translation is consonant with the biblical theology of revelation and inspiration. Languages are vehicles through which God speaks; all languages are capable of transmitting God's message to their speakers.

3. Missionaries have been in the forefront of translating the Scriptures. In the majority of cases--particularly in tertiary and quaternary language categories--they first reduced the language to writing and then translated the Scriptures for the people.

4. While there may be as many as seven thousand languages in the world, and while the Scriptures have been translated into only some two thousand (or fewer) of them, the Bible is available in the primary and secondary language groups spoken by about 90 percent of the world's people. If we add to these the translations of the minor language groups, the Bible--at least a portion of it--is theoretically available to 97 percent of all people

5. Another mark of the translation movement from earlier Christian eras to the present has been its concern to produce an affordable Bible for all people. The Bible societies and auxiliary agencies have been the major force in printing and distributing the Scriptures throughout the world.

6. The fruit of all Bible translating has been far-reaching; in some instances it has been remarkable. The vision and inspiration of John Wycliffe, for example, may have had a greater impact than his translation itself in that they gave rise to the Wycliffe Bible Translators centuries later. Thus the light he lit on the medieval paths of darkness has kindled a thousand candles as the WBT have translated the Scriptures in order to illumine the way to God for a thousand people groups in remotest places of the globe.

The translation of God's Word into the languages of humankind and its distribution throughout the world is simply a phenomenal missionary achievement in the power and providence of the Spirit of God. We are privileged to participate in this work now with the anticipation that one day we shall stand together before the throne of God with the countless multitudes of peoples from all nations, tribes, and tongues, singing in awe and worship, "Blessing and glory and wisdom and thanksgiving and honor and power and might, be to our God forever and ever. Amen" (Rev. 7:12 NASB; cf. 9-17).

ENDNOTES

1. See the bibliography in this publication for a complete list of articles and books by Dr. Ewert. At least a dozen items deal specifically with translation and/or transmission of the Bible.

2. W. Richey Hogg, "The Scriptures in the Christian World Mission: Three Historical Considerations," *Missiology* 12 (October 1984): 398. (Hereafter, Hogg, "The Scriptures," and page number.)

3. Guenther S. Wegener, *6000 Jahre und ein Buch* (Kassel: J.G. Oncken Verlag, 1960), pp. 149-51.

4. Pat Alexander, ed., *Die Welt der Bibel* (Wuppertal: R. Brockhaus Verlag, 1980), pp. 70-71; Wegener, *6000 Jahre*, p. 154.

5. Hogg, "The Scriptures," p. 399.

6. Cf. Hans Kasdorf, "The Reformation and Mission: A Bibliographical Survey of Secondary Literature," *Occasional [International] Bulletin of Missionary Research* 4 (October 1980): 169-75; "The Anabaptist Approach to Mission," in *Anabaptism and Mission*, ed. Wilbert Shenk (Scottdale: Herald Press, 1984), pp. 51-69.

7. Cf. Adolf Bach, *Geschichte der deutschen Sprache*, 7th ed. (Heidelberg: Quelle und Mayer, 1961), pp. 174-244; Eugene A. Nida, Toward a Science of Translating (Leiden: E.J. Brill, 1964), p. 24.

8. Alexander, *Welt der Bibel*, p. 72.

9. *Luther's Works*, Vol. 35:*Word and Sacrament I*, ed. E. Theodore Bachmann (Philadelphia: Muhlenberg Press, 1960), pp. 181-202.

10. Nida, *Science of Translating*, p. 15.

11. Hans Kasdorf, "Luther's Bible: A Dynamic Equivalence Translation and Germanizing Force," *Missiology* 6 (April 1978): 218.

12. *Luther's Works*, Vol. 35, p. 193.

13. *Luther's Works*, Vol. 35, pp. 213-4.

14. Richard William Frederick Wootton, "Bibeluebersetzungen in aussereuropaeische Sprachen," in *Theologische Realenzyklopaedie*, eds. Gerhard Krause and Gerhard Mueller (Berlin/New York: Walter de Gruyter, 1980), Vol. 2, p. 299. (Hereafter, *TRE*, and page number.)

15. Stephen Neill, *A History of Christian Missions*, rev. ed., revised by Owen Chadwick (Harmondsworth, Middlesex: Penguin Books, 1986), p. 193. (Hereafter, Neill/Chadwick, *History*.)

16. Cf. Arno Lehmann, ed., *Alte Briefe aus Indien: Unveroeffentlichte Briefe von Bartholomaeus Ziegenbalg 1706-1719* (Berlin: Evangelische Verlaganstalt, 1955), pp. 86, 89, 103; Wootton, "Bibeluebersetzungen," TRE, p. 300; Neill/Chadwick, *History*, pp. 177, 195, 216, 227.

17. Edwin Munsell Bliss, ed., *The Encyclopedia of Missions Vol. 2* (New York: Funk and Wagnalls, 1901), Vol. 2, p. 339.

18. Neill/Chadwick, *History*, p. 224.

19. Wegener, *6000 Jahre*, pp. 174-75.

20. Wegener, *6000 Jahre*, p. 177; Wootton, "Bibeluebersetzungen," p. 300.

21. Wegener, *6000 Jahre*, p. 177.

22. Edwin M. Bliss et al, eds., *Ecumenical Missionary Conference New York, 1900*, 2 Volumes (New York: American Tract Society, 1900), Vol. 1, p. 402.

23. Bliss et al, *Ecumenical Missionary Conference*, Vol. 1, p. 476.

24. Wegener, *6000 Jahre*, pp. 178-80; Hogg, "The Scriptures," p. 399.

25. Ethel Emily Wallace and Mary Angela Bennett, Two Thousand Tongues to Go (New York: Harper and Row, 1959), p. 31.

26. Wallace and Bennett, *Two Thousand Tongues*, p. 38.

27. Wallace and Bennett, *Two Thousand Tongues*, p. 51; cf. pp. 49-65.

28. *Wycliffe Book Catalog*, Huntington Beach: Wycliffe Bible Translators, [1987].

29. W. J. Culshaw, "United Bible Societies," in *Concise Dictionary of the Christian World Mission*, eds. Stephen Neill, Gerald H. Anderson, and John Goodwin (Nashville and New York: Abingdon Press, 1971), p. 621. (Hereafter, *Concise Dictionary*, and page number.)

30. Pat Alexander, ed., *The Lion Encyclopedia of the Bible*, rev. ed. (Berkhamsted, Herts: Lion Publishing Company, 1986), pp. 83-84.

31. Nida, "Bible Translation," pp. 130-39.

32. Klaus Wegenast, "Bibel V," *TRE*, Vol. 6, p. 104.

33. Ewert, *From Ancient Tablets to Modern Translations: A General Intro-duction to the Bible* (Grand Rapids: Zondervan Publishing House, 1983), pp. 250-51.

34. Cf. Harold K. Moulton, "Bible Distribution," *Concise Dictionary*, pp. 57-58; 122-23; Wegenast, "Bibel VI," *TRE*, Vol. 6, p. 104.

A BIBLIOGRAPHY OF BOOKS AND ARTICLES AUTHORED AND EDITED BY DR. DAVID EWERT: 1953-1987

Compiled by Herbert Giesbrecht

BOOKS

1961

"The Christology of the Apocalypse." Master of Theology thesis.St. Paul, MN: Luther Theological Seminary, 1961

1966

Creation from a Biblical Perspective. Hillsboro, KS: Mennonite Brethren Publishing House, 1966.

1967

An Approach to Problems of Christian Ethics. Winnipeg, MB: Canadian Conference of Mennonite Brethren Churches, 1967. (Also reprinted, as an insert, in *Mennonite Brethren Herald.*)

1969

"The Spirit and the Age to Come in Paul." Montreal, PQ: McGill University, 1969.

1973

Pilgrims and Strangers: The Story of Our Exodus from Russia and Settlement in Canada. Authored (in the original) by David Ewert, Sr., and translated and edited by David Ewert. Harrisonburg, VA: Issued by David Ewert, 1973.

1975

Stalwart for the Truth: The Life and Legacy of A.H. Unruh. Winnipeg, MB: Board of Christian Literature of the General Conference of Mennonite Brethren Churches, 1975.

How the Bible Came to Us. Winnipeg, MB: *Mennonite Brethren Herald* (reprint), 1975.

1978

Die Wunderwege Gottes mit der Gemeinde Jesu Christi: Praktische Erklaerungen des Epheserbriefes. Winnipeg, MB: Christian Press, 1978.

1980

And Then Comes the End. Scottdale, PA: Herald Press, 1980.

Called to Teach: A Symposium by the Faculty of the Mennonite Brethren Biblical Seminary. Edited by David Ewert. Fresno, CA: Center for Mennonite Brethren Studies, Mennonite Brethren Biblical Seminary, 1980.

1983

The Holy Spirit in the New Testament. Scottdale, PA: Herald Press, 1983.

From Ancient Tablets to Modern Translations: A General Introduction to the Bible. Grand Rapids, MI: Zondervan Publishing House, 1983.

1986

The Church in a Pagan Society: Studies in 1 Corinthians . (Luminaire Study Series), Winnipeg, MB: Kindred Press, 1986).

ARTICLES IN JOURNALS AND CHAPTERS WITHIN BOOKS
1953

"Repentance and Forgiveness in the Old Testament," *The Voice of the Mennonite Brethren Bible College* 2 (September-October 1953), 11-14.

"Der Begriff des Wortes 'Gnade' im Neuen Testament," *The Voice of the Mennonite Brethren Bible College* 2 (November-December 1953), 4-6.

1954

"The Dangers of Secularism (1)," *The Voice of the Mennonite Brethren Bible College* 3 (September-October 1954), 16-19.

"The Dangers of Secularism (2)," *The Voice of the Mennonite Brethren Bible College* 3 (November-December 1954), 17-20.

"Sanctification and its Relationship to Justification," *The Voice of the Mennonite Brethren Bible College* 3 (March-April 1954), 9-12.

"Some New Testament Teachings on 'the World,'" *The Voice of the Mennonite Brethren Bible College* 3 (January-February 1954), 6-9.

"Union with Christ: The Secret of Sanctification (1)," *The Voice of the Mennonite Brethren Bible College* 3 (May-June 1954), 6-9.

"Union with Christ: The Secret of Sanctification (2)," *The Voice of the Mennonite Brethren Bible College* 3 (July-August 1954), 4-6.

1955

"The Christian Pastor and His Flock: A Grammatical Analysis of Hebrews 13:17-19," *The Voice of the Mennonite Brethren Bible College* 4 (July-August 1955), 4-7.

"A Brief Presentation of Some of the Highlights of Bernard Ramm's *The Christian View of Science and Scripture,"* (Book Review) *The Voice of the Mennonite Brethren Bible College* 4 (May-June 1955), 14-17.

"Das Heil als Geschichtliches Erlebnis in der Paulinischen Theologie," *The Voice of the Mennonite Brethren Bible College* 4 (September-October 1955), 8-13.

1956

"Der Advent der Rettenden Gnade," *The Voice of the Mennonite Brethren Bible College* 5 (November-December 1956), 4-6.

"Fragen um das 'Fragliche' im Christenleben," *The Voice of the Mennonite Brethren Bible College* 5 (September-October 1956), 9-14.

"The Gentiles' Need of Divine Righteousness: An Analysis of Romans 1:18-23," *The Voice of the Mennonite Brethren Bible College* 5 (January-February 1956), 5-8.

"The Preeminence of the Person of Christ–Colossians 1:15-18," *The Voice of the Mennonite Brethren Bible College* 5 (March-April 1956), 6-9.

"Schools and Missions (1) and (2)," *The Voice of the Mennonite Brethren Bible College* 5 (May-June 1956), 12-15 and 5 (July-August 1956), 4-9.

"Das Heil als Geschichtliches Erlebnis in der Paulinischen Theologie," *Gemeindeblatt der Mennoniten* 87 (15 Maerz 1956), 30-1.

1957

"Building in God's Kingdom," *The Voice of the Mennonite Brethren Bible College* 6 (January-February 1957), 4-8.

"The Preservation of the Believer (1) and (2)," *The Voice of the Mennonite Brethren Bible College* 6 (September-October 1957), 7-11 and 6 (November-December 1957), 3-10.

"Revival and Missions (1) and (2)," *The Voice of the Mennonite Brethren Bible College* 6 (May-June 1957), 10-14 and 6 (July-August 1957), 9-13.

"Der Sieg des Kreuzes," *The Voice of the Mennonite Brethren Bible College* 6 (March-April 1957), 5-8.

1958

"Die Begegnung des Christentums mit der Religion: Ein Geschichtlicher Ueberblick," *The Voice of the Mennonite Brethren Bible College* 7 (September-October 1958), 9-12 and 7 (November-December 1958), 13-16.

"Die Bibeluebersetzung von Hermann Menge," *The Voice of the Mennonite Brethren Bible College* 7 (May-June 1958), 6-9.

"Er und Sie im Gottesdienst," *The Voice of the Mennonite Brethren Bible College* 7 (July-August 1958), 8-12.

"Die Freudige Zuversicht des Glaubens," *The Voice of the Mennonite Brethren Bible College* 7 (January-February 1958), 1-3.

"Der Sieg Gottes in der Weltmission," *The Voice of the Mennonite Brethren Bible College* 7 (March-April 1958), 6-10.

1959

"Ein Jeder in Seiner Sprache...," *The Voice of the Mennonite Brethren Bible College* 8 (March-April 1959), 7-11 and 8 (May-June 1959), 13-17.

"Jesus Shall Reign," *The Voice of the Mennonite Brethren Bible College* 8 (January-February 1959), 4-7.

"Martin Luther und die Deutsche Bibel (1)," *The Voice of the Mennonite Brethren Bible College* 8 (September-October 1959), 18-22.

"Missionsbibeln aus Alter Zeit," *The Voice of the Mennonite Brethren Bible College* 8 (July-August 1959), 15-19.

1960

"Reflections on Bible Reading in the Mennonite Brethren Church," *The Voice of the Mennonite Brethren Bible College* 9 (January-February 1960), 3-6.

"Martin Luther und die Deutsche Bibel (2)," *The Voice of the Mennonite Brethren Bible College* 9 (March-April 1960), 16-20.

"Martin Luther und die Deutsche Bibel (3)," *The Voice of the Mennonite Brethren Bible College* 9 (May-June 1960), 22-5.

"Martin Luther als Bibeluebersetzer," *The Voice of the Mennonite Brethren Bible College* 9 (July-August 1960), 15-20.

"Vollkommenheit," *The Voice of the Mennonite Brethren Bible College* 9 (September-October 1960), 8-11.

"Maintaining a Theological Balance," *The Voice of the Mennonite Brethren Bible College* 9 (November-December 1960), 8-13.

1961

"In Memoriam: A.H. Unruh, D.D., 1878-1961," *The Voice of the Mennonite Brethren Bible College* 10 (January-February 1961), 1-3.

"Die Lehre von der Demut," *The Voice of the Mennonite Brethren Bible College* 10 (March-April 1961), 13-17.

"Why Another New Version?" *The Voice of the Mennonite Brethren Bible College* 10 (May-June 1961), 6-10.

"Wie Soll Sich der Christ zum Humor Verhalten?" *The Voice of the Mennonite Brethren Bible College* 10 (July-August 1961), 24-5.

"Missionsmotive in der Paulinischen Theologie," *The Voice of the Mennonite Brethren Bible College* 10 (September-October 1961), 6-10.

"Jeremias' Suendenbegriff (1)," *The Voice of the Mennonite Brethren Bible College* 10 (November-December 1961), 15-19.

1962

"Jeremias' Suendenbegriff (2)," *The Voice of the Mennonite Brethren Bible College* 11 (January-February 1962), 16-19.

"Erweckung in der Stille," *The Voice of the Mennonite Brethren Bible College* 11 (March-April 1962), 7-10.

"Der Wille Gottes," *The Voice of the Mennonite Brethren Bible College* 11 (May-June 1962), 14-17.

"Gotteserkenntnis bei den Propheten (1)," *The Voice of the Mennonite Brethren Bible College* 11 (July-August 1962), 5-9.

"Die Erkenntnis Gottes bei den Propheten (2)," *The Voice of the Mennonite Brethren Bible College* 11 (September-October 1962), 10-13.

"The Transmission of Truth," *The Voice of the Mennonite Brethren Bible College* 11 (November-December 1962), 16-19.

"The Resurrection: Faith's Interpretive Center," *Mennonite Brethren Herald* 1 (April 19 1962), 1,6-7,12.

"What About Our Liberal Arts College?" *Mennonite Brethren Herald* 1 (August 24 1962), 11.

"'Credit' for Bible School," *Mennonite Brethren Herald* 1 (October 19 1962), 11.

1963

"Die Wertschaetzung des Alten Testament," *The Voice of the Mennonite Brethren Bible College* 12 (January-February 1963), 15-18.

"Predige das Wort," *The Voice of the Mennonite Brethren Bible College* 12 (May-June 1963), 13-16.

"The Problem of Leisure," *The Voice of the Mennonite Brethren Bible College* 12 (July-August 1963), 5-8.

"Das Versammlungshaus im Urchristentum," *The Voice of the Mennonite Brethren Bible College* 12 (September-October 1963), 12-15.

"Der Erste Tag der Woche," *The Voice of the Mennonite Brethren Bible College* 12 (November-December 1963), 10-13.

1964

"Der Geistliche Reichtum der Gemeinde"; "Die Goettliche Berufung der Gemeinde"; "Die Biblische Zucht"; "Heikle Fragen Einer Jungen Gemeinde"; "Der Rechte Gebrauch der Christlichen Freiheit"; "Die Christliche Frau in der Gemeinde"; "Die Einheit des Leibes"; "Das Hohelied der Liebe"; und "Mitteilungen und Ermahnungen", alle in *Das Ernste Ringen um die Reine Gemeinde*, verfasst von Heinrich F. Klassen. Winnipeg, MB: Christian Press, 1964.

"Men Whose Hearts God Touched," *Mennonite Brethren Herald* 3 (October 23 1964), 4-5.

"Altes und Neues," *The Voice of the Mennonite Brethren Bible College* 13 (January-February 1964), 1-4.

"Das Glaubensbekenntnis im Vaterunser," *The Voice of the Mennonite Brethren Bible College* 13 (March-April 1964), 16-20.

"But I Say Unto You," *The Voice of the Mennonite Brethren Bible College* 13 (May-June 1964), 19-21.

"The New English Bible" (book review), *The Voice of the Mennonite Brethren Bible College* 13 (July-August 1964), 21-3.

"The Earliest Christian Confessions" (book review), *The Voice of the Mennonite Brethren Bible College* 13 (November-December 1964), 23-4.

1965

"Teaching Absolutes in a Day of Relatives," *The Voice of the Mennonite Brethren Bible College* 14 (January-February 1965), 11-16.

"Sacred Times and Places," *The Voice of the Mennonite Brethren Bible College* 14 (March-April 1965), 1-3. Also appeared in *Mennonite Brethren Herald* 4 (June 4 1965), 8.

"Should the Mennonite Brethren Church Agree to Use the Same Version of the Bible?" *The Voice of the Mennonite Brethren Bible College* 14 (May-June 1965), 3-8.

"From the Exile to Christ" (book review), *The Voice of the Mennonite Brethren Bible College* 14 (July-August 1965), 22-3.

"Where Are the Preachers for Tomorrow?" *The Voice of the Mennonite Brethren Bible College* 14 (September-October 1965), 8-12.

"Tyndale Bible Commentaries. A. Cole: *The Epistle of Paul to the Galatians"* (book review), *The Voice of the Mennonite Brethren Bible College* 14 (November-December 1965), 20-2.

"What Shall We Do with the Old Testament?" *Mennonite Brethren Herald* 4 (January 8 1965), 4-5.

"Which Version Shall We Use?" *Mennonite Brethren Herald* 4 (June 25 1965), 4-6.

"An Approach to Questions of Christian Ethics," *Mennonite Brethren Herald* 4 (December 10 1965), 4-5.

"Biblical Guideposts in Questions of Christian Conduct," *Mennonite Brethren Herald* 4 (December 17 1965), 8-9 and 4 (December 24 1965), 4-5.

1966

"An Interview with the Author," *Mennonite Brethren Herald* 5 (January 14 1966), 6-7.

"Women in the Church," *Mennonite Brethren Herald* 5 (February 25 1966), 4-6.

"Love God and Do As You Like," *The Voice of the Mennonite Brethren Bible College* 15 (January-February 1966), 4-9.

"Eschatology and Missions," *The Voice of the Mennonite Brethren Bible College* 15 (March-April 1966), 10-13.

"Eschatology and Missions in the New Testament," *The Voice of the Mennonite Brethren Bible College* 15 (May-June 1966), 3-6.

"Missions and Eschatology in the History of the Expansion of Christianity," *The Voice of the Mennonite Brethren Bible College* 15 (July-August 1966), 13-17.

"Missions and Eschatology Prior to 'The Great Century'," *The Voice of the Mennonite Brethren Bible College* 15 (September-October 1966), 4-8.

"Missions and Eschatology in the Modern Era of Missions," *The Voice of the Mennonite Brethren Bible College* 15 (November-December 1966), 8-12.

1967

"The Biblical Concept of the Church," in *The Church in Mission*, edited by Abram J. Klassen. Fresno, CA: Board of Christian Literature of the General Conference of Mennonite Brethren Churches, 1967.

"The Disease of Contemporaneity," *The Voice of the Mennonite Brethren Bible College* 16 (January-February 1967), 1-3.

"In the Beginning God," *The Voice of the Mennonite Brethren Bible College* 16 (March-April 1967), 16-19.

"The Christian Use of Leisure," *Mennonite Brethren Herald* 6 (May 19 1967), 4-5.

1968

"The Work of the Holy Spirit in a Christian Academic Community," *The Voice of the Mennonite Brethren Bible College* 17 (May-June 1968), 7-15.

"Marks of the Holy Spirit's Presence," *Mennonite Brethren Herald* 7 (October 4 1968), 7-9.

"Saints and Faithful in Christ Jesus (Eph. 1:1)," *Mennonite Brethren Herald* 7 (November 29 1968), 8.

"Grace and Peace to You (Eph. 1:2)," *Mennonite Brethren Herald* 7 (December 13 1968), 13.

"Chosen of God (Eph. 1:4)," *Mennonite Brethren Herald* 7 (December 27 1968), 10.

1969

"The 'Spirit' in the Old Testament," *The Voice of the Mennonite Brethren Bible College* 18 (July 1969), 14-23.

"Foreordained to Sonship (Eph. 1:5-6)," *Mennonite Brethren Herald* 8 (January 10 1969), 9.

"Redemption Made Real (Eph. 1:7-10)," *Mennonite Brethren Herald* 8 (February 7 1969), 9.

"The Holy Spirit of Promise (Eph. 1:11-14)," *Mennonite Brethren Herald* 8 (February 21 1969), 7.

"A Prayer for Understanding (Eph. 1:15-17)," *Mennonite Brethren Herald* 8 (March 7 1969), 9,19.

"That You May Know (Eph. 1:18-23)," *Mennonite Brethren Herald* 8 (March 21 1969), 9, 23.

"The Human Predicament (Eph. 2:1-3)," *Mennonite Brethren Herald* 8 (July 11 1969), 8, 23.

"The Mystery of Salvation (Eph. 2:4-10)," *Mennonite Brethren Herald* 8 (July 25 1969), 9, 24.

"In the Darkness and Shadow of Death (Eph. 2:11-22)," *Mennonite Brethren Herald* 8 (August 8 1969), 8, 27.

"Reconciliation in Christ (Eph. 2:13-17)," *Mennonite Brethren Herald* 8 (August 22 1969), 9, 22.

"Unity in Christ (Eph. 2:18-22)," *Mennonite Brethren Herald* 8 (September 5 1969), 9, 21.

"The Mystery of Grace (Eph. 3:1-6)," *Mennonite Brethren Herald* 8 (September 19 1969), 9, 23.

"A Minister by God's Grace (Eph. 3:7-13)," *Mennonite Brethren Herald* 8 (October 3 1969), 9,21.

"I Bow My Knees (Eph. 3:14-21)," *Mennonite Brethren Herald* 8 (October 17 1969), 9, 20-1.

"The Nurture of Christian Unity (Eph. 4:1-3)," *Mennonite Brethren Herald* 8 (October 31 1969), 9, 23.

"The Foundations of Unity (Eph. 4:4-6)," *Mennonite Brethren Herald* 8 (November 14 1969), 7, 23.

"Diversity in Unity (Eph. 4:7-16)," *Mennonite Brethren Herald* 8 (November 28 1969), 8, 26.

"The Old Life and the New (Eph. 4:17-24)," *Mennonite Brethren Herald* 8 (December 12 1969), 6-7.

1970

"The Covenant Community and Mission," in *Consultation on Anabaptist-Mennonite Theology*, edited by Abram J. Klassen. Fresno, CA: Council of Mennonite Seminaries, 1970.

"The Resurrection Life," *The Voice of the Mennonite Brethren Bible College* 19 (April 1970), 3-8.

"The Covenant Community and Mission," *The Voice of the Mennonite Brethren Bible College* 19 (July 1970), 9-23.

"New Clothing (Eph. 4:25-32)," *Mennonite Brethren Herald* 9 (January 9 1970), 8-9.

"Walk in Love (Eph. 5:1-7)," *Mennonite Brethren Herald* 9 (January 23 1970), 8-9.

"Walk in the Light (Eph. 5:8-14)," *Mennonite Brethren Herald* 9 (February 6 1970), 8.

"Walk in Wisdom (Eph. 5:15-21)," *Mennonite Brethren Herald* 9 (February 20 1970), 6-7.

"Wives and Husbands (Eph. 5:22-33)," *Mennonite Brethren Herald* 9 (March 6 1970), 6-7.

"The Christian Household (Eph. 6:1-9)," *Mennonite Brethren Herald* 9 (March 20 1970), 6-7.

"The Warfare of the Church (Eph. 6:10-17)," *Mennonite Brethren Herald* 9 (April 3 1970), 7-8.

"Prayers and Blessings (Eph. 6:18-24)," *Mennonite Brethren Herald* 9 (April 17 1970), 8-9.

"Death and the Blessed Hope," *Mennonite Brethren Herald* 9 (March 6 1970), 2-4.

1971

"God the Creator," *The Voice of the Mennonite Brethren Bible College* 20 (January 1971), 9-18.

"Baptism and Church Membership," *Mennonite Brethren Herald* 10 (February 19 1971), 2-3,26-7.

"The Resurrection and Daily Life," *Mennonite Brethren Herald* 10 (April 2 1971), 2-4.

"An Approach to the Current Charismatic Question," *Mennonite Brethren Herald* 10 (November 19 1971), special insert.

1972

"Born of the Spirit"; "The Baptizing Work of the Holy Spirit"; and "Glossolalia in the Church Today", all in *Encounter with the Holy Spirit,* edited by George R. Brunk II. Scottdale, PA: Herald Press, 1972.

"The Spirit and the Age to Come," *Direction: A Quarterly Publication of Mennonite Brethren Schools* 1 (January 1972), 8-18.

"Is There a Future for MBBC?" *Mennonite Brethren Herald* 11 (August 10 1972), 21-3.

"Another Future for MBBC," *Mennonite Brethren Herald* 11 (September 22 1972), 16.

"December 25?" *Mennonite Brethren Herald* 11 (December 15 1972), 3.

1973

"Healing in the Apostolic Church," in *The Church, A Healing Community,* edited by John R. Mumaw. Harrisonburg, VA: Eastern Mennonite Seminary, 1973.

"The Unique Character of Christian Ethics," *Direction: A Quarterly Publication of Mennonite Brethren Schools* 2 (July 1973), 66-70.

"Revelation Interpreted for Today (1)," *Mennonite Brethren Herald* 12 (January 12 1973), 4-5.

"Revelation Interpreted for Today (2): The Church in the Last Hour," *Mennonite Brethren Herald* 12 (January 26 1973), 12-14.

"Revelation Interpreted for Today (3): The Seven Trumpets," *Mennonite Brethren Herald* 12 (February 9 1973), 12-13.

"Revelation Interpreted for Today (4)," *Mennonite Brethren Herald* 12 (February 23 1973), 4-6.

"Revelation Interpreted for Today (5): The Woman and the Dragon," *Mennonite Brethren Herald* 12 (March 9 1973), 6-8.

"Revelation Interpreted for Today (6): The Enemies of God and His People," *Mennonite Brethren Herald* 12 (March 23 1973), 12-14.

"Revelation Interpreted for Today (7): Visions of Assurance," *Mennonite Brethren Herald* 12 (April 6 1973), 8-10.

"Revelation Interpreted for Today (8): The Seven Bowls of Wrath," *Mennonite Brethren Herald* 12 (April 20 1973), 8-9.

"Revelation Interpreted for Today (9): The Mystery of Babylon," Mennonite Brethren Herald 12 (May 4 1973), 12-13.

"Revelation Interpreted for Today (10): The Fall of Babylon," *Mennonite Brethren Herald* 12 (May 18 1973), 4-5.

"Revelation Interpreted for Today (11): The Coming of Christ," *Mennonite Brethren Herald* 12 (June 1 1973), 6-7.

"Revelation Interpreted for Today (12): The Triumph of God," *Mennonite Brethren Herald* 12 (June 15 1973), 6-7.

"Revelation Interpreted for Today (13): The Heavenly Jerusalem," *Mennonite Brethren Herald* 12 (June 29 1973), 6-7.

"Revelation Interpreted for Today (14): The Consummation," *Mennonite Brethren Herald* 12 (July 13 1973), 4-5.

1974

"The Bible of Jesus and the Apostles," *Mennonite Brethren Herald* 13 (January 11 1974), 6-7.

"The Extra-canonical Literature," *Mennonite Brethren Herald* 13 (January 25 1974), 8-9.

"The Transmission of the Old Testament," *Mennonite Brethren Herald* 13 (February 8 1974), 7-8.

"The Formation of the New Testament Text," *Mennonite Brethren Herald* 13 (February 22 1974), 5-6.

"Transmission of the New Testament Text," *Mennonite Brethren Herald* 13 (March 8 1974), 10-11.

"Early Versions of the Bible," *Mennonite Brethren Herald* 13 (March 22 1974), 6-7.

"English Bibles Before the King James Version," *Mennonite Brethren Herald* 13 (April 5 1974), 7-8.

"The King James Version," *Mennonite Brethren Herald* 13 (April 19 1974), 5-6.

"From English Revised to Revised Standard Version," *Mennonite Brethren Herald* 13 (May 3 1974), 8-9.

"Major American and British Versions," *Mennonite Brethren Herald* 13 (May 17 1974), 6-7.

"Recent Modern Speech Versions," *Mennonite Brethren Herald* 13 (May 31 1974), 6-7.

"Poor, Yet Making Many Rich," *Mennonite Brethren Herald* 13 (April 5 1974), 32-3.

"The Private Reading of the Bible," *Mennonite Brethren Herald* 13 (October 18 1974), 2-3, 16.

"The Word Became Flesh," *Mennonite Brethren Herald* 13 (November 29 1974), 2-5, 30.

1975

"The Confessions of a Prophet (Jeremiah 15:1-21)," *Direction* 4 (October 1975), 383-8.

"Reflections on Pentecost," *Mennonite Brethren Herald* 14 (May 2 1975), 2-3,9.

"Law and Justice: The Minor Prophets" (Series of lesson expositions for adult Sunday School classes). *Mennonite Brethren Sunday School Materials. The Adult Quarterly* 41 (June-August 1975), 1-42.

1976

"Eschatology: What Are the Issues?" *Direction* 5 (April 1976), 3-7.

"The Presence of the Spirit in the Church," *Mennonite Brethren Herald* 15 (January 9 1976), 2-4.

"The Last Days," *Mennonite Brethren Herald* 15 (May 14 1976), 13-14,29.

"Death, and Then What?" *Mennonite Brethren Herald* 15 (November 12 1976), 6-7.

"At Home with the Lord," *Mennonite Brethren Herald* 15 (November 26 1976), 4-5.

"Scripture and the Language Game," *The Christian Leader* 39 (October 26 1976), 2-4.

"Being Biblical Today," *The Christian Leader* 39 (November 9 1976), 5-8.

"Difficult Bible Passages: The Creation Account," *Mennonite Reporter* 6 (November 1 1976), 5; 6 (November 15 1976), 5 and 6 (November 29 1976), 5.

1977

"The Battle for the Bible" (book review), *Direction* 6 (April 1977), 39-40.

"Now We Know in Part," *Direction* 6 (July 1977), 60-4.

"The Limitations of the Scriptures," *Mennonite Brethren Herald* 16 (February 18 1977), 4-6.

"Israel and the End Times," *Mennonite Brethren Herald* 16 (September 16 1977), 2-5.

"The Signs of the Times," *Mennonite Brethren Herald* 16 (January 7 1977), 2-5.

"Earth's Coming King: The Revelation" (Series of lesson expositions for adult Sunday School classes). *Mennonite Brethren Sunday School Materials. The Adult Quarterly* 44 (September-November 1977), 1-40.

"Now We Know in Part," *The Mennonite* 92 (November 15 1977), 664-6. Also appeared in *The Christian Leader* 40 (April 12 1977), 2-4.

"Israel in the New Testament," *The Christian Leader* 40 (October 25 1977), 2-6.

1978

"The Resurrection and Daily Life," in *The Way of the Cross and the Resurrection*, edited by John M. Drescher. Scottdale, PA: Herald Press, 1978.

"Born of the Spirit," *Mennonite Brethren Herald* 17 (April 28 1978), 4-6.

"The New International Version of the Bible," *Mennonite Brethren Herald* 17 (November 28 1978), 6-7.

"Resurrection from the Dead," *Mennonite Brethren Herald* 17 (March 17 1978), 4-7.

"Christ's Final Triumph," *Mennonite Brethren Herald* 17 (February 3 1978), 26-7.

"Die Letzen Tage. Vortrag Gehalten am 26 Januar, 1978, auf der Studienkonferenz ueber Eschatologie in Fresno, CA," *Die Mennonitische Rundschau* 101 (Maerz 22 1978), 14; 101 (April 5 1978), 6; 101 (April 12 1978), 6; 101 (April 19 1978), 6 and 101 (April 26 1978), 6.

"Werdet Voll Geistes (Ephesians 5:18-21)," *Die Mennonitische Rundschau* 101 (November 8 1978), 12-13.

"Christ's Final Triumph," *The Christian Leader* 41 (January 17 1978), 12-14.

"An Encounter with the Risen Christ: An Easter Meditation on Luke 24:13-34," *The Christian Leader* 41 (March 14 1978), 2-4.

"A Brotherly Reply," *The Christian Leader* 41 (February 28 1978), 10-11.

"Magnanimity ('Window on the Bible' column)," *The Christian Leader* 41 (March 14 1978), 19.

"Der Tag Rueckt Naeher (1)," *Gemeinde Unterwegs: Mennonitisches Gemeindeblatt* 5 (Dezember 1978), 135.

"Israel and the End Times (1): Israel in the New Testament," *Gospel Herald* 71 (January 24 1978), 57-60.

"Israel and the End Times (2): The Salvation of Israel," *Gospel Herald* 71 (January 31 1978), 84-5.

"Israel and the End Times (3): Israel and the New Testament," *Mennonite Reporter* 8 (January 23 1978), 5 and 8 (February 6 1978), 5.

1979

"Der Tag Rueckt Naeher (2)," *Gemeinde Unterwegs: Mennonitisches Gemeindeblatt* 6 (Januar 1979), 5-6.

"J.A. Toews: Tribute to a Leader," *Direction* 8 (April 1979), 35-8.

"In Praise of the Gospel Ministry: A Meditation on 2 Corinthians 4:1-6," *Direction* 8 (October 1979), 28-32.

"Baptism with the Spirit," *Mennonite Brethren Herald* 18 (February 2 1979), 2-5.

"Filled with the Spirit," *Mennonite Brethren Herald* 18 (May 25 1979), 2-4.

"Christ Gives Meaning to Life," *Rejoice* 14 (October 1-7 1979), 28-31.

"Christ Sets the Example in Service," *Rejoice* 14 (October 8-14 1979), 32-5.

"Christ Provides the Pattern for Growth," *Rejoice* 14 (October 15-21 1979), 36-9.

"Christ Gives Cause to Rejoice," *Rejoice* 14 (October 22-28 1979), 40-3.

1980

"Preparing Teachers at Seminary," in *Called to Teach: A Symposium by the Faculty of the Mennonite Brethren Biblical Seminary.* Edited by David Ewert. Fresno, CA: Center for Mennonite Brethren Studies, Mennonite Brethren Biblical Seminary, 1980.

"Memoirs of and by Mennonite Brethren," *Direction* 9 (July 1980), 36-40.

"Der Neue Bund," *Die Mennonitische Rundschau* 103 (Maerz 26 1980), 12.

"God's Word in the Language of the Day" (Letters to the Corinthians: Study 1) , *Mennonite Brethren Herald* 19 (October 10 1980), 10-11.

"A Divided Church: 1 Cor. 1:10-17" (Letters to the Corinthians: Study 2), *Mennonite Brethren Herald* 19 (November 7 1980), 8-9.

"The Paradoxes of God's Ways: 1 Cor. 1:18-2:5" (Letters to the Corinthians: Study 3), *Mennonite Brethren Herald* 19 (December 5 1980), 6-7.

"What Does the Bible Say About Homosexuality?" *Mennonite Brethren Herald* 19 (May 9 1980), 8-10.

"What Does the Seminary Teach?" *Mennonite Brethren Herald* 19 (August 29 1980), 2-5.

"Der Tag Rueckt Naeher: Christus der Herr Wird Wiederkommen!" *Die Mennonitische Rundschau* 103 (Oktober 22 1980), 2-4.

"Meet Your King: Matthew" (Series of lesson expositions for adult Sunday School classes). *Mennonite Brethren Sunday School Materials. The Adult Quarterly* 47 (September-November 1980), 1-40.

"Was Heisst es Heute Biblisch zu Sein?" *Gemeinde Unterwegs: Mennonitisches Gemeindeblatt* 7 (September 1980), 102.

"Jesus Begins His Ministry," *Rejoice* 15 (December 22-28 1980), 24-7.

"Let Your Light Shine," *Rejoice* 15 (December 29 1980-January 4 1981), 28-31.

"How Mennonite Brethren Are Different," *The Christian Leader* 43 (June 3 1980), 10.

"Water Baptism," *The Christian Leader* 43 (August 26 1980), 2-5.

"Born of the Virgin Mary," *The Christian Leader* 43 (December 16 1980), 2-4.

"The Bible and Homosexuality," *The Christian Leader* 43 (April 22 1980), 7-9.

1981

"Erasmus," in *A Cloud of Witnesses,* edited by John C. Wenger. Harrisonburg, VA: Eastern Mennonite Seminary, 1981.

"John A. Toews: In Memoriam," in *People of the Way: Selected Essays and Addresses by John A. Toews,* edited by Abram J. Dueck, Herbert Giesbrecht, and Allen R. Guenther. Winnipeg, MB: Historical Committee, Board of Higher Education, Canadian Conference of Mennonite Brethren Churches, 1981.

"The Wisdom of God: 1 Cor. 2:6-3:4" (Letters to the Corinthians: Study 4), *Mennonite Brethren Herald* 20 (January 2 1981), 8-9.

"Paul Looks at Servanthood: 1 Cor. 3:5-23" (Letters to the Corinthians: Study 5), *Mennonite Brethren Herald* 20 (January 30 1981), 7-8.

"Ministers of the Gospel: 1 Cor. 4:1-21" (Letters to the Corinthians: Study 6), *Mennonite Brethren Herald* 20 (February 27 1981), 6-7.

"Paul Teaches Church Discipline: 1 Cor. 5:1-13" (Letters to the Corinthians: Study 7), *Mennonite Brethren Herald* 20 (March 27 1981), 5-6.

"Thy Kingdom Come: A Blumhardt Reader" (book review), *Direction* 10 (April 1981), 38-9.

"A Cause to Live For," *Mennonite Brethren Herald* 20 (April 10 1981), 6-7.

"Christians and Lawsuits: 1 Cor. 6:1-11" (Letters to the Corinthians: Study 8), *Mennonite Brethren Herald* 20 (April 24 1981), 6-7.

"Liberty or License? I Cor. 6:12-20" (Letters to the Corinthians: Study 9), *Mennonite Brethren Herald* 20 (May 22 1981), 8-9.

"The Sanctity of Marriage: 1 Cor. 7:1-16" (Letters to the Corinthians,Study 10), *Mennonite Brethren Herald* 20 (June 26 1981), 8-9.

"On Personal and Family Matters: 1 Cor. 7:17-40" (Letters to the Corinthians: Study 11), *Mennonite Brethren Herald* 20 (September 11 1981), 7-9.

"Love and Knowledge: 1 Cor. 8" (Letters to the Corinthians: Study 12), *Mennonite Brethren Herald* 20 (October 9 1981), 4-5.

"The Danger of Indulgence: 1 Cor. 10:1-22" (Letters to the Corinthians: Study 13), *Mennonite Brethren Herald* 20 (December 4 1981), 6-8.

"Paul Restricts His Rights: 1 Cor. 9:1-27" (Letters to the Corinthians: Study 14), *Mennonite Brethren Herald* 20 (November 6 1981), 6-7.

"Build on the Solid Rock," *Rejoice* 15 (January 5-11 1981), 32-5.

"Proclaim the Kingdom," *Rejoice* 15 (January 12-18 1981), 36-9.

"Learn from the Lord," *Rejoice* 15 (January 19-25 1981), 40-3.

"Be Filled with the Spirit," *The Christian Leader* 44 (June 2 1981), 4-6.

"Evangelism by Lifestyle," *Mission Focus* 9 (December 1981), 78-82.

1982

"Can We Have Diversity With Unity? Unity and Diversity in the Body of Christ," *Direction* 11 (July 1982), 20-8.

"When Things Aren't Black Nor White: 1 Cor. 10:23-11:1" (Letters to the Corinthians: Study 15), *Mennonite Brethren Herald* 21 (January 15 1982), 27-8.

"Head Covering for Women: 1 Cor. 11:2-16" (Letters to the Corinthians: Study 16), *Mennonite Brethren Herald* 21 (February 26 1982), 8-9,18.

"The Lord's Supper: 1 Cor. 11:17-34" (Letters to the Corinthians: Study 17), *Mennonite Brethren Herald* 21 (March 12 1982), 2-4.

"Spiritual Gifts: 1 Cor. 12:1-11" (Letters to the Corinthians: Study 18) *Mennonite Brethren Herald* 21 (April 23 1982), 24-6.

"The Body of Christ: 1 Cor. 12:12-31" (Letters to the Corinthians: Study 19), *Mennonite Brethren Herald* 21 (May 7 1982), 7-8.

"The Greatest of These is Love: 1 Cor. 13:1-13" (Letters to the Corinthians: Study 20), *Mennonite Brethren Herald* 21 (June 25 1981), 7-8.

"Tongues and Prophecy: 1 Cor. 14:1-25" (Letters to the Corinthians: Study 21), *Mennonite Brethren Herald* 21 (September 10 1982), 7-9

"Worship in the Early Church: 1 Cor. 14:26-40" (Letters to the Corinthians: Study 22), *Mennonite Brethren Herald* 21 (October 8 1982), 6-8.

"The Gospel of the Resurrection: 1 Cor. 15:1-28" (Letters to the Corinthians: Study 23), *Mennonite Brethren Herald* 21 (November 5 1982), 6-8.

"And I Will Raise Him Up at the Last Day: 1 Cor. 15:29-58" (Letters to the Corinthians: Study 24), *Mennonite Brethren Herald* 21 (December 3 1982), 5-7.

"God Reaffirms His Promise," *Rejoice* 17 (September 27-October 3 1982), 24-7.

"God Established the Passover Rite," *Rejoice* 17 (October 4-10 1982), 28-31.

"God Forgives His People," *Rejoice* 17 (October 11-17 1982), 32-5.

"God Proclaims the Year of Jubilee," *Rejoice* 17 (October 18-24 1982), 36-9.

"God Speaks Through a Gentile," *Rejoice* 17 (October 25-November 1982), 40-3.

"Random Reminiscences on MBBC," *Mennonite Brethren Bible College Bulletin* 14 (Fall 1982), 2, 15.

1983

"The Spirit and the Blessed Hope," in *Spirit Within Structure: Essays in Honor of George Johnston*, edited by Edward J. Furcha. Allison Park, PA: Pickwick Publications, 1983.

"We Have This Treasure in Earthen Vessels," *Mennonite Brethren Herald* 22 (July 29 1983), 10.

"Martin Luther and His Bible," *Mennonite Brethren Herald* 22 (November 18 1983), 2-5.

"Christ and Our Fears," *Mennonite Brethren Herald* 22 (December 2 1983), 6-7.

"The Forgotten Father" (book review), *Direction* 12 (January 1983), 35-6.

"*Last Supper and Lord's Supper* by I. Howard Marshall" (book review), *Direction* 12 (January 1983), 34-6.

"*Testament of Love: A Study of Love in the Bible* by Leon Morris" (book review), *Direction 12 (January 1983), 36-7.*

"Instructions, Plans and Greetings,"*Mennonite Brethren Herald* 22 (January 14 1983), 8-10

"Word and Deed," *Mennonite Brethren Bible College Bulletin* 14 (Spring 1983), 2.

"Our Fortieth Year," *Mennonite Brethren Bible College Bulletin* 15 (Fall 1983), 2.

1984

"A Plea for Wholeness," *Mennonite Brethren Herald* 23 (January 13 1984), 23.

"Church Loyalty," *Mennonite Brethren Herald* 23 (April 20 1984), 23.

"Tradition--Good or Bad?" *Mennonite Brethren Herald* 23 (September 7 1984), 22.

"Love Yourself," *Mennonite Brethren Herald* 23 (October 19 1984), 22.

"A Spiritual Tune-up," *Mennonite Brethren Herald* 23 (December 14 1984), 6-7.

"The Way of the Servant," *Rejoice* 19 (March 26-April 1 1984), 24-7.

"Confrontation in Jerusalem," *Rejoice* 19 (April 2-8 1984), 28-31.

"In the Shadow of the Cross," *Rejoice* 19 (April 9-15 1984), 32-5.

"Crucified and Raised from Death," *Rejoice* 19 (April 16-22 1984), 36-9.

"Memorials of God's Goodness," *Mennonite Brethren Bible College Bulletin* 16 (Fall 1984), 2-4.

1985

"Texts, Versions, Manuscripts, Editions," in *Harper's Bible Dictionary*, edited by Paul Achtemeier (general editor). San Francisco, CA: Harper and Row, 1985.

"Why Do People Suffer?" *The Christian Leader* 48 (March 19 1985), 2-4.

"Schools and Missions: They Belong Together" (Issues in MB Education: Part 2), *The Christian Leader* 48 (February 5 1985), 16-17.

"Erfuellt mit dem Heiligen Geist," *Gemeinde Unterwegs: Mennonitisches Gemeindeblatt* 12 (Juni 1985), 61-3.

"To Fulfill Our Mission We Need Schools," *Mennonite Brethren Herald* 24 (February 8 1985), 7-8.

"Do We Need Theologians?" *Mennonite Brethren Herald* 24 (March 20 1985), 25.

"More Wheat and Less Straw," *Mennonite Brethren Herald* 24 (May 3 1985), 24.

"Yes and No," *Mennonite Brethren Herald* 24 (August 16 1985), 23.

"Passion Season," *Mennonite Brethren Bible College Bulletin* 16 (Spring 1985), 2-3.

"Things We Can Surely Believe," *Mennonite Brethren Bible College Bulletin* 16 (Summer 1985), 2-3.

"A Pageant of Triumph," *Mennonite Brethren Bible College Bulletin* 17 (Fall 1985), 2.

"Emmanuel--God is With Us," *Mennonite Brethren Bible College Bulletin* 17 (Winter 1985), 2-7.

1986

"A Biblical Model of the Third Way," in *Witnesses of a Third Way: A Fresh Look at Evangelism*, edited by Henry J. Schmidt. Elgin, IL: Brethren Press, 1986.

"The Resurrection and Daily Life," *Mennonite Brethren Herald* 25 (March 21 1986), 2-4.

"Magnanimity," *Mennonite Brethren Bible College Bulletin* 17 (Summer 1986), 1-2.

"The Fruit of the Spirit," *Mennonite Brethren Bible College Bulletin* 18 (Fall 1986), 1-3.

"Behold, I Make All Things New," *Mennonite Brethren Bible College Bulletin* 18 (Winter 1986), 2-4.

1987

"A Christian Approach to the Problem of Homosexuality," in *Festschrift for Berkeley Mickelson*, edited by David E. Aune. Grand Rapids, MI: William B. Eerdmans Publishing Company, 1987.

"Board of Higher Education: President's Report," *Mennonite Brethren Herald* 26 (May 29 1987), 18-20.

"Reading the Bible Through Coloured Glass," *Mennonite Brethren Herald* 26 (October 30 1987), 6-9.

"A Tribute to F.C. Peters," *Mennonite Brethren Herald* 26 (October 30 1987), 30.

"The Call to a Life of Obedience (Gen. 12:1-4)," *Mennonite Brethren Bible College Bulletin* 18 (Summer 1987), 2-5.

"God's Call to a Redemptive Ministry," *Mennonite Brethren Bible College Bulletin* 19 (Fall 1987), 2-5.

CONTRIBUTORS

1. **Victor Adrian** (Th.D., Concordia Theological Seminary, St. Louis, MO) is General Secretary of Mennonite Brethren Missions/Services and editor-in-chief of its official publication, *Witness: Mennonite Brethren in World Mission*. He was President of the Mennonite Brethren Bible College from 1967 to 1972.

2. **Myron G. Augsburger** (Th.D., Union Theological Seminary, Richmond, VA) is pastor of the Washington Community Fellowship in Washington, D.C. He is the author of many books and articles, including *Quench not the Spirit* and *Walking in the Resurrection*. For many years he was President and Professor of Theology at Eastern Mennonite College and Seminary in Harrisonburg, Virginia.

3. **Abe Dueck** (Ph.D., Duke University, Durham, NC) is Academic Dean and Associate Professor of Historical Theology at the Mennonite Brethren Bible College. He was chairman of the Editorial Committee of *People of the Way: Selected Essays and Addresses by John A. Toews* and has published articles in a variety of journals.

4. **David Ewert** (Ph.D., McGill University, PQ) has been President of the Mennonite Brethren Bible College from 1982-88 and previously served at this institution from 1953-1971. He is the author of many books and articles. (See bibliography in this *Festschrift*.)

5. **Herbert Giesbrecht** (M.A., San Francisco State University; M.L.S., University of Minnesota; M.A., University of Manitoba) is College Librarian at the Mennonite Brethren Bible College. His publications include *The Men-*

nonite Brethren Church: A Bibliographic Guide, chapters in several books, and articles in a variety of journals.

6. Hans Kasdorf (D. Miss., Fuller Theological Seminary, Pasadena, CA; Th.D., University of South Africa) is Associate Professor of World Mission at the Mennonite Brethren Biblical Seminary (Fresno, CA). His publications include: *Gemeindewachstum als Missionarisches Ziel: Ein Konzept fuer Gemeinde und Missionsarbeit* (1976); *Christian Conversion in Context* (1980); and *It's Sunrise in World Mission* (1984).

7. Elmer Martens (Ph.D., Claremont Graduate School, Claremont, CA) is Professor of Old Testament at the Mennonite Brethren Biblical Seminary (Fresno, CA) where he also served as President (1977-86). He is the author of several books including *God's Design* and the *Believers Church Bible Commentary: Jeremiah.*

8. Bruce Metzger (Ph.D., Princeton University, Princeton,NJ) is the George L. Collord Professor of New Testament Language and Literature, Emeritus, at Princeton Theological Seminary, where he taught for forty-six years. He is the author or editor of more than twenty-five books, several of which have been translated into German, Japanese, Korean, Chinese, and Malagasy.

9. Frank C. Peters (Ph.D., University of Kansas, Lawrence, KS; Th.D., Central Baptist Seminary, Kansas City, KS) passed away suddenly on October 7, 1987, after almost completing the manuscript of his essay for this *Festschrift*. He was a respected leader and educator in the Mennonite Brethren Conference and in the evangelical community as a whole. He taught at the Mennonite Brethren Bible College from 1957-65 and, more recently, was President of Wilfrid Laurier University in Waterloo, Ontario until his retirement.

10. John Regehr (Th.D., Southern Baptist Seminary, Louisville, KY) is Associate Professor in Contemporary Ministries at the Mennonite Brethren Bible College . He has served as pastor and preacher in a variety of congregations and denominations, and has contributed numerous articles to several publications.

11. *David Schroeder* (D. Th., Hamburg) is Professor of New Testament and Philosophy at the Canadian Mennonite Bible College (Winnipeg, MB) where he has served since 1959. His publications include *Learning to Know the Bible* and *Solid Ground: Facts of the Faith for Young Christians.*

12. *V. George Shillington* (Ph.D., McMaster University, Hamilton, ON) is Associate Professor of Biblical Studies at the Mennonite Brethren Bible College. He has written educational materials in Study Guides, and contributed many articles to various publications.

13. *Herb Swartz* (Th.D., Emmanuel College, Toronto) is Associate Professor of Biblical Studies at Eastern Mennonite Seminary (Harrisonburg, VA). He was Registrar and taught New Testament at the Mennonite Brethren Bible College from 1966 to 1971. He has contributed essays to a variety of journals and periodicals.

14. *John E. Toews* (Ph.D., Northwestern University, Evanston, IL) is Academic Dean and Professor of New Testament at the Mennonite Brethren Biblical Seminary (Fresno, CA). He has published essays in a variety of journals and was co-editor of the book *The Power of the Lamb*, to which he also contributed a number of chapters.

15. *Esther Wiens* (Ph.D., Northwestern University, Evanston, IL) is Associate Professor of English and Drama at the Mennonite Brethren Bible College. She has recently written a play entitled *Sanctuary* and compiled an annotated bibliography of church drama.